health
magazine

the
essential
women's
health
guide 2001

Oxmoor
House.

© 2001 BY TIME INC HEALTH
A DIVISION OF TIME HEALTH MEDIA INC.

Editorial Offices:
Two Embarcadero Center, Suite 600
San Francisco, CA 94111
(415) 248-2700

TIME INC HEALTH CUSTOM PUBLISHING

EDITOR-IN-CHIEF: John Poppy
ART DIRECTOR: Robin Terra
ASSOCIATE ART DIRECTOR: Margery Cantor
EXECUTIVE EDITOR: Eric Olsen
SENIOR EDITORS: Kim Olson, Annie Stine
ASSOCIATE EDITOR: Ellen Rush
COPY EDITORS: Peggy Nauts, Mike Mollett, Jacqueline K. Aaron
EDITORIAL RESEARCHERS: Krista Conger, Meredith Allen, Danielle Lazarin
PHOTO EDITOR: Caren Alpert
PHOTO RESEARCHER: Caroline Cory
LAYOUT & PRODUCTION: Tom Burleigh, Amy Feldman
PRODUCTION DIRECTOR: Linda K. Smith

Printed in the United States of America

This book is not intended to replace common sense or a doctor's advice.
Because differences in age, sex, and medical history affect health care
decisions, only your doctor can render a definitive diagnosis and
recommend treatment for you and your family. The *Women's Health Guide
2001* is as accurate as its publisher, authors, and medical consultants
can make it; nevertheless, they disclaim all liability and cannot be held
responsible for any problems that may arise from its use.

First printing: November 2000

ISBN 0-8487-2485-2

Oxmoor House®

contents

20

26

section two keep fit

section three stay healthy

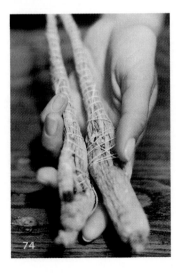

74

84

section four eat well

114

section five quick check

section six problems & solutions

68

The quotations in the section introductions on pages 11, 35, 67, and 113 are from the HealthMag.com discussion boards and from focus groups that HEALTH magazine has conducted as part of its Women in Motion research study. Names have been changed to protect the speakers' privacy.

Front cover photographs
VITAMIN E BOTTLE: SANG AN
WOMAN CLOSE-UP: AMY NEUNSINGER
RUNNING WOMAN: BROWN CANNON III
Back cover photograph
JIM WRIGHT

editor's **note**
so how are you?

A **sense of well-being.** Think for a moment what that means for you. For me, it's the feeling I get after a day when I've finally crossed at least a few things off my to-do list and I'm winding down with a steaming cup of tea. Or the way my muscles feel relaxed and my mind calm after I've actually made it to my yoga class. Or the sense of connection I feel when I get together with a friend to talk about absolutely everything under the sun—and laugh with her about the very things in my life that sometimes make me cry.

Often, though, our days seem too short to fit all the good stuff in. That's why the people you'll meet in HEALTH magazine's *Women's Health Guide 2001* are such great company: They know that taking care of themselves is the key to well-being, and they've discovered ways to achieve it with just a few tweaks to their daily routine. The truth is, nearly every moment of every day gives us opportunities to choose wellness. We can choose to eat a piece of fruit instead of a candy bar, choose to make time for a walk with a friend, and choose to react to a stressful situation by taking a deep breath—ahhh!—and seeing past the worry to a powerful solution.

Of course, a little help with your choices can't hurt. That's where this guide comes in. We separate fact from fiction about weight loss, fitness, and fatigue. On every page you'll find expert advice—and real-world strategies for putting that advice to work in your day-to-day life. Think the way to watch your weight is to hop on a scale every morning? Then you'll be pleasantly surprised by the far better test of success that starts on page 12. Uncertain about the herbal remedies being hyped for everything from insomnia to headaches? Flip to page 74 to find out what the researchers say. Think you lack the willpower to truly make a commitment to getting fit? You'll find good news on page 36 that could turn you into an exerciser for life.

A sense of well-being. It's what we all want, isn't it? I hope the advice you find in this guide will help you get there—every day. But first, take a deep breath . . . and pour yourself a cup of tea.

Barbara Paulsen

Barbara Paulsen
editor-in-chief
HEALTH magazine

look great

Don't take what people say so seriously.
And if you think you could stand to lose a few
pounds, do something about it! Get out,
go for a run, work out; that's the right way
to do it.   —kim

I take pride in who I see in the mirror now. I
had an eating disorder for a long time. And so
to be able to look in that mirror and say, "I'm
okay; my butt might not be what it looked like
when I was 18, but that's okay," I take great
strength from that.   —linda

I spent my twenties struggling and struggling,
trying to fit in. "Where do I go? Do I dye my
hair blonde and go this way? Do I dye my hair
red and go this way?" And then as soon as
I turned 30, it was like, phew, don't have to do
that anymore. I know who I am.   —fiona

trade in your bathroom scale for a
better body equation

Experts say measuring body fat is a much smarter way to improve your shape.

By Ingfei Chen

Twenty years ago, Carol Marchel was hardy enough to backpack the 2,000-plus miles of the Appalachian Trail. But in her late thirties, caught between a hectic university teaching career and nagging hip and knee injuries, she cut back on exercise.

Her weight gradually crept up to 195 pounds, way too much for her 5-foot-7 frame. She was headed for a size 18, far outgrowing her favorite dress—an elegantly slinky red number she used to wear to the symphony. And her once-prized fitness was gone. Even balancing on one foot to pull on her socks had become a demoralizing challenge.

Then, in September 1998, Marchel volunteered for a special exercise-and-diet study at Appalachian State University in Boone, North Carolina, where she teaches psychology. In lab tests, researchers found that she burned calories at an unusually slow rate, making it a struggle for her to shed pounds. They also measured her body composition to see how much was fat and how much was water, organs, muscle, and bone. Results showed that about 40 percent of her weight was flab.

It was a difficult moment of truth for Marchel, who still tended to think of herself as the active woman she had once been. "I thought, Holy smoke. When someone tells you almost half your body is fat, it gives you a different perspective," the 46-year-old says wryly. Freshly motivated, she began following the researchers' prescription and stuck to it for the next eight months: a low-calorie diet and five miles of walking every day. Midway through the study, she joined a gym and began lifting weights.

Early on, Marchel noticed she had a lot more energy. As the weeks went by, she found her blouses and pants were getting looser. Inches of fat were slowly melting away.

"After two months, I realized I needed new clothes." As she pared down, she was able to walk farther without aggravating her knee and hip injuries. By Christmas 1998, Marchel was much trimmer. She made a bet with her husband. If, come Valentine's Day, she could zip into her red evening dress again, he would wine and dine her at a fancy restaurant.

photographs

by david martinez

subtract fat,
ADD MUSCLE

Back in 1998, when 46-year old Carol Marchel joined an exercise-and-diet study, she wore a size 18 and struggled to get up a flight of stairs. The program, designed by exercise physiologist David Nieman at Appalachian State University in North Carolina, was no-nonsense—Marchel had to eat less and walk more. But it also took the emphasis off that number looming on her bathroom scale. The regimen is about losing body fat, not weight, says Nieman. Still, it helped Marchel shed 60 pounds and get down to a size 12 in just six months. On average, the women in Nieman's study lost about a pound of fat a week. But he's quick to warn: "This takes time, and it's a complete lifestyle change."

How many calories do you need? Women between age 30 and 60 can use this equation: Divide your weight by 2.2. Multiply that number by 8.7, then add 829. That final number represents the maximum number of calories you should eat in a day if you're working out and trying to lower your body fat.

What to eat? Nieman's eating plan is straightforward: 55 percent of your calories should come from carbohydrates, 25 percent from fat, and 20 percent from protein. Here's what a typical meal plan might look like for a woman who is limited to 1,400 calories a day:

> **BREAKFAST:** bowl of Raisin Bran with 1 percent milk; grapefruit half
> **LUNCH:** turkey sandwich with cheese, lettuce, and tomato; banana
> **SNACK:** apple; reduced-fat wheat crackers
> **DINNER:** stir-fry with tofu, broccoli, carrots; 1 cup of rice

What's the workout? In Nieman's study, participants wore pedometers to track the number of steps they took throughout the day. That was their baseline. Nieman had them walk two miles above and beyond that, seven days a week.

You can skip the pedometer and just tack two miles a day onto whatever you're already doing. The miles can be added in minidoses—a walk to the post office or grocery store, or a lap around the office at lunch.

Marchel went further. She began lifting weights. If you decide to follow in her footsteps, shoot for a program of 8 to 10 lifts, and do one to three sets of 8 to 12 repetitions for each move.

Yes, this is a lot to tackle. But look what it did for Marchel: Now she's down to a size 6, and her body fat is minuscule.

—JULIE CEDERBORG

Share your body-fat loss experience with other readers in the Diets, Weight Loss, and Working Out discussion group at www.healthmag.com.

When the study ended in April 1999, Marchel was one of its star achievers: She'd slimmed to a size 12 at 135 pounds—and pared her body fat to 17 percent. And the dress? She wore it with glowing pride to her reward dinner. "When we got to the restaurant, the waitress said, 'Oh, what a beautiful dress.' It was pretty cool," she says with relish.

Marchel's amazing success taught her something that most people don't know: Whether you're trying to get fit or trim, stepping onto a regular scale won't tell you how you're doing. Marchel did drop 60 pounds during the eight-month study. But in the year since the study ended, she has continued to firm up and reshape her body through resistance training, though you wouldn't know it from her bathroom scale. "My weight has stayed the same, but my fat-to-muscle ratio has changed," she says. At last check-in, she was down to a size 6, and her body fat was 13 percent.

"Women need to know how much of them is fat and how much is not, because that's what matters," says David Nieman, the exercise physiologist at Appalachian State University who led the study in which Marchel participated. He's also on the medical advisory board of Tanita, a manufacturer of body-fat scales you can use at home. More and more researchers agree that switching from an obsessive focus on the weight scale to smart use of this new breed of machine could help people finally get the body they want.

WEIGHT HAS ALWAYS BEEN A FLAWED YARDSTICK of a good body and good health. Yet for many women battling the bulge, the reading that flashes at their toes is all that counts. Even a single extra pound can ruin an entire day. Certainly, weight isn't a totally useless measure. Doctors weigh patients because it's easy, and because studies indicate that excess weight boosts the odds of developing heart disease, diabetes, high blood pressure, cancer, and osteoarthritis. By using weight-and-height charts or a related measurement called body mass index, your physician can see whether you're overweight for your stature.

But focusing on the scale can be misleading because not all pounds are equal. Personal trainers talk about seeing clients who are "skinny fat." These women don't have a weight problem, but because they don't exercise, they have little muscle and too much body fat. "A lot of women think that if they lose weight, they're going to look good and be more healthy. That's not always the case," says Pinaki Joadder, a personal trainer in San Francisco who routinely measures his clients' body-fat levels. "I tell people to throw their weight number out the window." While body weight is made up of both flab and lean mass, what people want to lose is the

lean lines
eat less and love it
Here's a satisfying reason to enjoy olive oil: Researchers in France say it may help you lose weight. People who lunched on meals made with monounsaturated oils, including olive and canola, were a lot less hungry later in the day than others who dined on the same dishes made with their polyunsaturated cousins, such as corn oil.

the smart way to
EAT AND RUN

Anyone who's ever tried to lose weight can tell you the magic recipe: Eat less, exercise more. But trying to do both at the same time can be tricky. You need to eat enough to fuel your efforts, but not so much that you get a side stitch or pile on more calories than you burn. Here are strategies that can mean the difference between feeling strong during your workout and finishing weak and unsatisfied.

Fill Up Before You Go

Eat something before working out if you want to lose weight. You'll exercise longer and harder—and burn more calories by doing so. If you have time before your morning jog, strive for between 100 and 200 calories in the form of fast-digesting carbohydrates. Have a fruit smoothie or a small bowl of cereal with a cup of skim milk. If you only have five minutes to eat before you run, have half a banana or a quarter bagel. Don't eat much more; it can leave you tired mid-workout.

Snack Aggressively

If you work out later in the day, have a 300-calorie snack about three hours ahead of time. Experts suggest combining carbohydrates and protein to keep you energized throughout your workout. Try a bagel and cottage cheese with fruit.

Snack this way consistently and you'll be on the most exercise-friendly diet of all—eating all day long. Eating four to six small meals throughout the day helps maintain even blood sugar levels, ensuring you'll have energy for an impromptu workout.

Trim the Fat

Remember to keep a lid on fat. Carbohydrates are digested the quickest, in one to two hours. Fat takes about five hours.

Power On Without Bars

Munching on one of these high-calorie bars during a workout could do your figure more harm than good—unless you're working out for more than two hours. If you find yourself fatigued, eat a few orange slices instead.

Finish With a Flourish

After a workout, you need carbohydrates to keep you from feeling washed-out and protein to sustain your energy and repair muscle. Eat a small snack with a carb-to-protein ratio of four to one.

Sleep Tight

If you exercise at night, following the above advice may force you to eat just before you head to bed. Don't feel like it? Don't worry. Eat light; just have a bowl of cereal or a cup of yogurt.

—MICHELE MEYER

fat. If they do it right, Joadder explains, they'll see the chubbiness dwindle away while they keep or even add to their muscles.

What many dieters don't realize, says Nieman, is that when they drop 20 pounds on a low-calorie plan, on average 5 of those pounds are muscle and water, leaving the body weaker. With fasting, as much as half of the weight that comes off is lean tissue. The distinction is crucial: A recent Columbia University study that tracked 4,621 people for up to 16 years found that those who lost body fat lived longer; but if the weight loss came at the expense of muscle, the risk of an early death increased.

Another difficulty with the scale is that being overweight doesn't necessarily mean a person is overfat. The body mass index can mislabel people, leading them to strive for an impossibly low weight goal, cautions Nieman.

"I've seen women who are 5 foot 5 and 150 pounds. I measure their body fat level and it's healthy." These women don't need to lose weight. They're heftier simply because they pack more muscle and bone—thanks to genes or rigorous exercise—than the average Jane does. Jackie Joyner-Kersee, the Olympic track star, is a good example. She's in fabulous shape. But because she's so muscular, conservative weight charts indicate she's too heavy.

How much body fat is too much? Most experts say it's unhealthy for women to be more than one-third body fat. Men are at risk if they're more than one-fourth flab. (Too little blubber can also be hazardous. Women should have at least 12 percent; men, 8 percent.) But even within the healthy range, a 5 percent drop can make a huge impact on the way you look.

lean lines
a hot new diet drink
The antioxidants in green tea that seem to protect against cancer and heart disease may also help you lose weight. A Swiss study found that drinking four or more cups a day can boost metabolism by about 4 percent.

FOR THE FIRST TIME, RELIABLE GIZMOS are available for tracking body-fat levels in the comfort of your own home. Until recently, the most precise methods were expensive and time-consuming. And they remind one of interrogation tactics banned by the Geneva convention: prolonged dunking in a tank of water or a full-body X-ray.

In contrast, new home fat-monitoring machines are convenient, trauma-free and relatively inexpensive. They send a tiny electrical current—so weak you don't feel a thing—through your body. The signal speeds through muscle and other lean tissue (which contain a lot of water and salt, allowing them to conduct electricity) but doesn't travel through fat (which lacks salt and water). So the more fat you have, the more resistance the current meets.

A built-in computer plugs the measurement into an equation that takes into account your age, weight, and height to predict your

how well do you
KNOW YOUR BODY?

When it comes to our bodies, we've all heard the folk wisdom. But how much of it is legit? Grab a pencil and take this quick quiz to see if you can tell fact from fiction.

1 Suppressing a sneeze can be harmful. TRUE OR FALSE

2 Lip balm is addictive. TRUE OR FALSE

3 Which of the following will soothe an upset stomach?
   a) milk   b) ginger ale
   c) honey and lemon   d) all of the above

4 Cracking knuckles causes arthritis. TRUE OR FALSE

5 Sleeping too much makes you tired. TRUE OR FALSE

6 Cutting hair makes it grow faster. TRUE OR FALSE

ANSWERS

1 True. The sneeze reflex creates a powerful blast. Plugging your nose forces air and mucus into delicate ear structures, potentially causing infection and, in rare cases, hearing loss.

2 False. Lip balm seems addictive because once it wears off, your lips feel dry in comparison.

3 B. Ginger ale is an effective tummy-soothing elixir, but only if it's made with real ginger—studies show that the pungent root can reduce seasickness and nausea and help digestion.

4 False. The popping sound in knuckles is made by the release of gas trapped between bones.

5 False. For healthy, happy people, it's not really possible to sleep too much. But oversleeping can indicate the onset of sickness or depression.

6 False. But shaving hair might cause a growth spurt. How? It irritates skin, stimulating blood flow.

body-fat percentage. The home fat-monitoring machines have a margin of error of approximately 3 percentage points. So if the reading says 25 percent body fat, for example, your actual level could be anywhere from 22 to 28 percent.

While the gadgets may not be 100 percent accurate, experts say they do give consistent readings. "Don't get too hung up on the exact number," says Kenneth Ellis, a medical physicist at the Baylor College of Medicine in Houston. "Follow the changes—that's more important."

lean lines

light bites The next time you reach for a mid-afternoon snack, opt for low-calorie fare like carrot sticks or fresh fruit. Crave more substance? Try a handful of protein-packed nuts or some cottage cheese.

Over weeks and months, body-fat testing can reveal whether you're losing the kind of pounds you want to lose, says Nieman. With the right strategy, as much as 90 percent of what you shed could be fat. Nieman recommends a daily diet of about 1,400 calories, depending on your start weight, and walking an extra two miles every day (see "Subtract Fat, Add Muscle," page 14).

Tracking your body-fat percentage can prove invaluable if you're lifting weights. Women who start pumping iron often get discouraged because they don't lose any pounds, says Joadder. But since muscle weighs more than flab, building up strength can offset any fat loss on a regular scale. Body-fat testing shows what progress you're truly making. "Your weight should stay about the same," he says, "but your fat measurement should go down."

That's exactly what happened to Carol Marchel. Today, the psychologist is still going strong with her walking and weight training. She gets her body fat measured every six months. "I want more strength," she says, "and getting on a regular scale won't tell me how I'm doing." Her dedication to fitness has certainly paid off. During a trip to Washington, D.C., last spring, she hoofed 11 miles in one day. Two years ago, she couldn't have done that. Says Marchel: "I've come a long way."

six ways to
rev your metabolism

Want a quick fix? Sorry, that's all hype.
But with a few simple tweaks to your daily
routine, you can lose a pound a week.

By Louise Rafkin

Though it has taken me three decades, I'm nearly ready to accept my fate. Despite somewhat elaborate and persistent fantasies, I'll never vaguely resemble Audrey Hepburn as Holly Golightly in *Breakfast at Tiffany's.* I'm built like a Clydesdale: thick, strong, good to go. My body, like that of many of my fellow Polish-Russian peoples, was engineered to survive Siberian winters and potato famines.

Measuring 5 foot 5 (just about!) and weighing in at 160 (approximately!), I don't think of myself as fat. Rubenesque? Yes. But now, at just over 40, I'm verging on stocky.

My build is good for some things. I can swim for miles, endure cold water, walk for hours, and go for days without food. Just don't ask me to sprint.

But that's at least one thing I have to do if I want to maximize my metabolism, says Janet Walberg Rankin, a professor of nutrition at Virginia Tech University and an expert on metabolism.

Lately, there's been a fair amount of chatter about "revving up" metabolism. The promise is that by speeding your resting metabolic rate (RMR)—the amount of energy you need to keep organs functioning and muscles fed—you'll burn more calories just sitting around. But keep an eye on the research, as Rankin has, and you'll realize there's no magic pedal to stomp on.

Your genes determine metabolism, says Rankin. In one study at the Laval University in Quebec, the range of calories stored by people doing the same workout varied by as much as 200 a day. In other words, you might need to walk an extra three miles a day to maintain the same weight as someone more metabolically fortunate than yourself.

But don't throw up your hands. Rankin believes that everyone can rev their metabolism, provided they take the right steps.

I'm already fairly fit. I just want to put some pep in my sluggish motor. I ask Rankin what works. She ticks off a list of proven metabolism-boosters: getting pregnant, getting a fever, and moving to a colder climate, to name a few. Despite my level of commitment, they all seem a bit extreme. Rankin does trot out six suggestions anyone can try, however. Some of them will push

photographs

by eric tucker

your metabolism toward hummingbird territory; others may not sound like much, but they add up.

one **pick a pepper**

A NEW STUDY CLAIMS that eating chile peppers can raise metabolism. Rankin explains that capsaicin, a compound found in peppers such as cayenne and jalapeño, stimulates metabolism by increasing the body's release of stress hormones like adrenaline. She'd like to see the results of this study repeated: Apparently, a group of Japanese women raised their metabolism by 30 percent after eating capsaicin-rich peppers with a meal.

I decide to aim for at least one pepper-laden meal a day and count on burning an extra 20 calories or so.

two **pump some iron**

I LOVE WHAT I DO FOR EXERCISE—surfing and karate—but Rankin says both my regimes fail as RMR chargers. I've built some muscle, but I plateaued years ago.

That's an even bigger concern now that I've hit 40. Not only do we grow less active as we get older, but starting in our thirties, we lose muscle at the rate of 1 percent per year. Without lifting

weights, a 150-pound person will lose on average a half pound of muscle a year. And because muscle at rest uses up more calories than fat, one's metabolism dwindles along with the muscle.

Rankin has a remedy, of course: resistance training with weights. Studies in the Netherlands show that lifting boosted RMR 9 percent over 18 weeks by adding four pounds of muscle mass. As a result, the people who participated in the study—all were men—burned more calories throughout the day, even during sleep. Rankin reckons that if I start lifting, by the time I've gained two pounds of muscle (which will take about three months), I will be burning about 65 extra calories a day—every day—on top of the 150 calories I burn on the three days I lift.

three have a cup of joe

RANKIN SAYS CAFFEINE INTAKE may trigger a slight upswing in metabolism. Drinking two strong cups seems to raise RMR an average of 12 percent (around 21 calories a day) over the three hours post-coffee.

Here's something I can really get behind. More java, please! What if I already drink two strong cups daily? Rankin warns that the metabolic benefits of drinking more than that probably don't outweigh the detrimental effects of loading up with caffeine. "Irritability, sleeplessness, a loss in calcium," she throws out.

A week later I notice in the news that green tea seems to boost metabolism above and beyond the lift from caffeine alone. Maybe I'll treat myself to a cup in the afternoon.

four start fidgeting

BECAUSE I WORK FROM HOME, my days are fairly sedentary. I sit at a desk, talk for hours on the phone, and occasionally venture into the backyard to throw a ball at the dog.

Rankin wants me to move around a bit more; fidgety people burn more calories than nonfidgeters, she explains. (This may account for some of the difference in calories burned seen in the Quebec study.)

How does it work? Rankin says the vast majority of calorie burning takes place when we're not exercising. My typical workout burns about 200 calories. Rankin figures I use up around 2,000 calories a day. Exclude exercise, and that's 1,800 during the rest of the day—watching TV, working, walking, sleeping. Trade some tube time for, say, more walking or gardening, and it's easy to see how my calorie usage would soar.

I'm not keen on developing tics, but I could move around while making calls. I also decide to walk the three-quarters of a mile to the gym (I hope I'll be able to walk home). While this doesn't

lean lines
train thyself If you could use some direction on strength training and stretching but can't afford a professional, pick up a copy of *How to Be Your Own Personal Trainer* (Ten Speed Press, $9). Author Fenn Starr offers straightforward moves that don't require that much equipment.

rating TV's
FITNESS GADGETS

D o you ever wonder how the miracle claims of those get-in-shape infomercials really hold up? Marc Rabinoff did. In fact, the human performance professor at Metropolitan State College of Denver devised a 24-point test to measure various fitness aids, rating everything from the accuracy of claims to product safety. Here's how three late-night television leaders scored.

PRODUCT	PRICE	PROMISE	SHILL	PASS/ FAIL	NOTES FROM THE PROFESSOR
Ab Rocker	$120	Rock your way to a firmer, sexier waistline	Jake (you know, the Body Jake)	Fail	"It will work your abs, but the infomercial ties it to losing weight and inches. It can't do that."
Tae-Bo	$60 (four videos)	Kickbox yourself into tip-top shape	Billy Blanks	Fail	"You can't learn martial arts in an instant. Without a trainer present, it could be dangerous."
Total Gym	$999	Get lean and mean on this workout machine	Christie Brinkley/ Chuck Norris	Pass	"It doesn't isolate one body part—it works everything. It delivers on its promise."

qualify as metabolism-boosting, per se, Rankin believes I'll go through at least 300 extra calories a day.

five watch your protein

RANKIN MENTIONS A DIETARY STRATEGY that seems a tad more doable than the chile peppers: increase my protein slightly. High-protein meals tend to leave you more satiated and less likely to snack. And though RMR rises a bit after any meal, it goes up more after eating protein because digesting it requires a few extra calories. However, she eschews the fad of very high protein plans. "Nutritionally speaking, I can't agree with diets that severely limit the intake of fruits and vegetables," she says.

I decide to swap my snacks, skipping carbo-based cookies for protein-rich tofu pups. Other options include low-fat cottage cheese and fat-free plain yogurt. I'll save about 20 calories a day.

six get a move on

RANKIN RECOMMENDS I try interval training on a stationary bike. Short, intense periods of exercise stimulate the release of adrenaline and other stress hormones, which in turn raise resting metabolism. Intervals also promote afterburn, the higher rate of calories used immediately following a workout.

lean lines
look in the mirror
Duke University researchers asked a group of over-weight men and women to work out for one hour, four times a week for three months. Each exerciser's weight held steady, but they lost, on average, six pounds of body fat.

While afterburn lasts only about half an hour, Rankin says I could still burn up to 70 extra calories postexercise. Not too bad. Better yet, new research suggests your body incinerates more fat when faced with high-intensity exercise. All told, I'll be chewing up about 300 to 350 calories three times a week.

what's it all mean?

IF I STICK TO THE PLAN, I'll burn an extra 3,800 calories a week (not counting the 150 I already get from coffee). And after three months of lifting, I can tack on the 455 calories a week from new muscle. To lose a pound of fat, I have to burn 3,500 calories or so.

so I did it

UNBELIEVABLY, IT WORKS: Two weeks later, I'm two pounds lighter. And I'm not hungry—adding more protein does help. During one midafternoon slump, I downed a couple of tofu dogs and was full until a late dinner. Chilewise, I peppered cayenne on my corn and on some salads.

I think it was mainly the exercise that tweaked my metabolism, although—and I hate to admit it—I couldn't stand the gym. But I found satisfaction in being able to lift more weight with each session.

As for Rankin's interval workouts, trying to watch the clock and take my pulse was challenging. I eventually plugged into the bike's preset interval program.

Hesitant to whine to Rankin about her specially tailored workouts, I E-mailed her news of my weight loss, threw back a tofu pup, and admitted—both to her and to myself—that I did feel better.

Unsure about the gym, I bought some free weights and will tack on lifting to my karate workouts. I'm also cranking up my dog walks to include stints of running.

This experiment has left me lighter and somewhat altered after only a few weeks, but the real proof will show up over the long haul. In chatting with a friend and fellow karate instructor, Coleen Gragen, I found the plan has plenty of promise.

Coleen has been following Rankin's advice for the last eight months. Her diet adheres to Rankin's slightly higher protein, low-fat balance, and she's committed to a three-times-a-week, aerobics-plus-weights workout.

At 46, she began this regime to strengthen her bones and heart as menopause approached. In the process, she nabbed an ineluctable bonus: She's dropped 20 pounds. "It was a great lesson. Doing this prevented me from being depressed about my age," Coleen says. "I've turned my fear of getting older into a strength."

Okay. I'm inspired. Tanked on coffee, fidgety, but indeed inspired. Check with me in eight months.

a chef's guide to
staying slim

Want a deliciously simple way to lose weight? Just learn a few cooking tricks from doctor-turned-chef John La Puma. Then get ready to taste success.

By Peter Jaret

When diet doctors pull out their prescription pads, it's usually to order a weight-loss drug. Not John La Puma. When he reaches for his, it's to write down a recipe. This Chicago-area physician loves to talk about good food. "Roasted butternut squash soup; you'll love it," he tells a woman who has come to him hoping to lose weight and lower her cholesterol. "Roast the squash for an hour—that intensifies the flavor. Then add thyme and garlic to the chicken stock," he says, jotting it all down on a prescription slip. "Mmm. This is making me hungry."

Don't know what a butternut squash looks like? (That's one on the facing page.) No matter: La Puma keeps a basket of vegetables on his filing cabinet. Don't know how to peel garlic? The good doctor demonstrates right on his desk. Think dieting means suffering and starvation? You'll change your mind after sampling some of the low-calorie dishes he teaches patients to make in a program called Cooking, Healthy Eating, and Fitness, or CHEF.

photograph

by scott peterson

La Puma witnessed the need for a new approach to dieting firsthand. Nine years ago, soon after he began practicing medicine, La Puma was amazed at how many of his patients had health problems associated with being heavy.

As a doctor, he knew he should advise them to cut back on calories and fat, eat more fruit and vegetables, and get more exercise. But because he was almost 35 pounds overweight himself, he also knew how difficult it was to follow such advice. In La Puma's case, he finally managed to slim down on a diet featuring rice cakes and grapefruit.

And he hated every minute of it.

"I love food. It's one of the great pleasures of life. If maintaining a healthy weight meant denying myself that pleasure, I knew I would never do it." So he did something radical: He traded in his stethoscope for a chef's knife, taking a sabbatical to study at one of the country's premier cooking schools.

Learning to make pastries and creamy sauces may not sound like the smartest way to stick to a diet. But La Puma had a special

mission. "I really wanted to learn the art of seasoning, the art of adding flavor without ladling on butter and cream," he says. "I wanted to learn to make dishes that are rich in flavor without being sky-high in calories."

These days La Puma is back to doctoring, though he still moonlights occasionally as a sauce chef at Topolobampo, a top Chicago restaurant. For his day job, he's taken what he learned as a chef to create a weight-control program unlike any other, one that emphasizes the delights of truly good food. The program includes one evening when La Puma dons an apron and teaches a cooking class in the home economics classroom at a local high school.

By transforming diffident home cooks into confident amateur chefs, La Puma hopes to encourage people to savor their food, not just scarf it down. "People in this program have struggled with their weight for years. And many have come to think of food as the enemy," he says. "I want to teach them to love it all over again."

Along the way, he also tries to shift tastes away from fatty and sugary foods to flavors that are bright and clean. Instead of asparagus covered in butter, he presents perfectly roasted spears with a squeeze of lemon. Rather than pasta with a cream sauce, he offers a delicious rosemary-infused polenta with zucchini and eggplant. La Puma's point is clear: You can lose weight by preparing delectable, healthy meals.

His students are getting the message. "I never knew vegetables could taste so delicious," says Deborah Boesch, as she oversees a pan of wilting escarole—part of the evening's cooking school menu, which also includes a double cranberry chutney and roasted spaghetti squash with feta cheese and fresh herbs. "I'm cooking vegetables at home now that I'd never even heard of before." In the five months since she started the program, she's lost 28 pounds.

For Carol Chesick, the goal is to keep her weight down, something she had never managed before. "I've tried dieting regimens with liquid protein drinks. But I always knew that was no way to live," says Chesick, who's lost 35 pounds in the past year. "Now I'm eating fresh food that's satisfying and delicious. I used to think of myself as perpetually on a diet. I don't think that way any longer."

Testimonials like that are a dime a dozen in weight-loss programs. But La Puma's approach has the numbers to back them up. In one study, participants in CHEF shed an average of 11 pounds and 10 percent of their body fat during a 21-week span. What's more, an exceptionally high percentage of the people who completed the program have stuck with what they've learned and kept the weight off.

Best of all, they've renewed a healthy love affair with good food. Just what the doctor ordered.

lean lines
put it in writing
To get a clear picture of your eating habits, write down exactly what you eat and the portion size every day for at least a week. Keeping a food diary is a great way to pinpoint which foods you overindulge in.

the new taste of lean

BELIEVE IT OR NOT, you can eat healthfully and enjoy every minute of it. Forget about those rice-cake diets and try one of these scrumptious, quick-and-easy entreés—they're low in fat and calories, and loaded with flavor.

Take a journey to the East with the spicy stir-fry below. (A cup of aromatic Thai tea complements the meal nicely.) In the mood for something hearty? The savory vegetable-bean ragout on page 31 won't disappoint you. It's the perfect choice for a lazy Sunday dinner. So dig in—your waistline will love you for it.

thai-style chicken & vegetable stir-fry

SERVES 4

2 cups water
1 cup uncooked long-grain rice
¼ to ½ teaspoon salt, to taste
1 bag precut vegetables (1 pound), such as mixed vegetable stir-fry
1 tablespoon canola oil
½ pound boneless, skinless chicken breast, cut into strips about ¼ inch
   thick and 1 inch long
¼ cup prepared spicy thai peanut sauce

■ Bring water to a boil in a medium saucepan; add rice and salt. Cover, reduce heat, and simmer 15 minutes or until liquid is absorbed. Remove from heat and keep warm.

■ While rice is cooking, pierce bag containing vegetables in several places. Microwave bag on high for 3 minutes. Let stand 1 minute before carefully removing vegetables from bag.

■ Heat a large nonstick frying pan or wok over medium-high heat until hot enough to evaporate a drop of water on contact. Add oil and chicken. Cook, stirring constantly, 2 to 3 minutes, until meat is cooked through with no traces of pink.

■ Add vegetables. Stir for 1 minute, remove from heat, and stir in peanut sauce.

■ Fluff rice with a fork; spoon onto plates. Top with chicken mixture.

Per serving: Calories 338 (16% from fat), Fat 6 g (1 g saturated), Protein 21 g, Carbohydrate 47 g, Fiber 2 g, Cholesterol 34 mg, Iron 3 mg, Sodium 927 mg, Calcium 52 mg

add flavor
CUT CALORIES

Slimming down doesn't have to mean suffering through one bland meal after another. Making just a few simple adjustments to the way you prepare food can really kick up the flavor quotient. And let's face it—the happier your taste buds are, the more likely you are to stick with a healthy eating plan. Here are some tips and tricks that you can use to perk up the flavor of your favorite dishes without adding a lot of unwanted fat and calories.

Think small with meat Slice and dice meat into tiny pieces to distribute its flavor throughout a dish. A small amount of beef, poultry, or pork goes a long way in a Chinese stir-fry; a single chicken breast can serve two people if it's chopped small and tossed with lots of veggies.

Make the most of vegetables Microwaving vegetables is fine if you're in a hurry, and steaming is a great way to cook them without adding fat. But for the richest flavor, try roasting them at around 450° until tender. Grilling is another tasty option. Brush asparagus spears, peppers, or quartered onions with a bit of olive oil and grill until tender.

Treat yourself to the finest ingredients Invest in quality ingredients to turn up the volume on taste. A mere drizzle of vinaigrette made with pungent balsamic vinegar and intensely fruity olive oil drenches salads with flavor. An aged parmigiano-reggiano delivers a much sharper taste than the canned variety, so you'll need less.

Remember parsley, sage, rosemary, and thyme Herbs and spices are the best way to add rich flavor without adding fat and calories. Physician and chef John La Puma's recipe for roasted spaghetti squash gets its zest from basil and minced italian parsley. A simple lentil soup simmered with fresh marjoram, sage, and a bay leaf makes a hearty meal.

Forget five a day La Puma recommends shooting for eight to ten daily servings of fruits and veggies. When you're cutting back on calories, it's important to make sure the foods you eat are concentrated with nutrients. What's more, fruits and vegetables are also packed with fiber, which makes low-calorie meals more filling.

Team up tastes Learn another secret of the pros: doubling up the flavors. La Puma's cranberry chutney uses both fresh and dried cranberries. His recipe for orange-glazed sweet butternut squash combines orange juice and a dash of orange-flavored liqueur.

—P.J.

PHOTOGRAPH: JONELLE WEAVER FOOD STYLING: KIMBERLEY ANSON

vegetable-bean ragout

SERVES 8

olive-oil flavored cooking spray
2 cups diced green bell peppers
1 ½ cups chopped onion
¼ teaspoon crushed red pepper
1 can (28 ounces) crushed tomatoes, with liquid
1 can (16 ounces) navy beans, rinsed and drained
1 can (15 ounces) no-salt-added chickpeas, rinsed and drained
¾ cup water
½ cup chopped fresh basil
1 teaspoon italian seasoning
½ teaspoon salt
¼ teaspoon freshly ground black pepper
2 teaspoons minced fresh flat-leaf parsley
1 clove garlic, minced
1 teaspoon grated lemon rind

■ Coat a dutch oven with cooking spray; heat over medium-high heat. Add bell peppers, onion, and red pepper; cook 8 minutes or until tender. Stir in tomatoes and next 7 ingredients (through black pepper).
■ Cover and cook over medium heat 15 minutes or until thoroughly heated.
■ Combine parsley, garlic, and lemon rind in a small bowl. Stir well and set aside.
■ Ladle ragout into bowls; sprinkle with the parsley mixture.

Per serving: Calories 256 (9% from fat), Fat 3 g (1 g saturated), Protein 10 g, Carbohydrate 46 g, Fiber 5 g, Cholesterol 0 mg, Iron 4 mg, Sodium 457 mg, Calcium 89 mg

glad you asked

Answers to your questions about looking good

I've started a weight-loss program, walking 3 ½ miles in an hour every day. What should my heart rate be?

As high as you can get it without becoming too winded to gab with a friend. The ideal flab-fighting workout is both long and fairly intense. You've already made a smart move by committing to walking a full hour. Anything less than 45 minutes won't get you the results you want. Similarly, if you don't walk fast enough, you won't burn enough calories.

To lose weight, experts suggest keeping your heart rate between 60 and 90 percent of your maximum. (To get those numbers, subtract your age from 220 and multiply by .6 and .9.) A heart-rate monitor can deliver helpful reminders when you need to take it up a notch.

I walk 45 minutes a day, and I'm thinking of adding 5-pound ankle weights to burn more calories. Is that a good idea? What about carrying dumbbells while I walk?

It's hardly surprising that a hard-core walker like you wants to take your workout up a notch. But loading yourself down with extra weights isn't the way to do it. Your body simply isn't built to carry additional pounds so far from its center of gravity. Strapping extra lead around your ankles could put undue strain on your knees and mess up your natural gait. And if you carry around dumbbells, you might end up with shoulder, neck, or back pain.

To add insult to potential injury, studies show that carrying weights makes a surprisingly small difference in the number of calories you burn. You could get just as much payoff—if not more—simply by walking a bit faster, climbing hills, or swinging your arms more vigorously.

Can my gym's steam room and sauna help me lose weight? And is there any risk to that sort of heat?

Sorry, but using a sauna doesn't lead to lasting weight loss.

While you may drop a pound or two, what's lost isn't fat but water from blood and muscles. You'll gain it all back once you quench your thirst. In fact, if you don't drink enough or you stay in too long, you could be asking for serious trouble. In either a dry sauna or a steam room, it's easy to deplete your water reserves by a quart or more per hour. That fluid loss puts extra stress on your heart and temporarily wreaks havoc with your blood pressure.

Does that mean you should swear off the sauna? No way. A 10- to 15-minute session can be very relaxing. Just be sure to down plenty of fluids. To get a rough idea of how much you need, weigh yourself before and after, then swig 16 to 24 ounces for each pound you've dropped.

I lift weights three times a week in addition to aerobics classes, but I don't like the muscles I'm developing. How do I slim down without bulking up?

For most women, the fear that lifting weights will turn us into hulks is unfounded. But some women *are* born with higher levels of hormones that trigger muscle growth.

If your biceps are bigger than you'd like but you still have fat around your midriff, you might want to crank up your aerobic exercise regimen—and take it a bit easier in the weight room.

Aerobic exercise burns off fat without making muscles bigger. That's because the muscles contract over and over but against little resistance, so the muscle doesn't suffer very much damage. Strength training, on the other hand, causes microscopic tears in muscle tissue. When the body repairs those rips, it adds a bit more muscle each time so it'll be better equipped for the next session.

Instead of cutting back on lifting weights, switch to lighter weights—just enough to keep the lean tissue you've gained. After all, muscles really are sexy. Plus, they burn a whopping 75 percent more calories than fat cells, even on a lazy day.

I'm an avid runner who makes it a point to wear a sports bra (or two!). But I still worry: Will all that bouncing make my D-cup breasts sag?

Don't worry about sagging. How your breasts hold up over the years is influenced mostly by genes as well as weight gain and loss. Gravity takes a toll, too, but all the jouncing in the world won't speed the rate at which your breasts lose their perk.

Comfort's another matter. Half of women athletes complain of breast pain during exercise. No surprise, since breasts—mostly fat—get little support from muscles.

A stretchy pullover sports bra may be comfy for women with an A or B cup, but larger women will find it too constrictive. Shop instead for a sports bra with separate cups, smooth seams, and snug, inelastic shoulder straps.

If you have trouble finding one you like, check the Title Nine Sports catalog for women (800/609-0092).

No matter how well I take care of my feet, I can't seem to avoid embarrassing perspiration and odor. Is there anything I can do?

Begin by scrubbing your tootsies daily with a washcloth and antibacterial soap, and drying them with a clean towel. Then sprinkle them with an odor-preventing foot powder to help stifle sweat. A spritz of antiperspirant can also help. Wear clean cotton socks or try a pair made of the new synthetic fibers designed to wick away moisture. Give footwear a 24-hour break between wearings to starve the odor-causing bacteria that call your clodhoppers home. If there's no improvement after two weeks, visit your physician; prescription foot soaks or antibiotics may be in order.

keep fit

I have a habit of being too lazy and not
prioritizing right. I can either do the laundry
or exercise. So I just do laundry. Lifting those
baskets, that's a workout. —*amy*

I like sports. I do everything, everything
and anything. I enjoy doing it, so I do it.
My age is 61. —*susan*

I have a swimming partner, and we meet
on Saturday mornings. We leave the house
at 7 A.M., which seems ungodly early,
but it's nice because everyone's asleep.
We stop afterward for lattes. —*helen*

prime yourself to
get hooked on exercise

Are you working out less than you'd like to?
Too busy? Too bored? Well, lace up those
sneakers, because we've got a plan for you.

By Christie Aschwanden

After hustling out the door at seven this morning, Linda Calvert spends eight hours fielding a stream of customer calls at the landscaping company she works for in Richardson, Texas. The workday behind her, she navigates a maze of snarled traffic on her way home. Her car vibrates to the beat of a stereo blaring nearby. A headache threatens as she squints at the glare flashing off the car ahead of her.

Overcome with relief as she walks through the front door, Calvert faces her first free moment all day. Few would fault her for slumping on the couch with a snack and the remote control. Instead, she laces up her walking shoes. "Exercise has become automatic for me," she says. "I just don't feel right if I don't do it."

To put Calvert's habit in context, some 25 percent of Americans are sedentary and nearly 60 percent don't exercise enough to improve their health. Surveys suggest that half the people who make New Year's resolutions to start working out give up by June. Daunting as these odds may be, Calvert is beating them. She's been walking for a half hour five times a week for two years, and she shows no signs of stopping.

How? Calvert adopted a program of "life change" designed by James Prochaska, a psychologist who heads the Health Promotion Partnership at the University of Rhode Island. Prochaska's model is one of psychology's great success stories; its unprecedented power to break addiction and alter behavior has been proved in hundreds of studies during the last 15 years, garnering Prochaska international acclaim. Yet the fitness world has only recently begun to incorporate his ideas. Chances are, the trainers at Calvert's local gym haven't even heard of him. Calvert only stumbled onto the program by volunteering for an exercise study at the Cooper Institute for Aerobics Research in Dallas.

Prochaska's methods (outlined in his book *Changing for Good*, Avon, 1995, $12.50) are startlingly simple. He invented nothing; he merely observed people who successfully overcame intractable behaviors such as smoking, overeating, and inactivity. Prochaska found that they all went through the same six stages along the way (for a list of the stages, see page 38.) What's more, he discovered

photograph

by cedric angeles

that by identifying which stage a person is in, he could prescribe techniques so she could eventually make a permanent change.

a plan in hand

FIFTY-SIX-YEAR-OLD HELEN FELDMAN was stuck in the second stage, contemplation, when she signed up. She had spent years thinking about working out. She knew exercise would make her healthier, but after several attempts she'd always end up back on the couch. "I joined a gym and told myself I was going to go for an hour four times per week. But all of a sudden it would be the end of the day and I hadn't gone. I was disappointed in myself," recalls Feldman.

She ended up feeling this way, explains Prochaska, because she made a common error: She skipped the stage between contemplation and action—preparation. If you don't have a detailed plan of attack that takes into account your schedule and abilities, he says, the likelihood that you'll stick with a regimen is slim.

Sheila Reynolds, then a counselor at the Cooper Institute, helped Feldman write up specific goals. Feldman started with two-minute walks, a far more realistic goal than working out for an hour at the gym. "Those walks made me see that I really could do this. Soon I started challenging myself to see how many I could do each day," she says.

six steps to
HEALTHY CHANGE

How many times have you tried to make a healthy change, only to fall back into an old pattern? Whether you want to stop smoking, start exercising, or ditch a drug habit, these are the six stages you must go through. If you want to learn more about this program, developed by psychologist James Prochaska, check out his book *Changing for Good* (Avon, 1995, $12.50).

1 **PRECONTEMPLATION** Unconvinced you need to change.
2 **CONTEMPLATION** Convinced but not committed.
3 **PREPARATION** Making a plan.
4 **ACTION** Doing it—the first six months.
5 **MAINTENANCE** Forming a habit.
6 **TERMINATION** Leaving the past behind.

keep fit

Feldman learned that you can't go from couch potato to athlete in one day. "When you assess people who say they suddenly made a big change, you find they'd been thinking about it for a long time," says Prochaska.

That's a concept our nation's exercise experts have yet to grasp. By relying on slogans designed to jolt people into immediate action, the health and fitness community is essentially asking us to quit our indolent lifestyles cold turkey. "'Just do it' is a great message if you're already doing it," says Prochaska. But the idea that they should be active hasn't even occurred to most sedentary Americans. For them, the current advice to "get some exercise" can be a turnoff, a recipe for failure, or both.

Evidence is emerging that Prochaska's message works for anyone. James Sallis, an exercise psychologist at San Diego State University, and his colleagues have designed a system doctors can use to determine a patient's stage. Doctors then give advice tailored precisely to a person's mind-set. In early results, six weeks after an initial doctor visit, more than 50 percent of those who had developed a plan were exercising regularly, compared with only 10 percent of those who had been told to "just do it."

time out

ALICIA ALVAREZ, 44, WAS DRAWN to the Cooper Institute study because of her father's poor health. He was battling illnesses that exercise can help prevent: diabetes and heart disease. But despite her familial risk, Alvarez thought that she couldn't spare the time; she was studying psychology and sociology while working full-time at an insurance company in Dallas.

People stuck in the contemplation stage say lack of time is the number one reason they don't work out, according to Prochaska. Often they just haven't considered what an excellent use of time exercise is, he says. There are at least 50 health benefits to regular activity. More immediate rewards, such as stress release and increased energy, can help convince someone who is run ragged daily.

After her counselor at the Cooper Institute filled in the picture, Alvarez was ready to make the time. Then she realized a solution had been staring her in the face all along: Her college offered dance aerobics and weight-training classes. She knew she wouldn't skip them, because they counted toward her degree.

making it work

SEARCHING FOR SOLUTIONS is key to the preparation stage. For Helen Feldman, starting with two-minute walks revved her engine, readying her for the ultimate goal of walking 30 minutes a day, five days a week. While time was still a concern, she had vowed to make exercise a higher priority, granting it the same amount of attention as, say, doing her errands.

overcoming
OBSTACLES

Obstacle #1 You aren't truly convinced it's important.

You plan to start exercising. But you're not sure how or where to begin, and time is an issue. You're in what psychologist James Prochaska calls the contemplation stage. People who have started and abandoned exercise often get stuck here. To get past this stage, make a convincing case to yourself for starting a fitness plan.

ENVISION A NEW YOU Imagine the clothes you'll be able to wear, the energy you'll have, the confidence you'll gain. Now imagine how you'll look and feel if you don't start.

ADD UP ALL THE PLUSES Working out has more than 50 benefits, from warding off disease to helping you lose weight to reducing stress.

RETHINK THE TIMING Ask yourself what you'd be doing if you weren't exercising. Watching TV? Reading the paper?

SEE THE POSSIBILITIES You'd happily join friends for a bike ride or a hike. "Imagine yourself taking part in life rather than watching it pass by," says Prochaska.

Obstacle #2 You don't have a realistic plan.

You decide to start exercising—this afternoon. Whoa. Before you begin, take the time you need to think things through. Starting to work out with no preparation, Prochaska says, is a big reason people fail.

PICK A DATE Choose a definite start date within the next month and don't put it off for anything.

SET THREE GOALS How often and how long will you exercise the first month, in six months, and a year from now? Start with small goals and work your way up.

WRITE IT ALL DOWN Get all of the details down on paper: What kind of workout most appeals to you? Where and when will you do it? How will you fit it in? How will you deal with potential roadblocks?

GO PUBLIC Let everyone know about your new exercise program, and don't be afraid to ask for help.

Obstacle #3 You don't know how to make exercise a habit.

You're working out, but will it stick? You're in the action stage. The first six months may be the trickiest. In the next phase, maintenance, chances are only an injury or a severe emotional blow will come between you and exercise.

TAKE CHARGE OF YOUR ENVIRONMENT If you plan to work out in the morning, lay out your gym clothes the night before. Should television's siren call prove too strong, move an exercise machine into the TV room.

REWARD YOURSELF If you stick to your plan for a week, treat yourself to a manicure. After two weeks, you've earned a massage.

FIND A WORKOUT PARTNER The more support, the better.

As you move from thinking to doing, remember that exercise can boost confidence, fight depression, and speed healing. Repeat this mantra: "I am an exerciser." Researchers are finding that "exercise identity" is key to making your habit stick. Forever.

The result? She found ways to work exercise into her schedule. "Now I see opportunities to walk all around me. Yesterday as I was shopping with my husband, I realized that our next stop was just down the street, so I walked over and met him there," Feldman says. When she goes to the grocery store, she walks every aisle before she grabs a cart.

As Linda Calvert journeyed from the preparation stage to the action stage, her adviser at the Cooper Institute suggested she think of ways to stay positive. "I put up notes on the refrigerator and around the house to encourage myself," she says.

Reinforcement is essential to getting through this six-month stage successfully, says Prochaska. Maintaining a good outlook will nurture your fragile new habit. Rewarding yourself helps as well, he says. One week Calvert promised herself a movie if she walked every day. Other times she gave herself a new book or magazine.

Calvert also enlisted outside support. Many people hesitate to announce their plans for fear of failure, says Sallis, but family and friends can really help. Calvert recruited a cheering section that included her husband and one of her close girlfriends. Knowing that people would be checking on her progress nudged her along when her own drive failed her.

in the groove

FOR ALL THREE WOMEN, the need for motivational tricks faded as they became more fit. "It's really given me a new attitude," Feldman says. "Last Thanksgiving my sister-in-law said I had an air of self-confidence that wasn't there before."

Alicia Alvarez says her exercise classes actually help her balance the demands of school and work. "I leave feeling revitalized. I absolutely need this."

For Calvert, walking is now part of her life. These days, it would take a serious blow—a major injury or severe emotional trauma—to derail her. Calvert doesn't walk for exercise; she *is* a walker. The distinction is crucial, and that's the mental shift that Prochaska wants people to make. Not everyone sails through the program the first time around. But once you see yourself as an exerciser, slipping a bit is no disaster, he says. You'll know how to get yourself back on track.

Feldman gained the maintenance mind-set some time back and now has reached what once seemed an impossible goal: Prochaska's pinnacle, the termination stage. Exercise is now as natural as brushing her teeth.

"When I started walking, I went for months without skipping a day because I was so afraid that if I stopped, I might not be able to start again," Feldman says. "But finally, I had a revelation. I know that I may not get my full session in today, but I'll make it up tomorrow. I'm not so hard on myself anymore. I just keep it up. That's what really matters."

the truth about
ten big fat fitness myths

So you work out but don't see any results?
We debunk ten fibs that stand between
you and a stronger, slimmer body.

By Christie Aschwanden

Going for a run on a hot day? Whatever you do, don't carry any water. Instead, take along some salt pills and pop a few when you feel thirsty. Twenty or so years ago, that was standard training advice, espoused by well-meaning coaches hoping to help their athletes better withstand the heat. That's a severely cracked notion, but don't laugh too hard. Fitness researchers say there are still plenty of exercise myths to debunk. Here's the lowdown on some of the most widespread ones.

fitness myth number one

Aerobic workouts help you lose weight by boosting your metabolism.

A KERNEL OF TRUTH LIES hidden in this tale. As you exercise, your muscles and organs need more fuel, generally speeding your metabolism—the rate at which you burn calories. After you finish, it takes awhile for your internal machinery to slow down, so you get a little afterburn effect. A one-hour walk will leave your metabolism elevated for a few more minutes.

But people hoping to burn more calories in their sleep will be let down by doing aerobic exercise only. You must add muscle to boost your body's 24-hour calorie burn. Muscle uses about four times as much energy as fat does. While aerobic activitiy does build some muscle, it doesn't add enough to substantially increase your resting metabolism. Lifting weights two to three times a week, on the other hand, will tack on a pound of muscle every month or two—and a pound of muscle devours 30 to 40 extra calories daily.

fitness myth number two

For a flat stomach, do crunches.

CRUNCHES WILL TONE the muscles in your belly, but they won't put a dent in the fat obscuring those muscles. "Try as you might, you simply can't direct your body to lose pounds in a specific

photographs
by brown cannon III

area," says Miriam Nelson, an exercise scientist and the author of *Strong Women Stay Slim.*

The only way to shed fat is to expend more fuel than you take in. That forces your body to burn fat held in deep storage—the hips, buttocks, and stomach, among other places. Your genes determine which of these areas shrinks first, but one thing is certain: The first regions to bulge are the last to slim down. The silver lining here is that women tend to lose fat from the stomach first. Create a calorie debt by using more fuel than you eat, and your tummy will begin to look better.

Try achieving that calorie debt by doing crunches and you'll just get very tired. Fifty sit-ups burns a measly 10 to 15 calories. On the other hand, a brisk half-hour stroll will leave you 200 calories lighter. But don't give up on crunches. They're just the ticket for shaping those newly visible stomach muscles—and helping you maintain good posture.

fitness myth number three

Slow, steady workouts are the best way to burn fat.

WANT EVIDENCE OF the undying appeal of this myth? Just take a look at the exercise machines at your local gym. You'll find that nearly every type, from treadmill to stair stepper, has a setting for "fat-burning zone." This program calls for a slower pace than others such as the "cardio-zone." In fact, at a slow pace—say, striding at about 3 to 4 miles per hour—your body burns a fifty-fifty mixture of fat and carbohydrates. Speed up to a 4- to 5-mph pace, and your body starts to burn more carbohydrates; fat makes up only about 33 percent of your fuel.

But the difference is an illusion. Sports physiologist Jack Wilmore of the University of Texas says cyclists spinning at a slow pace for a half hour use an average of 220 calories, 110 of them fat. If they ride at a faster pace for 30 minutes, they burn 330 calories—110 of them fat. The harder-working group uses up the same amount of fat, but it burns an additional 110 calories.

Sure, if the slow cyclists had ridden for another 15 minutes, they would have used the same number of calories as the fast group, and more from fat. But their odds in the weight-loss sweepstakes stay the same.

When you sit down to a meal following a workout, your body replaces lost carbohydrates first. If you don't burn many, the tank is quickly filled, and most of the rest of your meal gets stored as—you guessed it—fat. Do yourself and your tight schedule a favor by speeding up.

smart moves

a good start

Walking is the best way to kick off a fitness program, especially if you include stairs or hills, according to Edmund R. Burke, director of exercise science at the University of Colorado at Colorado Springs.

fitness myth number four

You have to do high-intensity exercise to get a "runner's high."

YOU MAY HAVE HEARD ABOUT ENDORPHINS—those magical mood-boosting chemicals that are released when athletes push themselves past mortal limits. The endorphin theory grew from the discovery that a hormone called beta-endorphin rises when people exercise strenuously. The hormone is the body's natural painkiller; it's released during childbirth, for instance. Researchers believed this could explain why people report feeling great after a workout.

In an underpublicized follow-up study, however, that notion was disproved. Scientists gave the test subjects a drug that blocked the endorphin's effects, and the exercisers went right on grinning. The theory took another hit when surveys showed that people routinely report a mood lift even from workouts that are far too gentle to raise endorphin levels.

"No one really knows why exercise makes people feel so good," says Jack Raglin, an exercise scientist at Indiana University. "It just does." And that's good news for fitness enthusiasts of every stripe. Run a marathon or walk around the neighborhood; either way you'll feel better.

understanding
BACK PAIN

Four out of five adults will suffer lower back pain at some point in their lives. See if you know the secrets of the spine.

1   Most back pain is caused by accidents or heavy lifting. TRUE OR FALSE

2   When excruciating back pain hits, what's the first thing you should do?
a) call your doctor   b) take aspirin or ibuprofen
c) apply ice packs

3   To heal faster, get out of bed as soon as you can, even if it hurts.
TRUE OR FALSE

4   If you decide to seek help in the first couple of weeks, who shouldn't
you visit?
a) physical therapist   b) chiropractor
c) back surgeon   d) osteopath

5   Everyone with back pain should get an X-ray. TRUE OR FALSE

ANSWERS

1 **False.** Experts say muscle spasms, brought on by inactivity or even emotional stress, are as likely a cause. Up to 85 percent of cases lack a definitive diagnosis.

2 **B.** Over-the-counter pain relievers reduce swelling. Next, start icing the sore area for 15 minutes every three hours. Call a doctor if your groin or legs are numb, if you lose control of your bowels or bladder, or if you still feel lousy after six weeks. Of those who don't see a doctor, 90 percent recover in two weeks.

3 **True.** For the first day or two, lying down may help. But staying in bed longer than that will weaken your muscles, slowing recovery.

4 **C.** Surgery works for just 1 percent of patients, and only as a last resort. What's more, studies suggest you can bypass physical therapists, osteopaths, and chiropractors, too; all offer little advantage over standard advice in back-care booklets.

5 **False.** Until recently, doctors routinely ordered spine X-rays. But the scans can be misleading, since most causes of pain don't show up.

fitness myth number five

You don't need as much exercise if you're thin.

FOR MOTIVATION, nothing beats the goal of dropping a few pounds. And with the experts so focused on the nation's ever-expanding waistlines, the thin get off easy, dodging the finger-wagging scorn of public health campaigns.

Yet there's a compelling reason why the trim should work out as hard as, or even harder than, their heftier brethren. Yes, exercise offers protection against ailments that strike the slim and the stocky alike, such as cancer, depression, and arthritis. But it's especially key in warding off osteoporosis, a disease that disproportionately strikes thin women.

To prevent the wasting of bone and lessen the risk of a broken hip, women should do weight-bearing workouts. For women on the heavy side, just about every step they take counts. If you're trim, you'll have to schedule plenty of walking, jogging, and resistance training. No one can afford to skip exercise.

smart moves
healthy habit
Research shows that people who are able to stick with a workout program for six months reduce their chances of dropping out by 10 percent.

fitness myth number six

You have to train for months before you start getting benefits.

NOPE. OH, SURE, it takes a month or two before those aerobic workouts start to get noticeably easier. Your lung capacity has to increase so the lungs can deliver more oxygen, via the blood, to your limbs. Your muscles must learn to store more energy and build more mitochondria, microscopic fuel-producing factories.

But not all the gratification is delayed. You'll start shaving pounds within a week. And your muscles will quickly snap to attention: Studies done at Ball State University in Indiana show that sinew responds to weight lifting after only four sessions. How's that for motivation?

A further look at the research reveals that there are plenty of immediate pluses to exercise: Reduced stress, a rosier outlook, more confidence, better sex, sounder sleep—all benefits that kick in with your first workout.

fitness myth number seven

Weight lifting will give you big, bulky muscles.

ONE LOOK AT A MISS UNIVERSE contest can keep women out of the weight room for life. But the truth is most women simply don't have the high level of hormones needed to produce that kind of muscle growth. So picture a different type of bodybuilder: "Marilyn Monroe was an avid weight lifter, and I wouldn't call her bulky," says Miriam Nelson. "To develop big biceps, you'd have to spend hours doing very specific workouts with weights so heavy you could lift them only once or twice."

Instead of bulking you up, weight lifting will make you leaner. The end result? A smaller you. That's because a pound of muscle takes up less space than a pound of fat.

"Fat is bulky and jiggly, but muscle is sleek and trim," says Nelson. Her studies show that women who lift weights, even those on vigorous programs, typically gain about 3 to 5 pounds of muscle and lose an equal number of fat pounds. Even if the scale doesn't budge, most women drop a dress size or two. And remember that a pound of muscle chews through up to 40 calories a day when you're just lying around. Do the math: Those extra pounds can add up to 200 extra calories burned daily. That will make it easier to keep off unwanted weight.

fitness myth number eight
If you stop lifting weights, your muscles will turn to fat.

THIS MYTH CAN LIKELY be traced to the plight of retired football players. Their chiseled muscles seem to transform into fat pouches overnight. The lesson is clear: Once you start lifting, never stop. But this belief is—physiologically speaking—akin to spinning straw into gold. There is no way to morph a cell. Muscle cells are muscle cells, and fat cells are fat cells.

Here's what really happens: When the players stop using the brawn they've built, their muscle fibers begin to shrink. That means these guys burn fewer calories at rest. If they don't compensate by eating less, they store that extra energy as fat.

As for the rest of us, we're not likely to build a massive musculature, and we don't eat as much as these bruisers. Which means if you stop lifting, adjusting your diet to avoid weight gain won't be as daunting. There's another way around this worry: Follow the experts' advice and make lifting a lifetime habit.

fitness myth number nine
The stair machine will give you a big butt.

THIS MYTH, POPULARIZED BY fitness infomercials, posits that you shouldn't exercise the body parts you want to shrink. Baloney, says exercise physiologist Edmund Burke: "It's ridiculous to specifically *not* target parts of your body." Infomercials claim that stair climbing and bicycling only increase the size of your hips and derriere. While these regimens don't add much muscle, they're great for burning calories, which will reduce the size of your hips and rear. The whole notion of hip-free workouts overlooks an important fact: How many aerobic workouts don't involve the hips?

fitness myth number ten
Exercise cranks up your appetite.

NOT TRUE. STUDY AFTER STUDY has confirmed a surprising truth: Unlike dieting, working out doesn't spur an automatic increase in appetite. As a matter of fact, intense physical activity can actually blunt your appetite over the short term, says Neil King, an exercise scientist at the University of Leeds in England.

Some research indicates that people who exercise actually have a better sense of how many calories they need than their less active counterparts.

As dietitians point out, we eat for a variety of reasons, and hunger is often not one of them. By exercising, you put hunger back at the top of the list.

And there's another advantage to exercising regularly: As you work out, you burn more calories, so as long as you don't start eating more, you're suddenly dieting and losing weight. Now wasn't that easy?

building strength for
a great body

You're confident. You know where you're headed. Congratulations! Now comes the next step: looking as great as you feel.

By Petra Kolber

Nearly all the women in my aerobics classes are over 40, and most say their body started to get softer at 35. I'm 36, and I'm fighting it. For women, the first things to go are the abs and the butt. Bellies and bums, we call them in England. It's certainly easy to let those first changes slip by without getting serious about exercise. But if you do, before you know it, you're 40 or 45 and gravity's truly begun to take its toll.

At this age, most women aren't obsessed with having a perfect body. They've come to accept themselves—and that's terrific. All I say is, Let's make that body the best it can be. Do the weight workout shown on the following pages three times a week. Do 30 to 45 minutes of aerobic exercise most days. And you'll start to see changes—quickly. The first week or two, you'll feel more energetic. In a month, two months at most, you'll see a more shapely body in the mirror. Clothes will fit better. Those little creaks you were getting used to? Most will go away.

photographs

by david roth

Cellulite is nothing mysterious. If you work out, it does go away. You may not have the body of a 20-year-old again, but you can certainly earn the body you had five or ten years ago. You'll look younger, thinner, and fitter—as if you'd turned back the hands of time.

It's a commitment, no question. Katherin Lautner, the model for this workout, does a strength-training regimen and an hour on exercise machines several times a week. At 40, she enjoys golf and yoga, and she struck me as being at peace with her body. She's not skinny, just healthy. "I have free weights at home," she says. "I work on everything, but I especially keep my upper body toned. I don't mind my chest muscles looking a little perkier!" She's getting what she wants from exercise—without spending all day at the gym.

Isn't that the point? Sure, you want to slip into those jeans or show off that swimsuit, but you also want enough energy to run after your kids and grandkids. You want to be Rollerblading at 60 or 70. At least that's what I want from exercise: the chance to take a good bite of life.

PETRA KOLBER (below, kneeling) created this better-body routine for HEALTH; she is a Reebok University master trainer. To really see the benefits of her weight-lifting moves, shoot for doing them three times a week. For each one, pick a weight that allows you to do 8 to 12 repetitions. With all of the exercises, it's important to go slowly and execute the move evenly throughout.

Include aerobic exercise three to four times a week for 30 minutes or more. Mix it up to avoid burnout and injuries—play tennis with a friend, or if you have kids, kick a ball around with them.

Then add stretching or yoga. Both improve posture and can make you look ten pounds lighter.

Obviously, this plan takes some effort. But if you look at it as a lifestyle choice that enhances the rest of your life, you're bound to stay motivated.

weighted lunge

HOLD A SET OF DUMBBELLS at shoulder level and take a step back with your left foot. Letting your left heel come off the floor, lower yourself, making sure your right knee doesn't travel past your toes. Slowly rise to the starting position. After 8 to 12 repetitions, switch sides.

calf raise

HOLD ONTO A WEIGHT BAR with a wide grip, feet shoulder-width apart. The bar should rest lightly on your upper back. As with all standing weight exercises, posture is important. Standing tall with your abdominals pulled in, slowly rise up onto the balls of your feet, then smoothly return to the starting position. If you don't have a weight bar, you can do this move holding a dumbbell in each hand at shoulder level, with the weights lightly touching your shoulders.

smart moves
water on the cheap
If your bottled-water habit is draining your bank account, try a sports bottle with a carbon filter in the cap. The filter rids tap water of chlorine as you drink.

dumbbell fly

PROP YOURSELF UP ON several pillows so your neck and upper body form close to a 45-degree angle with the floor. Bend your knees; keep your feet flat. Holding a dumbbell in each hand at arm's length above your shoulders, slowly open your arms until you feel a stretch through your chest, then pull back in (imagine hugging a tree).

learn to
LOVE THE GYM

If working out at home isn't the answer for you, the solution may be joining a health club. For many people the key to sticking to an exercise program is social support—which is built into a gym membership.

So what's holding you back? Perhaps some negative feeling about gyms you've been harboring for years. Or maybe it's a spotty track record at clubs in the past—you've joined with the best intentions, only to quit a month into your membership. But your hang-ups with gyms are probably much easier to deal with than you might imagine. For every one of your excuses, we've got an answer.

"Gyms are too expensive" Sorry, but purchasing a gym membership won't exactly break the bank. The average annual cost is $684, or a little less than two bucks a day. That's equivalent to what you plunk down for your daily latte. Still not convinced? Start thinking of it as insurance. Sure, you'll be doling out money every month for a gym membership, but there is a good chance your newfound fitness will help you save later in medical bills. While there aren't any guarantees, it makes sense to do everything you can to swing the odds in your favor.

"They don't feel welcoming" True, the whole gym atmosphere can be awkward. While everyone seems to be sweating away with a purpose, you feel completely out of place. Get a friend to join with you, and you'll instantly feel more comfortable. A workout buddy also creates accountability. When you know someone's waiting for you, it gives you that added push to get out the door. Or consider hiring a personal trainer for the first few sessions. She can provide you with company while showing you the ropes.

"It feels selfish" Talk to your family about why you need to go, and ask for their support. "People are more likely to succeed if the people close to them encourage the changes they're making," says Bess Marcus, a psychologist at Brown University who specializes in exercise motivation.

"Gyms are just plain boring" Then mix things up. When your routine starts feeling stale, step off the treadmill and get in on a class. Most gyms serve up a smorgasbord of offerings, from belly dancing to water ballet to yoga. It will give you a change of pace, and you might just stumble upon something you will love.

"It's hard to go to the gym every day" Then have a backup plan handy, suggests exercise physiologist Richard Cotton, a spokesperson for the American Council on Exercise. On days when you can't get to the gym, ride your bike or take a quick jog around the neighborhood. If you have a Plan B, you won't have any excuses not to exercise.

dumbbell **chest press**

IT'S HARD TO THINK OF a better upper-body exercise than the chest press. You'll feel it in your biceps, triceps, and chest. Start by lying on your back with knees bent and feet flat on the floor. Grasp a dumbbell in each hand, arms up at a 90-degree angle, thumbs facing each other. With your abdominals pulled in, push weights up, keeping the back of your shoulders on the floor. Return to the starting position.

smart moves
strong bones
Even if you drink milk and take calcium supplements, it may not be enough. *The Bone Density Diet,* by George Kessler (Ballantine, 2000, $25), details foods rich in the minerals needed to head off osteoporosis as well as bone-building exercises.

ab **crunch**

IF YOU HAVE STRONG ABS, everything else—standing up straight, lifting weights, going for a hike—will come easier. To do a simple crunch, lie on your back with your knees bent, feet flat on the floor. Cross your arms, keeping your neck relaxed. Contract your abdominals so that your shoulder blades come off the floor. Slowly lower. Start with 12 to 15; build up as they grow easier.

reverse dumbbell fly

POSTURE IS SOMETHING WE all need to work on. The reverse fly is great because it helps you stand straighter. Place one foot in front of the other and lean forward slightly, bending at the waist. Hold a dumbbell in each hand in front of you, elbows bent at 90 degrees, and open your arms. Pretend you are squeezing something between your shoulder blades as your arms extend. Then slowly lower your arms to the starting position. Do just one set.

a weighty matter
When lifting weights, the last few reps should be quite difficult. When your workout becomes a piece of cake, add more pounds. Push yourself to increase the weight every month or two.

dumbbell squat

SQUATS HELP YOU BUILD muscle mass throughout your lower body, boosting your metabolism. They also target those telltale glutes. Hold a dumbbell in each hand so that they lightly touch your shoulders. Stand with feet shoulder-distance apart. Squat as if to sit in a chair, then slowly rise to the starting position.

introduce yourself to
the pleasures of hiking

If you're a walker, you're already a hiker.
Just find a trail and stride your way to a
toned body and a renewed spirit.

By Judith Stone

I first took to hiking as a kid at Camp Metaka, thrilled to find an activity at which a klutzy shrimp could excel. Mercifully, it involved no ball: You just had to walk doggedly and know a lot of songs. I zigzagged up my first mountain when I was 11. I couldn't get over it. How long did it take? All 99 bottles of beer and a few choruses of "Three Jolly Fishermen." The climb was exhausting but exhilarating.

Even at that age I could appreciate the lessons of hiking. "If I can climb a mountain," I said to myself back then, "maybe someday I'll be able to calculate the volume of a cylinder without crying!" ("If I can drag myself up this trail," I say today, "then, by God, I can finish my taxes!") That's what I like best about hiking: the way its triumphs transfer to the rest of life. That and the fact I can burn hundreds of calories on the trail.

photographs

by steven lippman

getting serious

POST–CAMP METAKA, I HIKED SPORADICALLY. In high school, I trekked on family trips to the desert and joined girlfriends for gossipy assaults on the gentle foothills near home. In college, I became a desk potato until a backpacking boyfriend reintroduced me to hiking. Over the years, my interest continued to wax and wane.

Finally, about five years ago, I thought, Enough with the waning. I like hiking, it feels good, and it's not that hard. I don't need any sophisticated gear. I can do it with my jockish friends and relations; it challenges both the serious athlete and the person whose enthusiasm for fitness regimens comes and goes. It's a sport easy to start, or to start over.

So I started over, embarking on a beginner's workout designed by a personal trainer. My immediate goal was preparing for an inn-to-inn hiking trip on England's Devon coast, a birthday gift from my parents. They've become fiendish walkers, the fossils, and I didn't want to eat their dust.

My training plan was simple. The first week, I walked 15 minutes at a moderate pace on day one, 20 minutes on day two, 25 on

before you
HIT THE TRAIL

Hiking is such a beautifully simple activity that you might be tempted to just lace up your boots and head out the door with nary a thought. But a little pre-hike planning can help make the most of your trek—and keep safety hazards at bay. So before you take off, follow these easy tips and you'll be on the path to enlightenment.

Picking a hike Check your phone book for a list of local parks. Then get on the horn: Park employees can often recommend the best walks and send you a map. Out-door equipment and sporting goods shops can also be a font of local tips. For more suggestions, contact the American Hiking Society, *www.americanhiking.org*; the American Volkssport Association, 210/659-2112 or *www.ava.org*; or the Rails to Trails Conservancy, 202/331-9696.

BONUS TIP

Joining a hiking club can be a great way to meet other hikers and get to know some of the trails near you. To find one, contact any of the groups listed above.

Once you're walking Bring sunscreen, sunglasses, and a hat to protect yourself from the sun's rays, as well as a basic first aid kit. To loosen up, stride for five minutes and then stop to stretch your quads, calves, and butt. When you're back on the move, be sure to nibble throughout the hike. It's a rough world inside your daypack, so bring some snacks that can take the hit, like apples, bagels, hard cheese, and gorp. Be sure to drink lots of water—two to four quarts for a full day of hiking—to prevent dehydration. And remember that it's not easy to go downhill in comfort. Take small steps, and keep the pace slow to protect your knees.

BONUS TIP

Want to stave off sore muscles? Make sure you rest for 5 minutes or less—or 20 minutes or more—says Gary Nussbaum, an outdoors expert and professor at Radford University in Virginia. In-between amounts tend to trigger the buildup of lactic acid.

Leaning on friends It's easier and a lot more fun to tackle a long hike with a companion. After all, who else will point out that you've got the map upside down? Plus, there's safety in numbers. Before you set out, be sure to tell your family or a friend where you're going and when you plan to return.

BONUS TIP

For added safety, bring your cell phone along with you on the trail. Just make sure it's turned off.

—AMY RUTH LEVINE

day three, and 30 on days four and five. The next week I walked 30 minutes a day for five days; then I added five minutes a day until I hit an hour. (That's about a four-mile hike for me; I'm no speed demon.)

I started and ended each session with five minutes of slow walking and some gentle stretching. I hit the treadmill, the streets of New York, or the paths of Devil's Den Preserve in Connecticut when I could. Within two months I was ready to hit the trail.

shaping up

ON THE DEVON JAUNT, I managed to keep up with my parents (generally) and had a glorious time walking high above pirate coves, striding through fields of flax in blue bloom, and communing with moor ponies.

If the idea of venturing into nature conjures thoughts of snakes, stalkers, or the Donner Party, relax. Hiking is probably safer than walking in your neighborhood. Blisters may be the worst hazard.

What's more, the activity is almost laughably healthy. For starters, you can walk off 400 to 500 calories an

smart moves
dress the part
Don't get on the path without broken-in shoes and one more layer of clothing than you think you'll need, preferably one that repels wind and rain.

how to
STAY WELL FOR WALKING

All it takes: 6 to 12 minutes after your walk. What you do: A calf stretch, a shin strengthener, and a thigh stretch. In one month: Your legs will be looser and your step surer. In two months: Your risk of lower leg injury, from knee pain to shinsplints to tendinitis, will be drastically reduced.

CALF AND ANKLE STRETCH

A Hold the back of a chair. Bend your left leg and slide your right foot back—keeping your heel flat and foot straight—until you feel the stretch in your right calf. Hold for 30 seconds. Switch legs. Repeat up to four times.

B With your heel flat, slowly bend your right knee until you feel a stretch in the tendon just above the heel. Hold for 30 seconds. Do up to four repetitions on each leg. (These stretches help prevent calf pulls, tendinitis, and plantar fasciitis.)

SHIN STRENGTHENER

A Sit in a chair with your right foot flat on the floor and rest the heel of your left foot on your right, just above where the toes meet the foot.

B Raise your right forefoot—keep the heel on the ground—while resisting with your left foot. Hold for a count and lower. Repeat 12 times before switching feet. (Strengthening the muscles in your shins will help fend off shinsplints.)

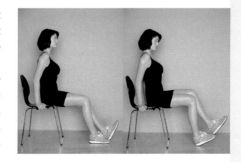

OUTER THIGH STRETCH

A Lie on your back, arms at your sides and your left leg in the air.

B With your hips flat, roll your left foot inward as you point your toes to the right. You'll feel the stretch down the outside of your thigh. Hold for 30 seconds, then switch legs. Repeat up to four times. (This keeps hip and knee pain at bay.)

—WORKOUT CREATED BY PETRA KOLBER

hour on a moderately challenging trail. That could add up to 2,000 calories—a week's worth of exercise—for a half-day hike. Besides improving your balance and flexibility, you're also working your entire lower body, toning your calves, hamstrings, butt, and quadriceps.

And you're working another important muscle: your heart. Studies show regular brisk walking lowers blood pressure and cholesterol levels and cuts a woman's risk of cardiovascular disease. It also reduces your odds of suffering from osteoporosis, breast cancer, or Type 2 diabetes. In fact, about the only bodily ill hiking won't prevent is a bad hair day.

changing my mind

BESIDES THE PHYSICAL BENEFITS OF WALKING, studies show that it fights insomnia and depression. And I find that a good hike clears out the mental cobwebs, refocuses my attention on what matters, and reminds me that my head and body live in the same ZIP code.

A few years ago, a colleague gave me a little guide to walking meditation by a Vietnamese Buddhist monk. The book recounts an anecdote in which someone asks Buddha what he and his disciples do.

Buddha says, "We sit, we eat, and we walk." The questioner responds that everyone sits and eats and walks. "Yes," Buddha replies, "but when we walk, we know we are walking."

Good point. To walk and know you are walking is to be fully present in your body and the surrounding landscape, not so mired in yesterday's regrets or today's anxieties that you miss the moment you're in.

I want to be present when I hike because there's so much I don't want to miss. Walking along California's central coast, I've seen otters floating with their abalone dinners balanced on their bellies. On a path in Ecuador, I came across a bundle of sticks with legs that turned out to be a farmer toting firewood. (My Spanish is excellent; I'm pretty sure he said, "Surely the frog seeks a bicycle pump.") In Thailand, I walked a trail winding through wild lemongrass, basil, and coriander that perfumed every step.

Hiking sweetens the soul, too. On a journey in the White Mountains of New Hampshire two summers ago, my sister the marathoner beat her sister the sloth to the summit of Mount Chocorua by an hour. But we enjoyed our solitary ascents under the spell of the trail, each slipping, at our separate paces, into a magical balance between relaxation and exertion—every grand vista something to be grateful for, each slap of foot to dirt adding to a slow-growing but lasting contentment. And we liked the chatty, companionable descent just as much. For old times' sake, of course, we sang "Three Jolly Fishermen."

glad you asked

Answers to your questions about keeping fit

I continue sweating long after my lunchtime workout ends. In fact, sometimes I'm still sweating after I've showered. Is there anything I can do?

Sweating is your body's natural way of cooling down after intense physical activity. But when your workout is over, you want to get dressed and go on with your day.

Here are some quick fixes to help halt the waterworks: Stop exercising two minutes early and sit still—outside, if it's cool. This gives your body a moment to power down before you hit the shower. Once you're in the shower, crank up the cold water and hold your head under the stream for a few seconds. Last, don't don a sweater, blazer, or other heavy clothing until you get back to the office.

Is running risky for knees? I run for 20 minutes three times a week and am worried I'll wear them out.

Not to worry. Though running does send powerful jolts to your knees, if you're healthy, just wear well-cushioned shoes and your knees should be fine. You'll get a great workout that actually helps strengthen the spongy cartilage between your joints.

Still, make sure to stop the minute you feel a twinge. If you have a history of knee pain or injury, check with your doctor before hitting the road. You may have a tear in the cartilage that needs treatment, or you could have osteoarthritis, a deterioration of the cartilage.

To avoid knee pain during exercise, stretch a bit after a brisk, five-minute warm-up walk. Try alternating a minute or two of light jogging with several minutes of walking. If possible, stick to dirt trails, which are softer than pavement. And if you develop any swelling or pain, cut out the running until your knee feels well again.

Some experts insist that I need to do two sets of 8 to 12 repetitions to get any benefit from weight lifting. Others say that one set is enough. Which is it?

Toss out the "two sets of 8 to 12 reps" mantra and adopt a less-is-enough attitude. By lifting slightly heavier weights, you'll find you're getting nearly the same payoff in half the time.

Studies have shown that adept weight lifters seem to glean as much from pumping one set as the rest of us do from three. The trick to earning that sort of return? Aim for failure. (In other words, give yourself permission to poop out.)

Start with a weight that burns on the eighth rep. When 12 reps at that weight are no longer a challenge, add a little more weight.

While it's okay to feel stiff the next day, your joints should never hurt. Muscle pain that lasts longer than 48 hours may mean you're hefting too much.

I walk faster than my friend jogs. Which one of us is getting the better workout?

You don't mention how fast you're walking, but at least one study shows that walkers who sped along at more than five miles an hour actually burned twice as many calories as runners traveling at the same speed. Most people, however, find it hard to keep up that pace without breaking into a run, which burns fewer calories because it's a more efficient motion. Chances are that your pace, though brisk, isn't quite that fast.

But forget about speed. To find out who's getting the better workout, you and your buddy should compare heart rates. It doesn't really matter whether you walk or run or hop along on one leg. Your goal, whatever your activity, is to reach a heart rate between 60 and 90 percent of your maximum, and to keep it revved that high for 20 to 30 minutes every day.

To figure out your desired heart-rate range, subtract your age from 220 and multiply the result by .6 and .9. Keep your heart rate within that range and—walking or jogging—you'll get a great workout.

I just turned 55 and want to begin an exercise program. Am I starting too late to get any real benefits?

First of all, congratulations! And in answer to your question: It's never too late to begin exercising. In fact, when it comes to fitness, the present means far more than the past.

A recent study of 2,400 men and women conducted by UCLA researchers showed that people who were active later in life cut their risk of developing heart disease and lowered their chances of dying early compared with those who worked out when they were younger. How's that for inspiration?

So even if you can't remember the last time you broke a sweat, you can change your destiny by getting in gear today.

DAVID MARTINEZ

Sometimes after I exercise, my blood sugar crashes, leaving me shaky and weak. Should I eat right before my workout?

The secret to avoiding that sinking feeling is to snack both before *and* after you work out, and to pick foods that will keep your blood sugar in balance.

During a strenuous bout of exercise, your working muscles can use up your body's store of glucose, a type of sugar produced when you eat carbohydrates. Since the brain runs on glucose, a short supply can make you woozy.

Eat before you work out—an hour or two beforehand if possible. You want to have food in your system but not sloshing around in your stomach. For a steady stream of energy, opt for a high-fiber, carbohydrate-rich food, such as oatmeal or vegetarian chili. Postworkout, have a sports drink or a bagel for quickly digested carbs, which will quell the shakes by topping off your blood sugar levels.

stay healthy

How do you motivate yourself to exercise?
I need to do it to break my fatigue cycle, but
when I get home from work, I'm dead on
arrival! I can't even push myself out the door
to take a walk down the street. —*marci*

You can do a lot. Get a bike. When you
need to go somewhere close by, instead
of driving your car, ride the bike. If you
need to get milk from the store three miles
away, save the gas and ride your bike.
Get a membership to the gym. (Hey, you
can ride your bike there!) —*tory*

Good advice! Reading good stuff like this
really gets me motivated. I feel like jumping
around, but I think I'll go eat first. —*amber*

tired of being tired?
rise and shine

Maybe your exhaustion isn't simply a lack of sleep. Find out whether you suffer from one of the six hidden causes of fatigue.

By Alice Lesch Kelly

photographs

by amy neunsinger

Last August was, for me, a lost month. First I couldn't doze off at bedtime. Then I started waking long before dawn. Eventually I was prowling the house, wide-eyed and desperate, most of the night. Exhaustion took over my days. I couldn't focus; thoughts clattered around in my brain with no place to settle. "I've got junk-drawer head," I told my husband. I was loony with fatigue.

Chances are, you know just what I mean. One in four Americans struggles at some time with a lack of energy that stretches a couple of weeks or more. What's surprising, experts say, is how many of these tired people get plenty of shut-eye. And even when insomnia seems to be the problem, it may actually be a symptom of a medical condition with a simple remedy. That was true for me. Could your fatigue be masking something, too? Consider the following mysteries and clues.

one restless sleep

AFTER LAUREN ERO, 39, HAD HER second child, she suffered the exhaustion of any new mother. But the lethargy stuck with her even after the baby started sleeping through the night. "I could fall asleep at a moment's notice, then wake up the next morning more tired than when I went to bed," Ero says.

Her doctor diagnosed depression, but antidepressants didn't help. "I was even falling asleep while driving," she says. Desperate, she sought a new doctor, who asked Ero if she snored.

"Horribly," she told him. An overnight visit to a sleep lab confirmed the second doctor's hunch: Like roughly 12 million other Americans, Ero had sleep apnea.

Loud snoring—the sound of struggle as she gasped for air— was the giveaway. During the night, Ero's upper airway would sag and periodically collapse. Though the disruptions never roused her completely, they kept her from falling into a deep sleep.

Sleep apnea occurs mostly in men, so doctors often miss it in women. Ero had other clues: Her brother snores loudly, and apnea runs in families. Also, she had kept her pregnancy weight—extra

pounds can put pressure on already sagging airways.

In mild cases, losing weight may relieve symptoms. New treatments involve trimming or shrinking flabby tissue at the back of the throat, but they can be painful and aren't always effective. Ero chose another solution: She wears a mask attached to a pump that forces air into her lungs as she sleeps. Though the mask took getting used to, waking up rested was worth it, she says. "Within a week or two, I felt like a different person."

two allergy time

EVERY SPRING AND FALL, Diahne Goodwin would start to sniffle and sneeze, and then her energy would drain away. "When the allergies really got going, I'd just be wiped out," says Goodwin, 35. She avoided over-the-counter drugs because they made her more tired. A year ago, her condition escalated to full-blown asthma.

There's no question that fatigue increases during allergy season: Histamine and other chemicals released during the allergic response have a soporific effect. Over-the-counter antihistamines trigger even more drowsiness. Allergic flare-ups can be worse in bed, where irritants such as dust mites are hard to avoid.

Luckily, the latest prescription antihistamines can dry up the nose and relieve itching and sneezing without making you tired. And prescription steroid sprays alleviate nasal stuffiness without disturbing sleep.

Another option, allergy shots, may appeal to people with severe symptoms. British researchers recently found that three to four years of such shots kept patients who were sensitive to grass pollen symptom-free for at least six years.

Goodwin's asthma finally forced her to see a doctor. She discovered that if she took a prescription antihistamine daily for a few weeks in the spring and fall, she could prevent even the initial symptoms of an attack. "It's made a huge difference," she says. "This year I've escaped asthma *and* the tiredness."

three tired blood

EARLY EVERY MORNING for years, before hopping the bus to her downtown job, Linda Smith enjoyed waking up with the birds on a two-mile walk around a eucalyptus-lined lake in her neighborhood.

But last summer, Smith, 47, just wanted to sleep late; even the oasis of fragrant trees and snowy egrets couldn't lure her from bed. A blood test found that her body's iron stores were low, making Smith one of 3.3 million women with iron-deficiency anemia.

Red blood cells need iron to be able to transport oxygen in and out of cells. Usually our bodies are able to absorb all we need from food. But among women of childbearing age, especially those with very heavy periods, uterine fibroids, or endometriosis, iron

health note

get down Doctors often urge people with asthma to avoid down bedding. But recent research turned up higher levels of lung-tickling dust mites and pet dander in synthetic pillows than in down versions. The densely woven covers designed to keep feathers in may also keep allergens at bay.

can run low. Besides feeling tired, such women may be sensitive to cold or notice that lips and fingertips have lost their rosy blush.

A simple blood test will detect this form of anemia. If iron levels have indeed dipped, your doctor may order further tests to try to discover whether you have internal bleeding caused by another condition such as an ulcer or even colon cancer. In Smith's case, all such tests were negative. Her doctor suspected that heavy periods, along with mild, recurring endometriosis, were to blame.

Smith took a ferrous sulfate supplement three times a day until her blood iron levels were normal, and soon she was tromping around the lake again. If you're tempted to pop a few iron pills yourself, don't—at least not until you've consulted a doctor. Too much iron can cause fatigue; worse, it can seriously hamper liver function and may raise your risk of heart disease.

four a misbehaving thyroid

WHEN INSOMNIA HIT LAST AUGUST, my doctor suspected clinical depression and referred me to a psychotherapist. I thought that seemed a little hasty; my melancholy and irritability had cropped up *after* a long string of restless nights, not before.

After doing some research on my own, I pushed the doctor to test me for thyroid problems. To his surprise, the small gland in the neck that plays a key role in spurring metabolism was pumping out only a fraction of the hormone I needed. Days after I started a replacement hormone, I had my life back. The insomnia and fatigue—and the hell that had shadowed them—vanished.

Patients with an underactive thyroid are typically female and about 50 years old; often they become cold, constipated, depressed, and sluggish as their metabolism winds down. Having too much thyroid hormone, on the other hand, usually makes people jumpy, but it also drains their energy, so they feel weak and spent. Either condition is difficult to diagnose without a blood test: Symptoms may be absent or they may come and go.

And fatigue's not the only danger. An overactive thyroid boosts a woman's chance of developing osteoporosis or an erratic heartbeat. There's new evidence that an underactive thyroid also poses a risk to the heart, probably by boosting cholesterol levels; in some cases, pumping up the thyroid can bring cholesterol levels

TEST YOURSELF

are you allergic
TO YOUR HOME?

People with allergies tend to put the blame for their troubles on the great outdoors, but the skyrocketing number of allergy and asthma cases may actually result from all the time we spend *indoors*. Find out how to clear the air in your home.

1 Indoor air quality is a concern mainly for people who've been diagnosed with breathing problems. TRUE OR FALSE

2 Which of the following may be allergenic?
   a) firewood   b) humidifiers
   c) houseplants   d) all of the above

3 You can rid sheets and pillowcases of allergy-causing dust mites by washing them in hot water. TRUE OR FALSE

4 You should avoid using roach spray. TRUE OR FALSE

ANSWERS

1 False. Even if you're healthy, poorly vented furnaces, gas appliances, and woodstoves can produce noxious gases that irritate your airways. Have such equipment cleaned and inspected annually. While you're at it, have your home checked for radon: This underground gas seeps into houses and can cause lung cancer.

2 D. Damp firewood generates mold spores. Houseplant soil harbors fungi; repot often. Humidifiers foster mold and dust mites; if you must use one, clean it weekly.

3 True. But few home water heaters are set high enough (130 degrees) to do the job. Try a Laundromat.

4 True. But while sprays can be an irritant, so can roaches, a leading cause of asthma in children. Use a boric acid roach killer and clean up thoroughly afterward.
—CASSANDRA WRIGHTSON

in line. When the gland is overactive, medication or a single dose of radioactive iodine can usually quiet the storm.

five the weight of depression

"SOMETIMES, IT'S REALLY AN ACT of courage to get out of bed in the morning," says Angela Dewey,* 37. From her teen years on, she was chronically tired no matter how much she'd slept. She had frequent headaches and some bouts of anxiety. A few years ago, after a bad breakup, she imagined jumping in front of a subway train. A therapist diagnosed depression.

Unrelieved sadness wears down the body even as it deflates the spirit. Long hours of restless sleep can signal depression, as can wee-hour wakefulness. The common theme: fatigue along with sadness, hostility, or loss of interest in formerly pleasurable activities. Roughly one in four women is diagnosed with depression; it may account for about half the cases of fatigue that doctors see.

Even deep melancholy can usually be eased by psychotherapy, alone or with medication. If symptoms persist, don't wait out the funk; untreated depression is more likely to intensify and recur.

In Dewey's case, therapy and a brief course of an antidepressant restored her equilibrium. Today she no longer needs the drug or the therapy. Her energy and resilience have returned.

health note

the pressure of a restless night

If you have sleep apnea, you may be at increased risk of high blood pressure. A National Institutes of Health study found that middle-aged and older adults with the disorder had a 45 percent greater risk of hypertension than did their well-rested counterparts.

six chronic fatigue syndrome

FIVE YEARS AGO, LISA PETRILLI came down with what she thought was the flu. But the 5-foot-2, 105-pound nurse lost 12 pounds in six weeks and didn't bounce back. The aches, pains, fever, and exhaustion lasted for years. Eventually she had to quit her high-stress job and go on disability.

Petrilli saw six doctors. Finally, one put a name to her symptoms: chronic fatigue syndrome (CFS).

The syndrome has no single cause. In some cases, an immune system abnormality may be the trigger; in others, it's a defect in the body's ability to handle stress. And there's no simple way to identify the disorder. Doctors must play detective and then treat symptoms one by one.

With CFS, memory loss, inability to concentrate, sore throat, and muscle or joint pain are common. The hallmark is fatigue that's lasted at least six months and that intensifies after exertion. Anyone can get CFS, but it seems to be twice as common among women as men and most often strikes adults aged 30 to 60.

Although not all CFS patients regain their health, about four out of five experience significant improvement within two years. Three years after her symptoms appeared, Petrilli began to feel better, and her recovery since has been slow but sure. She's delighted to be back at work in a new job: She visits homes to give follow-up care for newborns—and their exhausted parents.

* This name has been changed.

a smart woman's guide to
natural remedies

Confused about herbs? We'll
steer you toward the best ones—
and tell you how to use them safely.

By Sally Lehrman

A few months ago, allergies, PMS, and fatigue had me sneezing, wheezing, and clutching my stomach. My regular doctor tucked some prescriptions into my hand, but after reading up on my ailments I found myself visiting a traditional Chinese doctor. Why was I willing to trust his earthy-smelling concoctions but not my physician's HMO-sanctioned pills? For one thing, by the time he handed out his potions, the herbalist had quizzed me about every aspect of my life and explained his treatment plan in detail. What's more, his mysterious brown liquids seemed to work.

Of course, I didn't tell my regular physician. She'd just think I was a gullible fool. And I'm not alone in my secrecy. Most herbal users don't tell their M.D.s, even when they're going in for surgery or recovering from a life-threatening ailment.

But doctorly disdain isn't the only reason so many people keep mum. It's a good bet their physicians know as little as they do about herbs—or less. Plus, the medical establishment's inattention to botanicals helps convey the impression that they're harmless, so why bother to mention using them? Yet these remedies can, indeed, be powerful stuff. Side effects and cross-reactions can be just as serious as those associated with prescription medicines.

In an ideal world, doctors would collaborate with alternative practitioners. Until that happens, women need to educate themselves about what works, what doesn't, and what's downright dangerous. Here's what some of the country's leading herbal experts have to say about natural remedies for women's top health concerns.

photographs

by david tsay

feeling lethargic?

The experts' pick: ginseng

FINDING IT HARD TO GET OUT OF BED? Experts say no herb promotes energy more safely and effectively than ginseng (that's ginseng root at right). Scientists theorize that the Asian form, *Panax ginseng*, activates the adrenal gland, which in turn stimulates metabolism and endocrine function.

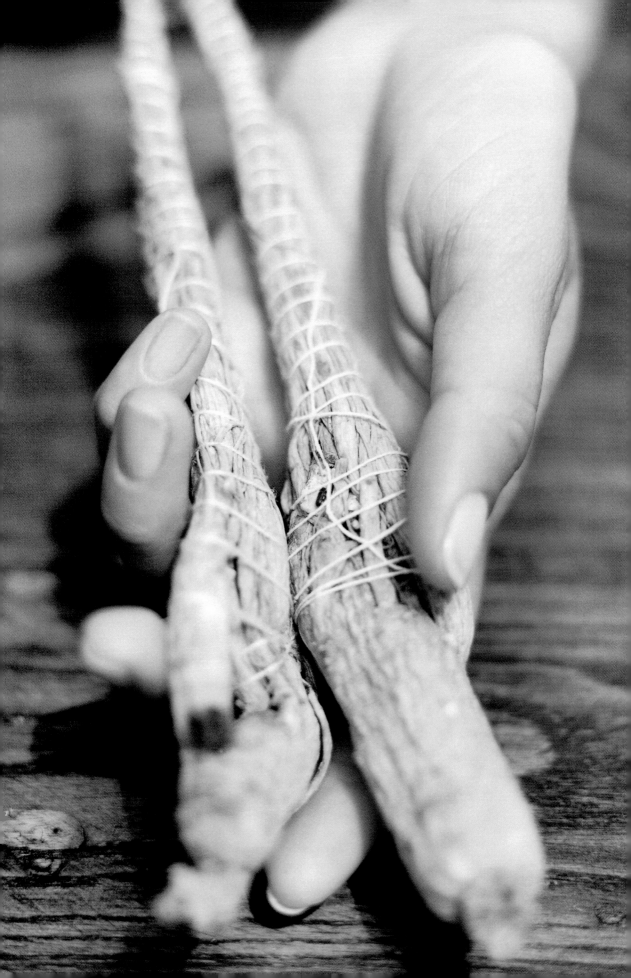

HOW TO TAKE IT: Follow the dosage on the label. In large amounts, ginseng can cause headaches, insomnia, diarrhea, agitation, and increased blood pressure. The root has been found to reduce glucose levels; it helped the mood and vigor of one group of 36 people with diabetes. But experts warn that it could affect the action of sugar-lowering drugs, including insulin and glipizide. Avoid ginseng if you have hypertension—it can elevate blood pressure—and note that it may interact with antidepressants that are monoamine oxidase (MAO) inhibitors. Children, pregnant or nursing women, and people on steroids should also avoid it.

OTHER OPTIONS: *Ma huang*, or Chinese ephedra, jolts the cardiovascular and nervous systems, boosting energy. But it can rev blood pressure to dangerous levels, particularly if combined with caffeinated beverages, other stimulants, or asthma medications. Side effects include dizziness and increased heart rate. In the FDA's database of herb-related complaints, one-third concern *ma huang*, including links to at least 34 deaths when the supplement was used in large quantities over a long period. People with cardiac problems, thyroid disease, or diabetes should be especially careful.

down in the dumps?

The experts' pick: saint-john's-wort

THIS HERB HAS BEEN HOT since 1996, when a review of 23 German studies found that it chased away mild to moderate depression as effectively as some drugs. Not only that, but *Hypericum perforatum* seems to produce fewer side effects than prescription antidepressants. But the herb's interactions with drugs can have serious consequences. Confused? Don't be. Saint-John's-wort is the best-studied alternative mood lifter and still holds first place on the experts' list. Just be very careful.

HOW TO TAKE IT: Saint-John's-wort isn't for severe depression. It can make you more sensitive to the sun, so use extra sunscreen. Most of all, be wary of combining the herb with other medications. It can weaken the effects of a number of drugs, including theophylline (for asthma), digoxin (for congestive heart failure)—even anesthesia during surgery. It also significantly compromises the effectiveness of indinavir (for HIV infection). Women on the Pill could have breakthrough bleeding, which could cause their birth control to fail. The herb can heighten the power of prescription antidepressants, increasing side effects such as confusion or dizziness. It can also intensify the grogginess caused by some cough syrups. If none of this deters you, buy an extract standardized for 0.3 percent hypericin, and take 300 milligrams three times a day.

OTHER OPTIONS: SAM-e (or s-adenosyl-methionine) shows promise as a treatment for mild depression and seems to have few side effects. But large-scale, long-term studies have yet to be done.

trouble sleeping?

The experts' pick: valerian

VALERIANA OFFICINALIS, which comes from a tall perennial that gardeners know as heliotrope, has been lulling people to sleep for more than a thousand years. How it works is unclear, but a number of human studies have demonstrated its mild sedative effect when taken over several weeks. Be aware that valerian won't help much if you use it just occasionally.

HOW TO TAKE IT: Experts suggest using 2 to 3 grams of the dried root to make tea. If you prefer an extract or pills, follow the dosage on the label. For maximum effectiveness, take valerian right before bed. Avoid combining it with other depressants, including sleeping pills, antianxiety drugs, antihistamines, kava kava, or alcohol.

OTHER OPTIONS: A few years back, melatonin was touted as a miracle supplement that would not only aid sleep but extend life. Now experts say it's effective only for special slumber problems, primarily jet lag and upset body clocks of night-shift workers.

herbal
RULES OF THUMB

Before herbs became hot, researchers paid little attention to how they interacted with conventional drugs—or with each other. Now scientists and regulatory agencies are scrambling to develop a fuller understanding of natural remedies before too many people get hurt. The bottom line, experts say, is to treat supplements as cautiously as you would prescription drugs. Here's their advice.

Don't double up It may be tempting to heighten the effect of a drug or an herb by taking another supplement that treats the same problem or has a similar effect on your body—say, kava kava with alcohol or antianxiety drugs. But instead of increasing the benefits, you double your risk of dangerous side effects.

Avoid multiherb pills Many herbs have more than one active ingredient—and the more you mix it up, the greater the potential for interactions and side effects.

Be especially careful with blood thinners Many supplements—including ginkgo, vitamin E, garlic, ginseng, ginger, and feverfew—work in part by making blood slower to clot. If you combine these supplements with each other or with aspirin or prescription anticoagulants like warfarin (Coumadin), spontaneous bleeding may occur. For a different reason, it's dangerous to combine coenzyme Q10, vitamin K, zinc, iron, or magnesium with warfarin: They all appear to decrease its effectiveness.

Stop all supplements before surgery Blood thinners could inhibit clotting, Saint-John's-wort can make anesthesia less effective, and other herbs may cause dangerous changes in blood pressure or even cardiac arrest. Quit taking supplements two to three weeks before going under the knife.

Buy from a reliable source The amount of active ingredient in a supplement varies widely from brand to brand, so make sure the preparation is "standardized." What's more, contamination with lead, arsenic, or mercury has proven a problem in some products from Asia. For help, check out *www.herbnet.com*.

Clue in your doctor She needs to know about any supplements you're taking, as well as prescription and over-the-counter drugs.

Tell your pharmacist, too Some drugstores are starting to keep track of drug-herb interactions and can alert you to problems.

Consult an herbal expert He can point you toward the most reliable brands and tell you whether you'd be better off with a pill, tea, or extract. He can also help you avoid allergic reactions or dangerous combinations your doctor may not know about. And he may be able to figure out why a remedy isn't working. —S.L.

no time to get ill?

IF YOU WANT TO STOP a cold before it stops you, try echinacea. Studies have shown that this botanical can snuff out the sniffles and soothe a scratchy throat (or at least ease your symptoms and shorten your agony by a day or so). But echinacea works only after germs have taken up residence in your body; it won't strengthen your immune system against every passing virus.

To do that, experts recommend *Astragalus membranaceus* (or *huang qi*), used in traditional Chinese medicine to fight colds, flus, and respiratory infections. Test-tube studies suggest that compounds in this pea-plant relative may have antiviral properties. Most experts, however, are waiting for studies on humans.

HOW TO TAKE IT: Swallow echinacea at the first sign of a cold, and follow the dosage on the label. The herb is a member of the ragweed family, so people with hay fever may want to avoid it. Also skip it if you have an autoimmune disease, as it could overstimulate your immune system and work against your medications. Astragalus comes in various forms, but experts say the root is most effective when it's cooked—say, in soup or stew.

OTHER OPTIONS: Vitamin C has gone in and out of style as an immune booster; the studies are not in its favor. What's more, doses higher than 2,000 mg may cause diarrhea.

---

health note
thumbs up for soy
Labels on soy products can now tout heart benefits. Find soy protein powder at major drugstores and markets, and mix it into milk, juice, and smoothies. Aim for three to four tablespoons a day.

---

splitting headache?

The experts' pick: **feverfew**

PRIZED SINCE THE DAYS OF THE ROMAN EMPIRE as a fever and headache reducer, feverfew is believed to muffle pounding in the head by influencing how blood vessels contract. Interest revived a decade or so ago when two British studies found that the herb decreased the number and severity of throbbing attacks. Research since then has been less favorable.

HOW TO TAKE IT: The usual dose is 100 to 125 mg a day. Buy a powder with at least 0.2 percent parthenolide, the active ingredient. But if you're allergic to ragweed, feverfew—a member of the same family—might trigger the sniffles or a rash. And it shouldn't be combined with supplements or drugs that thin the blood.

OTHER OPTIONS: Magnesium and vitamin B-2 also show promise as migraine treatments.

memory a blur?

The experts' pick: **ginkgo**

AMERICANS BUY MORE *Ginkgo biloba* than any other herb in hopes of recharging a failing memory. While it won't help you recall the details of your book group's latest novel, it will probably help if you're suffering some memory loss due to impaired circulation. Ginkgo is an antioxidant, protecting against damage by free radicals, plus it increases blood flow to the brain. In studies, it seems to slow the progress of Alzheimer's disease; research is under way to see if it can help normally aging brains stay sharp.

HOW TO TAKE IT: Try 40 mg of standardized extract three times a day at meals. In that amount, side effects are rare, though occasionally people report unusual bleeding and rashes. Don't take ginkgo with other blood thinners except with your doctor's okay.

OTHER OPTIONS: Megadoses of vitamin E slowed the mental decline of Alzheimer's patients in one 1997 study, but research has yet to show whether vitamin E supplements can help regular folks keep their marbles. Doses higher than 400 international units can

what to do for
COLD OR FLU?

Nearly all of us will battle a virus or two this winter. But as you pop echinacea or sip chicken soup, will you know which illness you're fighting? Take this test to find out.

1 **Fever is a sure sign of a flu virus.** TRUE OR FALSE

2 **Colds begin more mildly than the flu.** TRUE OR FALSE

3 **Nausea means it's the flu.** TRUE OR FALSE

4 **Take antibiotics for a cold when symptoms include**
  a) heavy congestion   b) tooth or facial pain
  c) uncontrolled sneezing   d) none of the above

5 **If the flu knocks you out for a while, talk to your doctor about taking the latest antiviral drug.** TRUE OR FALSE

ANSWERS

1 False. A cold virus can cause a fever, but a temperature above 103 usually points to the flu.

2 True. Colds appear slowly, with a sore throat, stuffy nose, and sneezing. The flu tends to strike suddenly, with chills, headache, cough, and muscle aches.

3 False. Influenza is actually a respiratory virus. In fact, "stomach flu" isn't a flu at all; it's caused by bacteria, usually food-borne.

4 B. Antibiotics are useless against viruses. But they can help if a cold turns into a sinus infection. Call your doctor if you have facial pain; left untreated, bacteria can do damage.

5 False. The newly approved antiviral drug Relenza must be taken within the first 48 hours after symptoms appear and even then doesn't always work. While no drug reliably treats the flu, you may be able to prevent it by getting a flu shot every year before flu season starts.

health note
cancer care
New research finds
that 70 percent
of cancer patients
use some sort of
alternative therapy.

cause headache, nausea, or stomach cramps; vitamin E is also a blood thinner, so don't take the supplement if you are taking an anticoagulant medication.

feeling stressed out?

The experts' pick: kava kava

THIS MUSCLE RELAXANT and mild depressant, from the roots of a plant in the pepper family, has long been used in Polynesia to induce calm and promote harmony. Unlike most tranquilizers, *Piper methysticum* extract seems to take the edge off without spacing you out. Two initially skeptical British scientists recently reviewed seven small but well-designed studies and concluded that the herb is relatively effective against mild anxiety.

HOW TO TAKE IT: Choose a formula standardized for kavalactone, which is believed to be the main active ingredient. Take 120 to 200 mg at bedtime only when you feel anxiety building; doses above 240 mg a day can produce a scaly rash. Stay away from other herbs that have a depressive or sedative effect, as well as alcohol and prescription antianxiety drugs.

natural-born
FAT KILLERS

Weight-loss supplements have become tremendously popular. But do they really work? And are they safe? Before you jump on the bandwagon, it pays to do a little homework. Here's how some of the best-selling supplements hold up under scientific scrutiny.

Chitosan

Chitosan, made from the shells of crustaceans, binds to fat. Supposedly, this prevents the body from absorbing the fat, so you can eat high-fat foods and simply flush the consequences away. But studies have shown mixed results. The consensus among obesity researchers is that it doesn't work. And nutritionists worry that while binding fat, chitosan may also be sucking up some important fat-soluble vitamins such as D, E, A, and K.

Chromium Picolinate

Chromium is a trace mineral that scientists think may influence appetite. When bound with picolinate, which increases absorption, chromium is reputed to aid in fat loss without harming muscle mass. Though there are studies that make chromium picolinate look good, many are linked to the maker of the product. If you try a supplement, don't go overboard. Headaches, sleep disturbances, memory problems, and mood changes have been reported with high doses.

Ephedra (or Ephedrine)

Ephedra, derived from the Chinese herb *ma huang*, stimulates the nervous system and heart. It has been shown to help fight flab, if moderately. Unfortunately, the risk is great with this stimulant. In people with cardiac conditions it can trigger a heart attack, stroke, or seizure. Other side effects include dizziness, headache, or stomach upset. Weight-loss experts suggest using ephedra only with the help of a watchful physician.

Garcinia Cambogia (Hydroxycitric Acid)

Extracts from this Indian fruit and its relative, *Garcinia indica*, compete with an enzyme needed during digestion. Advocates claim the herb reduces the amount of overeaten carbohydrates that get converted to body fat, dampens the appetite, and whisks away extra pounds. But studies show mixed results. While no unpleasant side effects have been reported, more research is necessary before declaring this herb safe.

Glucomannan

The supplements and chips containing this ingredient, from the konjac root, purportedly swell in the stomach and signal the brain that you're full. Two tiny studies point to improved weight loss, but neither obesity experts nor herbal experts are impressed. And the FDA took a capsule form of glucomannan off the market because of the danger that the fiber would swell up and cause suffocation.

OTHER OPTIONS: When it comes to relieving stress, most alternative practitioners prefer meditation and yoga over herbs.

sick at heart?

The experts' pick: garlic, vitamin e

EXPERTS SAY GARLIC SEEMS to maintain the flexibility of blood vessels while discouraging clotting. But garlic has many detractors, who say research is scant and contradictory. Bottom line: Gobbling it up won't do any harm—and may do good.

Until recently, vitamin E seemed to be the clear choice for anyone worried about heart health. Several long-term studies have suggested that this powerful antioxidant can reduce the risk of heart disease by improving blood flow, checking inflammation in blood vessels, and disarming LDL cholesterol before it can batter arteries. But a new Canadian study found that cardiovascular patients who took the vitamin over four years had just as many heart attacks, strokes, and heart-related deaths as those who popped a placebo. Still, many heart specialists remain fans of E.

HOW TO TAKE IT: Eat garlic raw; even light cooking can destroy its active enzyme. As an alternative, try 900 mg in powder or tablet form every day. Don't pair dried garlic with other blood thinners, and don't use it if you're taking the platelet inhibitor ticlopidine (Ticlid); it might heighten the drug's activity to dangerous levels.

If you prefer vitamin E, take 400 IU a day.

OTHER OPTIONS: Fermented red yeast—aka cholestin—has been used for centuries in China to keep the heart healthy. It contains a substance that is almost identical to the active ingredient in the cholesterol-lowering drug lovastatin (Mevacor). It's powerful, so take it under a medical specialist's supervision.

having hot flashes?

The experts' pick: black cohosh

NATIVE AMERICAN WOMEN have long used *Cimicifuga racemosaa* to chill out when hot and bothered by the approach of menopause. In one study, German researchers found it to be as effective as estrogen in treating the sudden sweats, low spirits, and disrupted sleep associated with hormonal fluctuations. What's less clear is how it works.

HOW TO TAKE IT: Stick to the usual dose—40 mg a day in tablet or extract form—to avoid stomach upsets, dizziness, headaches, or joint pain. If you're on hormone replacement therapy, some experts recommend skipping black cohosh.

OTHER OPTIONS: Isoflavones, estrogenlike substances found in soy products, promote overall menopausal health, but supplements appear to be of little benefit.

second thoughts from
the hormone debate

Is the news on estrogen giving you hot flashes? We cast a cool eye on the latest research into HRT's risks and benefits.

By Susan Freinkel

Until a year or two ago, the biggest question most researchers had about hormone replacement therapy was why more women weren't taking advantage of it. After all, here was a treatment that was known to stave off some of the worst illnesses and indignities of age: brittle bones and soaring cholesterol, not to mention hot flashes and other annoyances of menopause. And it was believed to have the power to prevent heart disease and Alzheimer's. Yet only about a third of women who might benefit were availing themselves of HRT.

How things change. Now a number of unsettling new studies have experts asking a whole host of questions. For starters, they're wondering whether estrogen does indeed protect the heart—or actually harms it. They're wondering if its brain benefits are all they're cracked up to be. And more are questioning whether HRT's breast cancer risk has finally proven to be so high as to outweigh its benefits.

As if matters weren't complicated enough, most women considering HRT come to the table with more than a single issue to throw into the mix. What if you're at risk for osteoporosis *and* heart disease? What if you're suffering horrendous hot flashes, but you also lost a mother and a sister to breast cancer? These days, you need more hands than a Hindu goddess to juggle all the relevant factors.

Enter Nananda Col, a congenial Boston internist with a new approach for navigating the HRT dilemma. As a resident, she'd been frustrated by her inability to advise patients who wondered if they should be taking hormones. "All I could say was, 'I don't know,'" she recalls with a laugh.

Over the next three years, she and her colleagues sifted through more than a hundred studies to develop a mathematical model to predict how any given woman may fare with, or without, hormone replacement therapy. To determine that, Col enters a woman's medical history into her computer. After churning it through the database, the computer spits out a personalized report predicting the woman's odds of developing heart disease, breast cancer, or a hip fracture in the next ten years and over the

photographs
by heidi wells

Linda Birdsong

stay healthy

course of her lifetime—and how HRT might raise or lower those odds. The report doesn't make recommendations; its primary purpose is to help women discuss the decision with their doctors, says Col, who plans to make the program available to physicians.

Col's model isn't perfect, drawing as it does on research that is less than perfect. "We're only now doing studies that should have been done 30 years ago," says V. Craig Jordan, an eminent hormone researcher at Northwestern University Medical School. The biggest study—the Women's Health Initiative, which is tracking 27,000 women taking either hormones or placebo pills—should bring some of the sorely needed answers. But its results aren't due until 2005 at the earliest.

Sadly, we can't put our bodies on hold for four years until science catches up. So in the meantime, we decided to follow three women who turned to Col for help in sorting out the pros and cons of hormone replacement therapy.

linda birdsong

LINDA BIRDSONG'S PERIODS began to taper off when she was 47. At first she just had an occasional hot flash or two, but soon she was waking at night drenched in sweat, visiting the dry cleaners a couple of times a week, and stocking her home and office with paper fans. Then came the loss of her libido. "My husband and I used to have super-duper sex," she says. "Now I have to work a lot harder at it."

Still, while she could live with what menopause was doing to her body, she couldn't bear what it was doing to her psyche.

"I was nuts," says Birdsong. "I've never had a nervous breakdown, but I think that's how it must feel." A confident, optimistic, even boisterous person by nature, she became increasingly insecure, withdrawn, and mistrustful. She wept for no reason, accused coworkers of plotting against her, and picked fights with her husband. Finally, her doctor suggested one of the standard hormone regimens, and within weeks she felt nearly her old self again. "I hate taking pills," she says, "but this one is my salvation."

That kind of turnaround is typical for women with severe menopausal symptoms; nothing quells hot flashes and mood swings like estrogen. (The hormone also treats problems like vaginal dryness and incontinence, but once a woman stops taking it, those symptoms return.)

Birdsong had some nagging concerns about the treatment's possible health dangers, however, so she turned to Col. According to her report, Birdsong is unlikely to ever find herself with heart disease (she has a 12 percent risk of developing it in her lifetime) or breast cancer (8 percent). She also learned that she has a 26 percent chance of fracturing a hip as she gets older, and that long-term hormone therapy could reduce that danger to a less-worrisome 14 percent.

How did all that add up? Birdsong could benefit from short-term use of HRT to alleviate symptoms of menopause but could postpone long-term use.

Even critics say HRT is safe to use short-term. The breast cancer risks don't kick in unless you take it for five years or more.

And because of recent discoveries about how estrogen acts on bones, Birdsong didn't need to commit herself to HRT for the long haul to stave off osteoporosis. One of the most exciting findings of the last few years is that women can delay treatment and their bones will still benefit.

"The ideal time to consider doing something is around age 65," says Bruce Ettinger, a researcher at Kaiser Permanente in Oakland, California. "That's close to the point when fractures start, but it leaves enough time for HRT to have a significant effect on bone density." Another reason to wait is that it's now become clear that the bone mass gained with estrogen lasts only five to ten years after a woman stops taking it. So if you start on hormones at 50, you'll have to stay on them a good long while if protecting your skeleton is the goal.

Anne Coviello

These findings have prompted a new therapy strategy: short-term use for symptoms, then periodic reevaluations as risks change over time. Breast cancer, heart disease, and osteoporosis are all less likely to strike the average woman when she's in her fifties than later in life. The risk for heart disease only begins to climb in her sixties, and it isn't until her seventies that bone fractures begin to loom as a significant danger. Ettinger's recommendation: Reconsider your decision to use long-term hormone therapy every ten years.

That approach works for Birdsong, especially since Col's report said she's not in any immediate danger. For now, she's happy to have found something that gets her safely through the first few crazy-making years of menopause. "It was reassuring to have someone say, 'Linda, it's okay to take the HRT.'"

anne coviello

AROUND THE TIME Anne Coviello first realized she was entering menopause, her older sister discovered she had breast cancer. "You already feel lousy when you're

mind over
MENOPAUSE

These days, women bothered by menopausal symptoms tend to travel down one of two paths. They either talk to their doctors about hormone replacement therapy, or they visit an alternative practitioner or a health food store to stock up on black cohosh and other nonmedical treatments.

But the Mind-Body Medical Institute in Boston offers the best of both worlds. Over the course of ten weeks, women get advice on everything from hormones to midlife crises. During one session, a physician covers HRT; in another, a dietitian demonstrates how to add plant estrogens to your diet with soy smoothies and tofu stir-fries.

"We offer it all," says Alice Domar, the Harvard psychologist who founded the program. "Medical advice, tips on diet and exercise, stress relief, and emotional support through services like group therapy and prayer."

In the late 1980s, Domar began running mind-body seminars for infertility patients. She was stunned when women started getting pregnant: 34 percent of them, at a time when the average success rate was around 18 percent. (In Domar's most recent study, an astonishing 55 percent of couples conceived.)

Soon after, she decided to offer a three-week trial program for women experiencing menopause. "The patients loved it so much, they insisted on a fourth session," Domar says. Even in that short a time, their symptoms improved.

Eventually, Domar took a closer look at the effect of relaxation on 33 menopausal or perimenopausal women, each of whom was suffering at least five hot flashes daily. (None of the women were using HRT.) Domar had some of the women listen to a relaxation tape each day, while others read for the same amount of time, and still others (the controls) made no changes at all. After seven weeks, the women practicing relaxation techniques experienced a nearly 30 percent drop in the intensity of their hot flashes and a significant decrease in tension, anxiety, and depression.

How does relaxation quell hot flashes? No one knows for certain. Physiologically, hot flashes look similar to the fight-or-flight response that can be triggered by stress. Your heart pounds, your breathing speeds up, and stress hormones course through your body. "These same things happen during a hot flash," Domar says, "and we also know stress can induce hot flashes. So it seems logical that relieving stress might make them less intense—or even keep them from occurring."

Studies have shown that relaxation techniques may ease insomnia, moodiness, and other menopausal symptoms. Domar's program also offers targeted psychological help for women whose menopause triggers a deeper emotional crisis. Often these troubles are compounded by what's going on in a woman's life—career frustrations, say, or an aging and increasingly needy parent.

"Many women are down on themselves when they come in here," explains Ann Webster, a health psychologist and codirector of the program. "Their bodies are changing, and they don't like how they look or feel. Our goal is to help these women weather the transition."

—ALICE LESCH KELLY

going through menopause," she says. "But with my sister's situation on top of that, I started wondering if the sun would ever shine again."

Her sister did not survive. After that, Coviello's hot flashes worsened until they were coming every 20 minutes around the clock. But when her doctor suggested hormone therapy, Coviello said no. She'd also lost an aunt to breast cancer, and she was convinced she'd be next. "The risk was just too great," says the 56-year-old suburban Boston homemaker.

Indeed, fear of breast cancer is one of the main reasons women shun estrogen. How serious is the danger? Experts have been debating that for years. As early as 1992, evidence showed that going on estrogen raises a woman's chances of developing the disease. But today many women take estrogen with another hormone, progestin. Progestin protects against estrogen's cancer-causing effects in the uterus, and many experts had hoped it might work the same trick in breast tissue as well.

No such luck, according to recent studies. Last spring, after interviewing 1,900 postmenopausal breast cancer patients and 1,600 postmenopausal healthy women, University of Southern California researchers announced that those who had used the combined therapy for more than five years had a 24 percent higher risk of breast cancer compared with women who had taken no hormones—nearly four times that of the women taking estrogen alone. Another study pegged the risks even higher.

The numbers sound scary. But Col says the increase is actually quite subtle. A woman at average risk for breast cancer has an 11 percent chance of developing the disease over the course of her lifetime. A 24 percent jump pushes that risk to only about 14 percent.

It may be another story, however, for someone whose risk starts out higher than average. Few experts would recommend HRT for a woman who's already had breast cancer, for instance. And they might hesitate if she has several of the recognized risk factors, such as delayed childbearing (or having had no children), early onset of menstruation (before age 11), or first-degree relatives (a mother, sister, or daughter) who had breast cancer before reaching menopause.

Coviello was happily surprised to learn she wasn't in that category. Partly because her aunt was a second-degree relative and her sister was 64 when she was diagnosed, her lifetime chances of developing the disease were only a little higher than average, at 16 percent. According to Col's model, HRT could raise that risk to 22 percent. "I still know breast cancer is in my family," Coviello says, "but it's not like I'm next."

Equally surprising, Coviello discovered her most significant risk was one she hadn't considered. According to Col's report, she stands a 34 percent chance of breaking a hip, which HRT could reduce to 19 percent.

Several factors put her at risk for osteoporosis, starting with her age and the fact that she's Caucasian. (Anyone who is underweight, smokes or drinks heavily, or has a family history of the disease is also at risk.) But the most significant factor is a 1991 bone scan that showed signs of thinning in her bones.

That doesn't mean Coviello has to take immediate action. Like Birdsong, she has the option of delaying hormone treatment. What's more, recent findings have prompted Ettinger and others to start putting patients on lower doses of estrogen—about half, or even a quarter, of the amount typically prescribed. Such doses won't tame hot flashes, he says, but they do protect bones.

And these aren't the only alternatives available to women. The last few years have seen the arrival of estrogen mimics—drugs like raloxifene—that deliver many of estrogen's benefits but with few of the risks. Raloxifene has been shown to raise bone density by 2 to 3 percent (about half as much as estrogen), reduce the incidence of bone fractures by 40 percent, and improve cholesterol levels. And in one study, it actually cut the risk of breast cancer by a stunning 76 percent. So-called bone-only drugs, like fosomax and the nasal spray miacalcin, also build up bones that are already dangerously thin.

Coviello hopes none of these medications is in her future, and she's doing everything she can to strengthen her bones without them: taking calcium and vitamin D, eating better, and going for daily walks. (Luckily, her hot flashes have died down.) But she also plans to have another bone scan to see if the thinning has gotten worse. "If it looks like a hip fracture is a real possibility," she says, "that's when I'll consider HRT."

judy frazier

LONG BEFORE HER PERIODS STOPPED, Judy Frazier became interested in hormone therapy because of reports touting its power to protect the brain. Staying sharp is critical to Frazier, a nurse who oversees nutrition research. Also, while the women in her family tend to live long, her mother spent her last years in a fog of stroke-induced dementia. "I'm single," explains the 53-year-old Frazier. "I want to stay cognizant enough to take care of myself."

There's been much debate about whether estrogen actually protects the brain, however. There are data suggesting that women who take the hormone can cut their risk of Alzheimer's by 40 to 60 percent. And the notion makes sense: Among other things, estrogen seems to boost levels of chemicals that help neurons live longer and that deliver messages between brain cells.

But researchers were disappointed last spring when a study showed that estrogen didn't delay the progress of Alzheimer's in women with the disease. "That was a surprise," says Stanley Birge, an Alzheimer's researcher at Washington University School of Medicine in St. Louis. But it's not the end of the story, given the pile of data suggesting other brain benefits. And, of course, all eyes remain on the Women's Health Initiative.

While Frazier's initial interest in hormone therapy was spurred by her concerns about dementia, her report from Col turned up some revelations about other health risks. For one thing, it showed she runs a 34 percent risk of sustaining a hip fracture. Frazier wasn't overly concerned. "I'm tall, I'm not lean, I move around a lot, and I've taken calcium for decades," she says.

Another risk, which she didn't dismiss so easily, was heart disease. Heart attacks had claimed all the men on her father's side and both grandparents, plus aunts and uncles on her mother's side. Also, she had gained 30 pounds in the last ten years, and her cholesterol levels had crept way up.

Frazier knew her family history, of course, and she was well aware of her increasing pants size. But there's knowing and there's *knowing*, so the report from Col was jolting. "I didn't think I had that kind of risk, but the numbers tell the story," says Frazier. And the story was that she had a 17 percent chance of developing heart disease. By Col's reckoning, hormone therapy could lower that to 11 percent.

Or could it? Of all the factors in the HRT calculation, the one involving heart disease has become the most controversial.

For decades, researchers were convinced estrogen was a woman's best chance of protection against heart disease, thanks to its ability to improve the ratio of good to bad cholesterol and to dilate

do you have a
STRONG SKELETON?

After examining more than 1,200 postmenopausal women, scientists at Merck and Company discovered that just six questions could determine who would most benefit from a bone scan. If you're worried about brittle bones, take this test.

Are you African American? Though not all experts are convinced, many studies suggest that African Americans are at lower risk.

Yes	0
No	5

Do you have rheumatoid arthritis? This condition, along with the corticosteroid drugs used to treat it, can deplete bones.

Yes	4
No	0

Have you had a fracture of the wrist, hip, or rib since you turned 45? In older women fractures at these vulnerable spots may indicate bone trouble, but in younger ones they may simply result from an active lifestyle.

I'm younger than 45.   0

I'm older, but haven't had a fracture since age 45.   0

I'm older than 45, and I've had at least one break at ___* of these spots.
   *Multiply this number by 4 and enter here: ___

What is your age? _____* The older you get, the likelier you are to have thin bones.
*Multiply the first digit by 3 and enter here: ___

If postmenopausal, have you ever taken supplemental estrogen? This hormone helps shore up bone.

Yes	0
No	1

ADD UP YOUR SCORE TO THIS POINT: _____

What is your weight? _____* At last, a reason to love your love handles: Bone density is directly proportional to weight in women of all ages.
   *Divide this number by 10, round to the nearest whole number, and
   subtract it from the subtotal above for YOUR FINAL SCORE: _____

If you scored higher than 6, ask your doctor about a bone density scan. But don't panic: In Merck's study, only half of those with a high score had osteoporosis. On the other hand, a low score doesn't guarantee sturdy bones. (For one thing, the test omits risk factors that may be more influential in younger women.) Whatever your score, the sooner you start tending to your bones, the longer they'll last.

blood vessels and keep them supple. The idea helped explain why women tend to develop heart disease 10 to 15 years later than men. And according to more than 30 observational studies in which researchers looked at causes of death among women who took hormones and those who didn't, it appeared that estrogen could decrease the risk of heart disease by as much as 50 percent.

So experts were shocked two years ago by the results of the so-called HERS study, the first randomized clinical trial of hormone therapy. HERS researchers asked 2,700 women with heart disease to take either hormones or a placebo for four years. The finding: The women who were on hormones had just as many heart attacks, strokes, and other coronary complications as did the ones who weren't. "We were so surprised that we asked a lab to analyze the pills we were sending out to make sure we hadn't made a mistake," says one of the authors, Deborah Grady, an epidemiologist at the University of California at San Francisco.

The conclusion was backed by another study last spring that compared images of the arteries of women with heart disease who were taking HRT with those who were taking a placebo. There was no significant difference between the groups in how much the women's heart vessels narrowed over a three-year period.

Of course, the more important question is whether estrogen can protect healthy women like Frazier from developing heart disease. Unfortunately, early results from the Women's Health Initiative are not encouraging.

Last spring, researchers announced that participants taking hormones suffered a slightly higher number of heart attacks, strokes, and blood clots during the first two years of the study than did those not on hormone replacement therapy. But the increase seemed to level out after the two years, according to the study's codirector, Jacques Rossouw, who insists it's still too early to draw any conclusions about HRT's long-term heart benefits.

Others are increasingly dubious, though. Why push this unproven approach, they ask, when there are risk-free ways to reduce your chance of a heart attack? A woman can always try statins, for instance, a class of drugs that have been proven to safely lower cholesterol. Or better still, says Francine Grodstein, an epidemiologist at Harvard University School of Public Health, "if you can exercise, eat healthy, and not smoke, you can get the benefits attributed to HRT."

What ultimately made Frazier decide against HRT was her history of blood clots. It's long been known that estrogen can raise the risk of clots about threefold, and the condition can be fatal.

Twenty-five years ago, Frazier suffered a clot deep in her left leg when she tumbled off her bicycle. She remembered how painful it felt and wasn't willing to chance another, especially one that might lodge in her lungs or her brain. For now, she says, she'll rely on exercise and diet to protect her heart and mind—and wait for better pills.

the protective power of the
disease-fighting four

Which supplements work? As vitamins
spill off the shelves and health claims fly,
experts target the real guardian angels.

By Peter Jaret

If you've shopped for a bottle of vitamins lately, you know
the problem. Never mind that you have to choose between
tablets, capsules, and liquids made for men, women, children, or vegetarian athletes who've turned 50. You're quickly
confronted with products like Mega-Life Plus Advanced Formula
II and Mother Nature's Eco-Sensitive Vitamin Support System.
Beside those stand jar upon jar of not-quite-identical multivitamins. Peering at the fine print, you find that some contain 100
percent of the recommended daily doses, while others hold 150,
300, 500 percent, or more.

So what's best? The old thinking about meeting your body's
needs doesn't apply anymore. "We used to set levels just high
enough to prevent nutritional deficiencies," says Robert Russell,
associate director of the Human Nutrition Research Center at Tufts
University in Boston. "Now we know that some vitamins at higher
doses may help lower the risk of many chronic diseases." Among
these illnesses are cancer and heart disease—the nation's leading
killers. Experts have raised the dose for folic acid, a B vitamin,
from 200 to 400 micrograms in light of evidence that it prevents
certain birth defects.

Yet some supplement makers tout outlandish benefits—and
charge accordingly. A month's supply of basic multis may cost less
than your morning coffee, while a jar of pumped-up pills can run
as much as a high-class dinner, with wine included.

Just which vitamins are worth your hard-earned dollars? If
you're seeking optimal protection, based on the latest and best
studies, you may want to reach for more than one pill. It all depends on who you are and how you live. But there are four that
you'd do well to consider.

a daily multivitamin

IF YOU AREN'T ALREADY TAKING ONE, stop and ask yourself
why. Yes, the best policy is a smart diet packed with whole grains,
fruits, and vegetables. But focus for now on just the B vitamins
that come loaded into every multi. Researchers have learned that

photographs
by james worrell

how to buy
VITAMINS

When it comes to supplements, it's easy to be suckered in by the promise of more: extra ingredients, larger doses, bigger health benefits. But what looks like a bonanza may really be a bunch of untested substances that serve only to empty your wallet. How to avoid the hype? Follow these tips for shopping wisely, and you could save enough in a year for a flight to Hawaii or a new dishwasher.

Check leading pharmacies They frequently offer the best deals to be had in any store, especially if you buy in bulk. You should be able to find 250-pill bottles of no-frills multivitamins for as little as $9. That's about a dollar a month, or less than four cents a pop. But reach for the fanciest formulations, and you could end up paying as much as $36 a month—a pocketbook-slimming $430 a year.

Log on to the Web But first browse at your favorite drugstore. Comparing supplements on the Internet can be confusing and frustrating because it's difficult to study labels side by side. So find a brand at the store with the right nutrient levels, then search the Web for a better deal. Good places to start are *www.drugstore.com*, *www.planetrx.com*, and *www.vitaminshoppe.com*. When you compare prices, be sure to factor in the cost of shipping and handling.

Skip the extras Avoid paying more for add-ons, such as beta-carotene (several large studies have shown that beta-carotene supplements don't deliver any health benefits) or arrays of fancy-sounding herbal extracts.   —P. J.

folic acid not only prevents birth defects but also helps keep down levels of homocysteine, an amino acid in the blood that's been linked to an added risk of heart attack and stroke. And while folic acid is the star, B-6 and B-12 also play significant roles.

Yet one in three women falls short on the Bs—and possibly pays a steep price. According to one recent study, older women whose blood levels of vitamin B-12 ran low were more likely than others to show hearing loss. Folic acid, meanwhile, may also fend off colon cancer. In a Harvard University study of 89,000 nurses, women who took supplements with folic acid for at least 15 years cut their colon cancer risk by 78 percent. You could pop a B complex, of course, but a multivitamin ensures that you're covering many nutritional bases.

WHAT'S BEST Choose a once-a-day with 100 to 150 percent of the recommended daily values for vitamins A through E, including folic acid. Heftier doses cost more, and if you need higher amounts of some nutrients, you're better off buying specific pills (read on about vitamins C, D, and E).

vitamin C

IF YOU CAN'T REMEMBER THE LAST TIME you peeled an orange, you may want to add a vitamin C tablet. The official advice calls for 75 milligrams a day for women, 90 mg for men, yet researchers now say we need more. The evidence comes from studies showing a diminished risk of stomach, colon, and lung cancers as well as lower heart disease rates among people who eat at least five servings of fruits and vegetables a day. The magic five, it turns out, deliver roughly 200 mg of C, says Mark Levine, a vitamin C expert at the National Institutes of Health.

Levine warns against relying on supplements, since the people who fared best in most of the cancer studies got their protection from vitamin-rich foods. Few of us, however, eat even four servings of fruits and veggies a day. If breakfast is coffee and a muffin, and lunch is a bagel with cream cheese, you'll almost certainly fall short of 200 when the day is done—whether you take a multi or not.

What else might sufficient C do? In 1997 researchers at Tufts University in Boston reported that women who took vitamin C for at least ten years were 77 percent less likely to show early signs of cataracts. There's also evidence that extra C can cut diabetics' heart disease risk and help people with asthma breathe easier in ozone-polluted air.

WHAT'S BEST Vitamin C is widely available in 500 mg pills, but it's worth hunting for 250s or chopping the big ones in half. Why? Because your body can use C only a bit at a time. Pop the smaller dose and you get all of it; swallow 500 mg of the stuff and you pee out a fourth of it. Besides, it's wise to be cautious. In 1998 the journal *Nature* reported that doses of vitamin C above 500 mg can damage D N A, raising concerns about cancer in people who take large amounts every day.

vitamin E

IF YOU'VE HAD MORE THAN YOUR SHARE of colds this year, you might want to swallow a vitamin E pill along with your multivitamin. In a 1999 study by Simin Meydani of Tufts University in Boston, people over 65 who took at least 200 international units (IU) of E a day for eight months were less likely than those who didn't to report coming down with colds and other infections.

What's more, a number of studies have shown that people who consume plenty of vitamin E are less likely to develop heart disease. The vitamin's value for those who already have the illness is debatable, however. A recent study of British women and men with cardiovascular disease found that subjects who took 400 to 800 IU each day cut their risk of having a second heart attack by 77 percent. But a long-term Canadian study found that E did *not* prevent heart attacks in people

what about
MINERALS?

Y ou don't need to think about most of them—even if your diet is less than saintly. But four deserve special attention. It's tough to get what you need from food and multivitamins, yet a shortfall could put you at higher risk for brittle bones, high blood pressure, anemia, and even cancer. To protect your health, think about boosting your intake of these key mineral warriors.

Calcium

DEFEND YOUR BONES Typically, a woman's diet delivers about half the calcium she needs in a day. Multivitamins often contain a small amount, but to hit the recommended daily 1,000 to 1,200 milligrams, you'll need a separate supplement. If you're over 65, take a pill composed of both calcium and vitamin D; they work together to protect bones. If you already get enough D (a multi plus two glasses of milk a day does the job), a cheaper alternative is to take an antacid such as Tums or Rolaids twice a day; check the label for the amount of elemental (usable) calcium in each tablet.

Iron

PUMP UP YOUR BLOOD Although the amount of iron in the usual multi—18 mg, or 100 percent of the daily value—is adequate for most people, women who are pregnant or nursing may need more (see your doctor). After menopause you may need *less*. Look for multivitamins designed for people over 50; these supplements usually have little or no iron. Some caution is warranted: One in eight Americans has a gene that causes its carrier to absorb extra iron from food—iron that can build up and raise the danger of a heart attack or organ damage. A blood test can tell you if you have this problem.

Potassium

CUT DOWN THE PRESSURE If you have high blood pressure, you may want more potassium than most multis offer. A review of 33 clinical trials showed that people with hypertension who take a potassium supplement can drop their readings by four or five points. If your blood pressure numbers are elevated, check with your doctor about whether you should take two 500 mg pills a day—one in the morning, one at night—to be sure you get at least 3,500 mg altogether.

Selenium

FIGHT AGAINST CANCER In a 1996 study at the University of Arizona, men and women who took 200 micrograms of selenium a day were less likely than others to get lung and colon cancers; the men also reduced their risk of prostate cancer. Though doubts persist, scientists recently reported that extra selenium cut lung cancer risk by up to 60 percent in a group of men and women in Finland. Some multis supply a smidgen; to get much more, you'll have to take a supplement. But don't go overboard. More than 800 mcg a day can cause fatigue, nausea, vomiting, and hair loss.   —P.J.

with heart disease. Even so, a daily 400 IU of E may still benefit the disease-free masses.

The official recommendation for vitamin E stands at 33 IU, and that's what most multivitamins supply. No single multi is big enough to hold much more, nor is it possible to get extra in food unless you guzzle vegetable oil or gobble nuts by the pound.

WHAT'S BEST Several studies point to 200 to 400 IU as the optimal daily dose. Some brands contain natural E, identified in the fine print as d-alpha tocopherol. Made from vegetable oil, natural E is absorbed more readily than synthetic, or dl-alpha tocopherol. The natural kind costs more, though. And since virtually every study showing benefits from vitamin E used the synthetic form, it's probably the wisest choice.

vitamin D

IF YOU'RE NOT AN AVID MILK DRINKER, you may need more vitamin D than you absorb from meals and multivitamins. Your bones will certainly support you in your decision. Get too little of the vitamin, and your body can't use the calcium in your food. What's more, D helps you hang on to the calcium that keeps your skeleton strong.

Milk, of course, is fortified with D, and your skin manufactures plenty when exposed to sunlight for just 10 to 15 minutes a few times a week. But if you're one of the many Americans who shun milk—and you live where the winters are dark and cloudy—you may sometimes run short. The likelihood rises as you age, since the body's ability to make vitamin D declines over time, passing a critical point at around 50.

A supplement can make a big difference. In a study at Johns Hopkins University School of Hygiene and Public Health, 389 men and women over 65 who for three years took vitamin D (700 IU per day) along with a calcium supplement (500 mg) significantly lowered their risk of suffering bone fractures.

WHAT'S BEST A standard multivitamin holds 400 IU of vitamin D, or about two-thirds of your daily requirement if you're one of the people at higher risk. The easiest way to make up the shortfall—and to cover your calcium needs—is to take a calcium supplement with 200 IU of vitamin D added. If you're sure you don't need the extra calcium, hunt for a jar of 200 IU vitamin D pills. (Try a health food store or shop online.)

Avoid taking a mix of supplements that adds up to more than 600 IU of D a day. At high levels it can lead to headaches, fatigue, kidney stones, and even calcified heart valves.

health note

bananas for bones

Calcium has a fresh sidekick. A new study concluded that people with the highest potassium intake had stronger bones than those who ate the least. Bananas, potatoes, spinach, and yogurt can help you reach the daily goal of 3,500 milligrams.

arm yourself with facts to
fight cancer

What you don't know *can* hurt you.
So find out the latest on the big three
cancers: colon, ovarian, and breast.

Cancer. The word lands on the page with a thud. But the illness itself is stealthy, often giving no clear sign of its presence until it has spread too far to be easily treated. So how do you fend off this intruder? Begin by learning as much as possible about the danger signals and the steps you can take to protect yourself.

Just by making some simple lifestyle changes, you may be able to improve your odds against certain forms of the disease, including one of the most common—colon cancer. Starting on this page, you'll see tips on how to do that.

There's less information on preventing ovarian cancer, and the tests for it are imprecise or invasive. You may need help figuring out your risk so that you can decide whether and how to be screened. On page 104, we shed some light on the risk factors for the disease and the pros and cons of available tests.

Although mammograms and self-exams for breast cancer are helpful detection measures, they aren't foolproof. Researchers continue to improve prevention methods, tests, and treatments. You'll find their latest discoveries on page 108.

Reading about cancer may be difficult. But think of it this way: A few minutes now may add years to your life.

photograph

by david martinez

keys to preventing
colon cancer

NO ONE LIKES to talk about colon cancer, but the statistics practically scream. About 48,000 Americans die of the disease each year, making it the second deadliest cancer overall. Among women, only lung and breast cancers take more lives.

As if that's not bad enough, last year doctors learned that their most highly touted dietary weapon against colon cancer is probably a dud. For years medical experts insisted that high-fiber diets lowered the risk of this disease. But in 1999, after examining the diets of almost 89,000 female nurses, scientists at Harvard found that the amount of fiber the nurses ate *didn't* affect their risk for developing colon tumors. And other studies showing that fiber does not prevent colon cancer soon followed. (It's not time to give

up your bran muffins, though; fiber still guards against heart disease.)

Ready for some good news? There's a lot of it. Screening tests for the disease are so sensitive that they can detect growths in the colon, called polyps, before they turn cancerous. Even better, though fiber turned out to be a false hope, scientists have identified crucial lifestyle changes that do lower the odds of getting colon cancer. The big payoff: If all Americans were regularly tested, and if they followed the preventive tips outlined below, the number who die of this cancer would be cut in half.

jump out of your chair

ACTIVE PEOPLE ARE LESS LIKELY than couch potatoes to develop colon tumors. Why? No one knows for sure, but the link between lack of exercise and a higher risk of colon cancer could be certain hormonelike compounds called prostaglandins. Sedentary people have higher levels of prostaglandins in their colons than do people who exercise, and colon polyps and tumors contain high levels of the substances. It's possible that these compounds may stimulate cancer growth. A daily half-hour jog, one-hour walk, or similar regimen is all it takes to keep prostaglandin levels in check.

pop a key pill

RESEARCHERS ASKED THOSE SAME 89,000 nurses about their use of multivitamins and came to an astonishing conclusion: Women who popped one each day were 75 percent less likely to develop colon cancer than women who didn't. Of the two dozen or so vitamins and minerals packed into a typical multi, one stands out as the probable wonder-worker: folic acid. Several studies support the theory that this nutrient prevents genetic mutations that lead to the formation of cancerous cells. You can get folic acid from a number of foods—orange juice, leafy greens, and fortified grains and breakfast cereals are good sources—but taking a daily multivitamin guarantees a large, steady dose of this stellar nutrient.

eat less of this

STUDY AFTER STUDY shows that eating too much red meat increases your odds of developing colon cancer. The culprit? It could be the saturated fat in red meat or the carcinogens that are produced when meat is cooked at a high temperature, or both. If you do eat lamb, beef, or pork, make it an occasional treat: no more than three small servings per week.

stay healthy

pour yourself a tall one

CALCIUM APPEARS TO BIND with carcinogens in the intestines and escort them out of the body. So get plenty of this mineral from milk and other low-fat dairy products, or take 1,200 milligrams a day in supplements.

Other substances also appear to affect risk. Women on estrogen replacement therapy have lower rates of colon cancer. And there's evidence that drinking a lot of water cuts your odds of getting the disease. People who drink alcohol or smoke, though, have higher rates of colon cancer than do teetotalers and nonsmokers.

don't be shy

ONLY A SMALL MINORITY OF WOMEN—less than one-third—gets screened for colon cancer. That's too bad, because such tests offer a double benefit. First, finding malignant tumors at an early stage dramatically improves the odds of survival. And second, during two of the tests, doctors can identify and remove benign polyps before they turn malignant.

The standard recommendation is to have two tests on a regular basis, starting at age 50. The simplest is the fecal occult blood test, which screens for traces of blood in the stool, a possible sign of polyps or tumors in the colon. This exam alone can reduce the risk of dying from colon cancer by 33 percent; you should do it every year.

Every five years you should also have a flexible sigmoidoscopy. In this indelicate procedure, for which you may be lightly sedated, a doctor inserts a lighted scope to view the lower colon. Any suspicious growths are removed and examined. According to one study, this procedure cuts the incidence of colon cancer by 42 percent and the risk of death by half.

If the results of either test hint at disease, your doctor will probably order a colonoscopy or a barium enema. The former is like a sigmoidoscopy, except that it allows a view of the entire colon; because it's more invasive, you'll be more heavily sedated. The latter involves an X-ray exam that looks for unusual masses in the colon. (You'll be given an enema beforehand containing barium, a metallic compound, to make those masses visible.)

As an added precaution, most guidelines suggest getting a colonoscopy or a barium enema every ten years after age 50. People with a close relative (a sibling or a parent) who has had colon cancer should start tests earlier than age 50—some experts say as young as 35. Doctors also like to keep a close eye on colon cancer survivors, using a colonoscopy as often as every three years.

These tests are nobody's idea of a good time. But think what a few moments of discomfort every five or ten years can buy you.

—TIMOTHY GOWER

should you be tested for
ovarian cancer?

OVARIAN CANCER is particularly frightening—for good reason. Symptoms of the illness are vague, and the tests for it are unreliable. Yet in the United States, ovarian cancer strikes one woman in 58, and more than half of those who get it die within five years. It kills more women than all the other gynecological cancers combined. That doesn't have to be the case: If the disease is caught in stage I, when it's confined to the ovaries, a woman has a 95 percent chance of long-term survival. But only about one case in four is detected early, and that's usually due to luck.

Most often, symptoms appear only after the cancer has spread through the abdomen or beyond, when survival rates drop steeply. About 60 percent of women diagnosed with ovarian cancer have advanced disease, and only 28 percent of them are alive five years later. Clearly, women at high risk should consider being tested for the illness. The question is, how do you know you're at risk? And how do you decide which tests are appropriate?

assessing the danger

AFTER DECADES OF RESEARCH, scientists still don't know what causes ovarian cancer, but they surmise that it has to do with incessant ovulation. Every month an ovary erupts, releases an egg, and heals. If a woman has no children and doesn't use birth control pills, she will weather perhaps 444 rupture-and-repair cycles by her 50th birthday. In some women the repair mechanism may break down, enabling abnormal cells to grow.

There are a few suspected risk factors. Women who have never or rarely given birth are more likely to develop ovarian cancer (but those who have used oral contraceptives for five years appear to cut their risk of the disease by half). Women whose mothers or sisters had the disease are at a higher risk. Breast cancer doubles the risk. And ovarian cancer is most prevalent in women over 55.

The vagueness of symptoms remains one of the biggest barriers to detection and survival. Fatigue, a generally lousy sensation, feeling full after eating very little—these "warning signs" are also common in healthy women. Even abdominal swelling, pelvic pressure, and gastrointestinal problems are easily ignored.

To add to the bad news, there is no good test for the disease. The problem is rooted in anatomy: The ovaries are small, well-armored organs floating in a cavernous space. A healthy ovary in a premenopausal woman measures about 5 cubic centimeters, roughly the size of an almond with its shell; an ovary in a post-menopausal woman is a little smaller. A cancerous ovary, even one that contains a billion cancer cells, may swell only to the size of a walnut. So it's little wonder that a routine pelvic exam rarely catches early-stage disease.

Pap smears don't pick it up, either. Even a surgeon looking at an ovary can't tell whether it's cancerous. The only way to know is to remove the ovary and send it to the lab for testing. Most women aren't willing to take such a draconian step.

evaluating the tests

IN FACT, THERE ARE TWO TESTS for ovarian cancer—a blood test and a vaginal ultrasound exam—but they aren't recommended for the average woman because they often give erroneous results.

The blood test measures levels of the CA-125 protein, which is secreted into the bloodstream by ovarian cancer cells. As it happens, though, CA-125 levels can be elevated by any number of factors, including pregnancy and menstruation. That's one of the frightening drawbacks of the test: It can convince healthy women that they have ovarian cancer. Some women get their ovaries taken out, in a procedure called an oophorectomy, only to find that they didn't have cancer after all.

The test's other major shortcoming: CA-125 levels can look normal in women who do have the disease. Studies have shown that the test detects early-stage ovarian cancer less than half the time.

Reliability of the blood test goes up if it's paired with an ultrasound exam. The procedure is much like the sonogram women have during pregnancy, except that instead of resting atop the belly, the probe goes into the vagina to get closer to the ovaries.

The ultrasound is better than CA-125 at detecting early-stage disease. But it can't distinguish between a malignant tumor and a benign growth. In one study, nine out of ten women who had their ovaries removed based solely on ultrasound results turned out not to have cancer. It's unclear, though, how many of those surgeries were truly unnecessary. Many of the "benign" growths showed signs of being precancerous. And without testing, far more cases of ovarian cancer would be missed.

shaking the family tree

JEWISH WOMEN OF EUROPEAN DESCENT, known as Ashkenazi Jews, are far more likely than other women to have a mutation in one of two genes, called BRCA-1 and BRCA-2 (for breast cancer 1 and breast cancer 2), which can predispose them to breast and

how to
TALK WITH YOUR DOC

Conversation, like the practice of medicine, is an art. And how well you've honed that art is critical when you're talking with a time-conscious doctor: You'll want to present information as efficiently and effectively as possible. To get the most from every doctor's exam, follow these tips adapted from *Don't Let Your HMO Kill You*, by Jason Theodosakis (Routledge, 2000, $15).

Make eye contact Your doctor may walk into the room reading your chart. Don't start talking until he or she looks up.

Paint the big picture When you describe your symptoms, always start with the general and then narrow down to specifics. That is how the doctor has been taught to think.

Begin with feelings Move from subjective information (what you feel) to the objective (facts you can see, count, or touch). Your doctor's thoughts move in this direction, too.

Describe the effects Be sure to talk about how your problem affects your life; if it interferes with work, sleep, relationships, or anything else that's important to you, let your doctor know. Doing so will help bring out the doctor's com-

passion and remind him that he's treating a person, not just an illness.

Take a breath or two Pausing every so often as you relate your medical history will give you time to collect your thoughts and your doctor time to take notes and ask questions. A note on note-taking: Just because your doctor's scribbling frantically doesn't mean she's not listening. It's actually a good sign that the information you're offering is useful. On the other hand, she might not take notes while you are talking about sensitive subjects. Don't worry; maybe she's just being sympathetic.

Don't expect reassurance Doctors don't say, "It's going to be okay," or "I'm sure it's nothing," until they're certain that's the case. They don't want to allay your fears only to have to break some bad news to you later.

ovarian cancers. Ashkenazi women with a family history of these cancers may want to have their genes checked.

The tests for this mutation are not for everyone. For one thing, they are expensive—$2,400 for an examination of every bit of the BRCA genes and $450 for a view of the section likely to hold a genetic error in an Ashkenazi woman.

Aside from the expense, the tests' results may present a woman with a torturous decision. If she has the faulty gene, she must consider prophylactic oophorectomy, taking out the ovaries before cancer has a chance to strike. Drastic as that seems, anyone with the mutation faces alarming odds if she relies on screening alone. For example, a recent study in England tracked 20,000 postmenopausal women who got blood tests for seven years, with ultrasound follow-up of abnormal results. Of 16 women in whom the tests found ovarian cancer, 11 already had advanced cases.

expanding the options

GIVEN THE FLAWS OF THE CURRENT screening tests for ovarian cancer, it's no surprise that many women choose to forgo these detection methods—and that some have their ovaries removed simply because they're in danger of getting the disease sometime in the future. But tests now under study may offer better choices.

One of the most promising is a simple blood test that measures levels of a protein called lysophosphatidic acid (LPA). Studies suggest that LPA is necessary for the growth of ovarian cancer cells, and it looks as if the protein can be detected early in the life of the cancer. Oncologist Maurie Markman, of the Cleveland Clinic, tried the blood test in 165 women with ovarian cancer. It flagged all the women whose cancer had spread and nine out of ten whose cancer was still confined to the ovaries.

Another sort of exam may someday ensure that no woman has her ovaries removed only to find they were healthy. The so-called ovarian pap smear is the brainchild of David Fishman, director of the Ovarian Cancer Early Detection Program at Chicago's Northwestern University Medical School. The test requires scraping the ovaries during laparoscopic surgery, then examining the cells under a microscope. Fishman and his colleagues recently collected tissue samples from 60 women who'd had their ovaries removed because of cancer or benign conditions. The researchers sent the ovaries to one pathologist and the scrapings to another. In each case, the diagnoses matched.

The ovarian pap smear is too invasive to become a routine test. But it could let women at high risk for the disease keep their ovaries intact.

—ALEXIS JETTER

<aside>
health note
a pill with punch
Acetaminophen may have an unexpected benefit: In one study, women who took the analgesic daily for ten years halved their odds of getting ovarian cancer. Though more research is needed, women at higher-than-average risk for the disease may want to consider this regimen.
</aside>

keeping current on
breast cancer

WHENEVER YOU HEAR of a friend diagnosed with breast cancer or chastise yourself for being late with a mammogram, you think: Why don't researchers figure this disease out?

Well, little by little, they are. Improvements ranging from sharper tests to better-aimed treatments are making their way out of the labs. Most of the progress involves tweaking methods already in use, but brand-new approaches are on the horizon as well. And even the steps that appear to be small can make big differences in detection and care.

In other words, there's plenty to get excited about. We asked the American Cancer Society, the National Cancer Institute, the Radiological Society of North America, and the Susan G. Komen Foundation to update us on the most encouraging developments of the last year.

sharper **mammography**

THE FOOD AND DRUG ADMINISTRATION has approved digital mammography, in which an X-ray image is converted into bits and bytes so that it can be viewed on a computer screen. The new technique appears to do as good a job as standard mammography of picking up cancer, and it produces fewer false positives—that is, it's less likely to suggest cancer where none actually exists. Experts hope that eventually digital mammography will also lower the number of cancers that radiologists miss. Another big advantage: It will allow women from remote areas to have their mammograms E-mailed to cancer centers, where they can be read by expert eyes.

earlier **early detection**

A WOMAN WHO HAS a high risk of breast cancer faces difficult decisions, such as whether to take tamoxifen, which can prevent a precancerous cell from multiplying but which carries real risks (it may increase the incidence of uterine cancer, cataracts, and blood clots, and in pregnant women it may harm the fetus). If she *knew* that her breast cells were starting down a wayward path, it might help her decide. A new test called ductal lavage may offer such information by gathering cells from the milk ducts, where all breast cancers originate. In the exam, a doctor checks to see whether any of a woman's ducts contain fluid; if one does, the doctor "washes" the duct with a salt-water solution, collecting a sample of breast cells that can be checked for precancerous changes. Ductal lavage should be avail-

---

health note
bonding to beat breast cancer

Women with breast cancer who join a support group improve their chances of beating the disease. These women appear to have lower levels of the stress hormone cortisol, which dampens the immune response, and higher amounts of a breast cancer antibody than do women without support.

stay healthy

able for high-risk women in up to 40 breast centers by the time you read this.

The test was developed by a team that included breast surgeon Susan Love, who discusses it in the latest edition of *Dr. Susan Love's Breast Book* (Perseus Publishing, 2000, $20).

better aim

SUCCESS RATES FOR BREAST CANCER drugs are going up as experts learn how to target treatments. Case in point: In 1998, clinicians started using an antibody called Herceptin for women with advanced cancer. Herceptin counteracts the effects of the HER2 gene, which produces a protein that speeds the growth of breast cancer cells. Recent studies, however, have found that the drug most benefits women with a lot of extra copies of the gene. Now doctors encourage such women to take Herceptin, but they warn others who have fewer copies of the gene that the drug probably won't help much. Herceptin is also being tested in women with early-stage cancer who produce a lot of the HER2 protein, in hopes of improving their chances of survival.

prevention equality

ONE LIMITATION OF the big tamoxifen prevention study of a few years back was that it included relatively few African Americans, leaving open the question of whether the drug is as effective for black women as for Caucasians. So researchers went further and analyzed nine studies in which tamoxifen therapy was given to breast cancer survivors—including a representative number of African Americans—with the aim of preventing cancer in the unaffected breast. The drug proved equally effective in black women and white. This finding reassures doctors that the use of tamoxifen should be race-blind when it comes to preventing the first occurrence of breast cancer as well.

help for hot flashes

WHEN BREAST CANCER SURVIVORS suffer from hot flashes—as a side effect of treatments, from chemotherapy-induced menopause, or during normal menopause—they often go without the relief of estrogen, the most effective remedy. The hormone is off-limits because of concern that it might promote a recurrence of the cancer. Other options may be on the way, however. This year, two small but promising studies found that the antidepressants Paxil and Effexor reduced the number and severity of hot flashes by at least 60 percent—greatly improving quality of life.

—LAURIE TARKAN

glad you asked

Answers to your questions about staying well

What's the best time to take vitamins and minerals—in the morning or at night? And should I take them with food or without?

The short answer: Whenever you'll remember to take them. The benefit of regularly swallowing a vitamin far outweighs that of timing it right. But if you can keep to a schedule, here are a few tips.

Taking a multivitamin with a meal helps your body absorb the nutrients. Iron pills, which are hard on the stomach, should also be taken with food. You'll retain more fat-soluble vitamin E if you wash it down with something slightly fatty, like a glass of milk. And divide calcium into small doses (300 milligrams or less); you'll soak up an extra 10 percent by taking it with a meal—*if* you avoid spinach, green beans, and wheat bran, which block absorption.

I've read that some candles have lead in their wicks. Is burning them risky?

It can be—especially if you have children.

Some candlewicks are stiffened with a strip of metal to ensure an even burn. That's fine if the metal is zinc or tin, but about 3 percent of candles sold today use lead.

The fumes pose the most risk to a child's developing brain. As lead burns, tiny bits waft through the air and are either inhaled or settle on objects that toddlers may then touch or put in their mouths. A recent study found that burning a lead-wicked candle for three hours in a poorly ventilated room produced enough lead to raise the level in a child's blood past the safety zone.

Luckily, it's easy to spot metal in the wick. You may end up tossing some candles, or you may opt to call the manufacturer to find out which type of metal's been used.

If you do burn candles with metal wicks, be sure that the room is well ventilated (but not drafty) and that kids don't play there.

I do the laundry for my family, and I was wondering: Can I get sick from handling dirty clothes?

Yes—if you're washing diapers or the clothing of someone who's sick. Germs can often survive warm and cold wash cycles.

E. coli and other nasty bacteria spread through feces can thrive inside home washing machines. And the machines tend to spread germs from one piece of clothing to others.

Washing clothes in hot water gets rid of bugs, but most people don't use the hot-water cycle. Your dryer kills most of the critters, though, so you're at the highest risk when you transfer a load of wet clothes from the washer to the dryer.

To reduce risk, wash underwear and baby clothes separately, and add a cup of bleach. Use the hot cycle when you can, and wash your hands after handling laundry. Finally, make your last load a bleach load to leave the washer disinfected.

A friend of mine suggested that I try acupuncture to treat my headaches. I'd like to try it, but I don't know much about it. Is it dangerous?

People most often ask whether acupuncture works, not whether it will injure them. But take heed: The technique does carry risks.

Researchers reached that conclusion after scouring the medical literature for cases in which patients were seriously hurt by the procedure. They discovered more than 110 serious injuries and four fatalities. The most frequent problem: the piercing of a patient's lung or tissue around a lung.

The news is not as bad as it sounds, however. The study covers 30-plus years, and all complications were caused by the practitioners' lack of skill. Major errors should virtually disappear as training and credentialing become more rigorous; most states now require practitioners to pass an exam.

You can do a lot to avoid becoming a statistic. First, seek a licensed practitioner who is a physician or has trained at an accredited school. Then ask how much experience the practitioner has with the desired procedure. Last, to avoid infectious diseases, make sure the practitioner uses disposable needles.

When I was cleaning out my cabinets, I found some medications that are slightly past their expiration dates. Are they still potent?

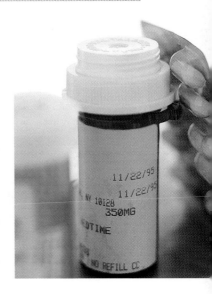

Maybe. The FDA recently tested drugs in the military's stockpile of expired medicines, and found that many of the drugs were safe and effective long past the dates on the bottles.

But before you start popping old pills, hold on a moment. Your drug-storage habits probably don't meet military code. The FDA tested only drugs that had been stored in ideal (cool, dry) conditions and had never been opened; in most homes, medicines are kept in steamy bathrooms or stashed in a purse.

So for now, stick to the dates; aside from losing potency, some drugs become dangerous over time. Other safety tips: Get rid of the cotton; it can become a haven for fungus. Clean out the medicine cabinet monthly. If you've got curious kids or pets, don't put unused drugs out with the trash. And don't flush them down the toilet. Instead, take them to your pharmacy for safe disposal.

DAVID PRINCE

I've heard that holding a grudge can actually be harmful to your health. Is there any truth to that idea?

It sounds odd, but if you don't let go of hurt feelings, you may end up hurting your heart.

One recent study tracked subjects' blood pressure and heart rate as they discussed being betrayed by a parent, friend, or lover. As interviews started, blood pressure shot up for all participants. But the levels for those who had forgiven soon returned to normal; grudge-holders' readings stayed high, placing strain on their hearts. Curiously, women were more likely than men to be unforgiving.

So next time you harbor a resentment, remember: Forgiveness is not only good for your mind—it's also good for your body.

PHOTOGRAPH BY AMY NEUNSINGER

eat well

We're a big Italian family. We cook;
there's no microwave stuff. We buy it.
We clean it. We cook it. There's 14 of
us for dinner every Sunday. It's all fresh,
all Italian stuff, to keep the tradition
going. It's very important to us. —*tina*

I used to hate water. New York water,
Mississippi water, North Carolina
water, I don't care what type of water.
I hated water. But now I put a little
fresh-squeezed lemon juice in, and
I drink it. —*martha*

I take myself out to dinner and order
whatever I want. Fanciest restaurant I can find.
I get a really good meal, a really good glass
of wine. It's just me. Nobody's yipping, yapping.
It's fulfilling. —*christine*

from china and its neighbors,
the healthiest diet

The simple, delicious meals Asians have eaten for centuries hold disease-fighting secrets we can all take to heart.

By Ingfei Chen

Salem, Massachusetts, is vintage New England, with its prim colonial houses, a harbor teeming with sailboats, and fresh lobster and seafood to whet your appetite everywhere you go. It isn't quite the first locale that would leap to mind, though, if you happen to be craving a taste of chow mein or moo shu pork. But step inside Nina Simonds's cozy red brick home, and you'll find you've come to just the right place.

Simonds, a sociable 47-year-old with a husky voice, is an authority on Asian cuisine. In 1972, at age 19, she journeyed to Taiwan for several years of study in Chinese food, language, and culture. It was the start of a lifelong love affair—one that has inspired her to write seven cookbooks.

On this particular evening, Simonds has prepared a small feast for her husband and a few hungry guests. Company includes Walter Willett, head of the nutrition department at the Harvard School of Public Health, who's nibbling on boiled *edamame,* or soybeans. Willett and his associates run the influential Harvard nurses' and health professionals' nutrition studies.

Helping himself to grilled shiitake mushrooms is Guohua Cao, a biochemist at the USDA Human Nutrition Research Center on Aging at Tufts University in Boston. A native of southern China, Cao works in a lab that grinds up fruits and veggies to study potential disease-fighters called phytochemicals.

Willett and Cao have come here not only to enjoy a fine meal, but to hash over a subject dear to Simonds's heart: the health benefits of Chinese and other Asian cuisines. In the land of the Great Wall and its neighbors, meals go light on fat and oil. Dishes typically showcase neither steak nor chicken breast, but humble vegetables transformed with a dash of spices. In short, Asian kitchens hold an ancient secret that could benefit us all: how to eat more veggies, less meat, and less artery-clogging fat with meals that are quick, simple—and mouthwatering.

The rewards go well beyond satisfying anybody's inner gourmand. According to a long-running study by researchers at Cornell University in Ithaca, New York, the traditional cuisines of Asia have helped to protect its peoples from many kinds of chronic ill-

photograph
by brooke slezak

nesses. Indeed, Cornell nutritional biochemist T. Colin Campbell, the project's director, thinks that the Asian style of eating is even more healthful than the much-touted Mediterranean diet.

SCIENTISTS HAVE KNOWN FOR YEARS that the most troublesome health problems plaguing westerners—heart disease, diabetes, obesity, and cancers of the breast, colon, and prostate—are far less common in China and Japan. For every five American women who die of heart trouble, only one Chinese woman suffers the same fate. The disease kills 17 times more middle-aged men in the United States—and roughly 9 times more men in Italy or Greece—than in China. And China has the lowest rate of breast cancer in the world.

These differences aren't just a matter of having the right genes. Asians born in the United States wind up with about the same health risks Americans face.

The rigors of farming life in China no doubt keep the body trim and hale, and even city office workers there pedal their bicycles everywhere. But if activity helps keep Asians healthy, diet also plays a crucial role.

In China, for instance, eating foods in the proper combination is seen as the key to health. "Food is a passion in Asia," says Simonds. "What fascinates me is this idea of balance in the diet." And with that, she ushers her guests into a comfy dining nook where a tasty salmon salad waits. She then tosses together a stir-fry of bok choy hearts (for the recipes, see page 120).

The Chinese style of eating is known as *fan tsai*. The heart of each meal is the *fan,* typically rice or wheat noodles. Side dishes of steamed or stir-fried *tsai,* or veggies, liven up the repast. Meat is used sparingly.

In the early eighties the Cornell scientists wondered whether fan tsai dining could explain China's lower rates of certain cancers. Campbell and Chen Junshi, a nutritionist from Beijing, realized rural China was the perfect place to find out. Most rural Chinese ate the same simple fare all their years. Coastal dwellers were blessed with fresh seafood, and a minority of northerners supped on beef and dairy foods. Rates of cancer and chronic illnesses varied considerably between counties.

In 1983 and again in 1989, Campbell, Chen, and colleagues at Oxford University surveyed 6,500 households in 65 counties across China. (The second sweep added 1,900 people in Taiwan.) The first survey revealed that about 70 percent of calories come from carbohydrates and only 15 percent from fat. By comparison, the American diet is about 50 percent carbs and 34 percent fat. The Chinese consume three times more fiber and a third less protein than Americans do; in addition, 89 percent of their protein is from plant sources, whereas 70 percent of ours is from animal foods other than fish, such as meat and milk.

table talk

don't be bitter Do you shun strong-tasting fruits and vegetables? Too bad, since they're loaded with protective compounds. Now there's reason to try again: Researchers report that as women age, they're more receptive to bitter flavors, from greens to grapefruit.

LEIGH BEISCH

eat well

Comparisons among regions showed that the more fruits, veggies, and grains at the table (and the less meat and animal protein) the lower the rates of breast cancer and heart disease. When the intake of vitamin C and beta-carotene went up, the odds of getting lung and stomach cancers went down. While rural residents had an average cholesterol count of just 127—far below the U.S. level of 203—adding even a little meat to the diet tugged the levels upward. And though Chinese women got about half as much calcium as Americans do, osteoporosis was fairly uncommon.

The second survey confirmed the earlier numbers but also revealed a dark new trend: With the invasion of fast-food joints and TV, cities are seeing a rise in heart disease, obesity, and diabetes—the diseases of nutritional extravagance, as Campbell sees it. "China is really under threat," says Banoo Parpia, a research associate who works with Campbell.

SUPPER IS IN FULL SWING. Making the rounds are the bok choy in a hot and sour sauce, and spicy stir-fried chicken nestled in fresh lettuce leaves. Meanwhile, Simonds has passed a big serving bowl of white rice down the table.

"There is one aspect of Asian diets you have to be careful about," says Willett. "And that's the high carbohydrate intake."

Willett himself is a proponent of the olive-oil-drenched cuisine of Greece and Italy. In 1994 he helped build the traditional Mediterranean diet pyramid, which has since become a pillar in the dogma of good nutrition. A rival plan—an Asian diet pyramid based largely upon Campbell's work—made its debut in 1995.

Though Willett and Campbell disagree on which ethnic menu is better, both diets are clearly far healthier than the standard American one. Each is grounded in a wide base of grains, such as noodles, breads, and rice, and calls for generous daily servings of vegetables, legumes, fruits, and nuts. Both urge major cutbacks on red meat, which is a prime source of saturated fat and which

foods for
LIFELONG HEALTH

In ancient Chinese philosophy, foods are yin (cooling), yang (warming), or neutral, and the right mix is vital to good health. Nina Simonds, author of several Asian cookbooks, says this idea adds up to a balanced, flavorful way of eating. Peek inside her pantry of Asian staples for some age-old wisdom on food's healing powers—and a modern take from current research.

yin

CABBAGES Ancient wisdom: Aid digestion and calm inflammation, rashes, and eye irritation. Cooked cabbage helps stomachaches; bok choy broth soothes ulcers.

New view: Cabbages are loaded with tumor-fighting compounds. Sulforaphane cranks up production of enzymes that help rid the body of carcinogens, and indole-3-carbinol may slow the abnormal growth of breast cells.

SOY Ancient wisdom: Fermented black soybeans are used to treat lung and digestive problems. Tofu is given for vomiting, intoxication, and high blood pressure.

New view: Soy seems to lower high cholesterol levels and may help explain Asia's low rates of breast and prostate cancer. Soy's isoflavones, plant estrogens with antioxidant powers, also may strengthen bones and ease menopausal symptoms.

TEA Ancient wisdom: Helps digestion, purges toxins, and clears the mind. Given for colds, diarrhea, and hangovers.

New view: Tea compounds may ward off cancer and heart disease. In one study, precancerous mouth sores shrank in patients treated with tea; in another, drinking black tea daily nearly halved people's odds of getting severe atherosclerosis.

yang

CHILES Ancient wisdom: Hot foods boost appetite and stimulate the heart, spleen, and stomach. A paste of pepper and ginger is applied to calm swollen, arthritic joints.

New view: Capsaicin from peppers is used in creams to relieve arthritis pain. It defuses carcinogens and slows growth of cancer cells. Chiles stimulate digestive juices that may shield the stomach lining from damage.

GARLIC Ancient wisdom: Healthful for the stomach, lungs, and spleen. Chewing raw garlic guards against the effects of eating tainted food.

New view: Garlic juice kills microorganisms and may lower cholesterol, ease blood pressure, and prevent blood clots. Its sulfur compounds may nip cancer in the bud.

GINGER Ancient wisdom: Eases digestion and motion sickness, and sweats out colds. Ginger tea is often given for headaches, nausea, and stomachaches.

New view: Ginger powder wards off seasickness and lessens nausea and vomiting after surgery and during pregnancy. Ginger may also reduce inflammation and fever.

MUSHROOMS Ancient wisdom: A longevity tonic and a remedy for vomiting, coughing, and urinary troubles. Shiitakes are prescribed for impotence and heart disease.

New view: A shiitake ingredient called lentinan may rev up production of immune cells. Eritadenine, also from shiitakes, may lower cholesterol.   —I.C.

may also open the door to certain cancers. The Asian approach allows for beef or pork just once or twice a month, or more often in small amounts as a garnish; seafood is welcome every day, eggs and poultry a few times a week. Dairy foods are optional.

Where do the two dining scenarios diverge? Mediterranean fare is higher in fat because of its penchant for olive oil, which raises good HDL cholesterol but not the bad LDL kind. The calories from the Mediterranean olive oil are essentially replaced by calories from rice and other starches in the Asian version.

But for many Americans, Willett says, splurging on starchy foods is unwise. Couch potatoes in particular are prone to blood glucose surges and a condition called insulin resistance that raises heart disease and diabetes risk. Still, Willett's not too worried about anyone who's active and lean, because it's usually extra pounds that foster insulin resistance. Furthermore, the Asian diet's fruits and vegetables serve up loads of fiber, which gloms on to starches in the gut, delaying their absorption and leveling out the glucose response.

There's another clear solution, too: Favor brown rice and whole grains, which are digested more slowly and don't set off extreme glucose surges. Indeed, until recently most Chinese ate lightly processed rice because white rice was too expensive.

The experts' worries shouldn't keep you from experimenting with what is perhaps the best lesson of Asian cuisine: its use of ginger, garlic, and other herbs to jazz up vegetable dishes. In recent years, researchers have begun homing in on the phytochemicals that lend fruits and veggies their power to ward off all kinds of illness. Yet Americans haven't been stampeding to the produce aisle. "Roughly half the people in this country eat hardly any green leaves," says Willett. "Spinach has been one option that people are sort of familiar with, but by itself it's not very interesting. So to be able to prepare greens in a variety of ways that are attractive and tasty, that's an important thing."

SALEM ISN'T SUCH A STRANGE PLACE for a Chinese dinner, after all. It's partly thanks to the seaside town that the spices of Asia first landed in this nation. In the late 1700s, local sea captains sailed their ships to the Far East loaded with New World molasses, beef, rum, furs, and tobacco. They returned with silks, ceramics, tea—and ingredients such as ginger, cloves, and cinnamon. Two centuries later, we have the luxury of deciding whether our taste buds will swirl in pasta primavera, dance a salsa to peppery fajitas, or exult in the flavors of hot and sour bok choy.

Take Simonds. She eats cereal and yogurt for breakfast, and loves salads and corn on the cob. But mostly, she cooks Asian. "I've taken the essence of the Asian diet and translated it in a way that adapts it to my lifestyle," she says. And if Simonds can do it, why not you? Chop up some bok choy, fire up the wok, and stir up a little Chinese magic.

seared salmon salad with cilantro dressing

SERVES 6

PREPARATION: 40 MINUTES

COOKING: 10 MINUTES

marinade

3 tablespoons soy sauce

3 tablespoons mirin*

1 tablespoon minced fresh ginger

1 ½ teaspoons dark sesame oil

1 ½ pounds salmon fillets, with skin

⅓ pound thin rice stick noodles, softened in hot
  water 20 minutes and drained

3 ½ cups grated carrots

3 ½ cups leaf lettuce, shredded

2 cups bean sprouts, rinsed and drained

cilantro dressing

10 tablespoons soy sauce

½ cup japanese rice vinegar

1 ½ tablespoons dark sesame oil

1 ½ tablespoons sugar

1 ½ tablespoons rice wine or sake

9 tablespoons fat-free, low-salt chicken broth

8 tablespoons chopped fresh cilantro

table talk

new fish story

Omega-3 fatty acids, the heart-healthy fats found in fish such as salmon and tuna, may also keep eyes healthy. An Australian study found that people who ate fresh or frozen fish one to three times a month got a type of blindness associated with old age about half as often as those who ate less.

SCOTT PETERSON

- In a medium-size bowl, combine marinade ingredients. Add salmon fillets and turn gently with your hands to coat. Cover with plastic wrap and refrigerate at least 30 minutes, turning often.
- In a large stockpot, heat 2 quarts of water until boiling. Add softened rice stick noodles and swirl. Cook 10 seconds, or until just tender. Drain in a colander and rinse under cold running water. Clip noodles, if desired, into 3-inch pieces, and spread on a deep serving platter. Arrange carrots, lettuce, and bean sprouts in concentric circles over noodles, leaving a space in middle for grilled salmon.
- To prepare dressing, combine all ingredients except cilantro in a small bowl, stirring to dissolve sugar. Transfer to a serving dish, and stir in cilantro.
- Prepare a hot fire for grilling, or heat a heavy skillet. Brush a little oil on grill or skillet. Place salmon fillets about 3 inches from heat source and grill, covered, 4 to 5 minutes on each side, brushing with remaining marinade. If using a skillet, sear salmon, covered, over medium-high heat, 4 to 5 minutes on each side. Remove and cut fillets in half along grain of fish; using your fingers, break into small pieces.
- Arrange salmon in middle of salad. Serve with dressing on the side.

Per serving: Calories 338 (21% from fat), Fat 8 g (1 g saturated), Protein 26 g, Carbohydrate 39 g, Fiber 3 g, Cholesterol 57 mg, Iron 3 mg, Sodium 2,009 mg, Calcium 77 mg

*A kind of sweetened rice wine available in Asian markets.

hot and sour bok choy

SERVES 6

PREPARATION: 15 MINUTES

COOKING: 10 MINUTES

2 pounds baby bok choy, or hearts of bok choy, stem end and
    leaf tips trimmed
3 tablespoons finely shredded or minced fresh ginger
3 tablespoons finely shredded or minced scallions

dressing

⅓ cup light soy sauce
2 to 2 ½ tablespoons chinese black vinegar* or worcestershire sauce
1 ½ tablespoons sugar
1 tablespoon minced garlic

■ Trim tough outer leaves from bok choy. Rinse and drain. Cut
leaves in half lengthwise. Cut halves into 2-inch sections. Using your
hands, toss ginger and scallions with bok choy in a medium-size
bowl. Arrange bok choy mixture on a heat-proof plate, a piece of
parchment paper, or wax paper; place in a steamer basket.
■ In a small bowl, mix together dressing ingredients; set by stove.
■ Fill a pot or a wok with several inches of water, and heat to boiling.
Place cabbage in steamer, and steam 5 to 6 minutes or until cabbage
is tender. Lay vegetables on a platter, and spoon dressing on top.

Per serving: Calories 50 (6% from fat), Fat 0.3 g (0 g saturated), Protein 4 g, Carbohydrate 8 g, Fiber 1 g, Cholesterol 0 mg, Iron 2 mg, Sodium 496 mg, Calcium 131 mg

*Available in Asian markets.

—RECIPES BY NINA SIMONDS

top ten anticancer foods

Potent disease fighters are waiting for you in the nearest produce case. Why not put them to work in your kitchen tonight?

By Peter Jaret

In the bustling heart of Seattle's Pike Place Market, Tamara Murphy scoops up a handful of ripe roma tomatoes and inhales their fresh scent. "Wonderful," she pronounces them. And then—why resist?—she pops one into her mouth, savoring its sweetness.

"Whenever I come here I feel like a painter with a box of paints," says the acclaimed chef, looking over bins full of the harvest's best and brightest: inky purple eggplants and red-stemmed swiss chard, fragrant round oranges and spiky green artichokes. "I'm thinking, 'How can I use this? What can I do with that?'"

A similar passion for produce brings another of Seattle's leading lights to this same market. But John Potter, director of the cancer prevention program at nearby Fred Hutchinson Cancer Research Center, shops at Pike Place with a plan for lowering his chances of contracting the nation's most dreaded disease.

A few years ago, he and a team of scientists reviewed more than 4,500 studies to find out just how much food choices influence cancer risk. A lot of the evidence came from countries where the daily fare includes ample portions of fruit, vegetables, beans, and grains—and where many malignancies that beset Americans are amazingly rare. "The bottom line is that a few simple changes in the way most people eat could cut the risk of cancer in general by one-third," says Potter. "Nothing else we know of, besides not smoking, will make as big a difference in your cancer risk."

Recent lab studies confirm that any produce stand contains an arsenal of protective compounds. "Substances in fruits and vegetables can lower the risk of cancer at virtually every step in its development," says Potter. And here Potter's and Murphy's passions merge: The scientist's work helps us choose the top cancer-fighting foods; the chef tells us great ways to eat more of them.

photograph

by scogin mayo

tomatoes

IN ONE OF POTTER'S REVIEWS, tomatoes showed up as a cancer fighter in more than 70 percent of the studies. Tomatoes are full of vitamin C and are the richest source of the pigment lycopene,

which guards against malignancies of the lungs, cervix, prostate, and mouth.

Slices of truly ripe tomatoes become a gourmet salad with just salt and pepper plus a splash of extra virgin olive oil and red wine vinegar, with perhaps some chopped fresh basil. Warm that same mixture quickly in a nonstick skillet to form a superb pasta sauce.

Whatever you do, don't put fresh tomatoes in the refrigerator; it spoils their flavor and texture. If they need to ripen, leave them in a cool spot for a day or two.

strawberries

"DOUBTLESS GOD COULD HAVE made a better berry," William Butler said of the strawberry, "but doubtless God never did." Actually, it's hard to imagine even a heavenly hand improving on the sweet, tart, luscious juiciness of a fat, fresh strawberry.

A Harvard School of Public Health study found that strawberry lovers were 70 percent less likely than those who rarely ate the fruit to develop cancer. Cranberries, raspberries, blackberries, and blueberries are also high in cancer-fighting phytochemicals.

Dozens of desserts feature strawberries. But for an especially classy and exotic dish, Murphy suggests that you serve bowls of hulled and sliced fresh strawberries sprinkled with top-quality balsamic vinegar.

"On the other hand," she says, "when berries are really ripe, supersweet, and juicy, you may not want to do anything but savor them just the way they are."

oranges

THE NAME *orange* evolved from the Sanskrit word *naranga,* derived from a root word meaning fragrant. Known for their aromatic oils and vitamin C content, oranges also contain more than 170 phytochemicals, including many antioxidants. Substances called limonoids appear to be particularly active. No wonder citrus lovers show comparatively low rates of stomach and lung cancers.

Don't stop at orange juice with breakfast. You can make an elegant salad by alternating avocado slices and orange sections on small plates. Scatter on shavings of red onion, and top with a vinaigrette of olive oil, wine vinegar, and orange juice.

garlic

"A NICKEL WILL GET you on the subway," New Yorkers used to say, "but garlic will get you a seat." It could also be your ticket to longevity. The sulfur compounds that give the bulb its pungent flavor neutralize carcinogens and slow the growth of tumors.

table talk
grow for it
Love homegrown vegetables but don't have a big yard? A deck or rooftop is all you need when you plant in pots. Cherry tomatoes, beans, peppers, and lettuce are among the varieties that thrive.

In fact, the Iowa Women's Health Study found that women who ate garlic at least once a week showed a 32 percent lower risk of colon cancer than garlic avoiders.

It's easy to ease more garlic into your meals without repelling your family and friends. Mellow it by baking whole heads in a covered dish or aluminum foil to create a spread for toast or bread. To whip up a sauce for roast chicken or pork, puree peeled roasted cloves in beef or chicken broth, add a dash of worcestershire and some fresh rosemary, thyme, or basil, then simmer until reduced by half. For a zingy cold soup, puree together 2 peeled seeded cucumbers, 1 cup nonfat yogurt, 1 clove garlic, and pinches of salt and pepper.

tea

TEA BEGAN AS A REMEDY, and now its disease-fighting powers are being rediscovered. Studies at Rutgers University have shown that mice that lap up green tea along with their regular water are far less likely to develop cancer than animals given only water.

Tea-guzzling humans may be just as lucky. In a 1998 Japanese study, researchers took detailed histories of women with several kinds of cancer. The disease appeared almost nine years later in life among those who drank more than ten cups of tea a day than it did among those who drank less than three.

Tea is rich in antioxidants called polyphenols. One recent study found that certain of these compounds, called catechins, appear to keep newly formed tumor cells from growing out of control. And you don't have to lose sleep to benefit: Tea now comes in decaffeinated varieties with its polyphenols intact.

whole wheat

"'A LOAF OF BREAD,' the walrus said, 'is what we chiefly need.'" Make that whole wheat bread, and Lewis Carroll's silly pronouncement will bring cheers from cancer experts. Whole grains have many of the same phytochemicals as fresh produce.

In early 1999, scientists from the University of Minnesota reported that the more whole grains in a woman's diet, the lower her risk of cancer. Reviewing 40 studies on 20 kinds of cancer, the same researchers found that grain lovers ran one-third the risk of people who rarely ate whole grain bread or cereal.

Try serving oven-warmed hunks of crusty whole wheat bread instead of the usual white rice or potatoes. Or brush toasted whole wheat triangles with olive oil, rub with a cut garlic clove, and top with salted diced tomatoes.

carrots

IN MEDIEVAL EUROPE carrots were typically red, purple, or black. It wasn't until the 17th century that the carrot as we know it—

simplify the
SALAD BAR

You may be tempted to fill up on disease-fighting veggies and beans at a salad bar instead of starting from scratch with produce from the fruit stand or market. But beware: You may pay a hidden price for the convenience of carryout. The dressing and other extras you pile into that clear plastic box could actually be clogging your arteries and widening your hips instead of reducing your cancer risk and protecting your heart and bones. Try these tips to get the light meal you were looking for.

PILE ON THE GREENS, REDS, AND YELLOWS. Remember that colorful vegetables pack the most cancer-fighting phytochemicals, so go for variety. When you can, choose romaine lettuce over iceberg.

SPRINKLE ON NUTS AND SEEDS. Yes, they're high in fat, but they're rich in heart-healthy vitamin E and fiber. Just don't overdo it. Two tablespoons of sunflower seeds come with 95 calories.

PICK FETA OR COTTAGE CHEESE OVER JACK OR CHEDDAR. The crumbly cheeses have 30 to 90 percent less fat than the others. And when cheese is part of the ensemble, lighten up elsewhere.

AVOID BEANS, OLIVES, AND MUSHROOMS THAT HAVE AN OILY SHEEN. It's your warning that they've been steeped in vegetable oil. When in doubt—it can be hard to tell with red beans and garbanzos—ask whether they've been marinated.

SCOUT OUT THE WHITE MEAT. Shredded roast turkey and chicken sound light, but the dark portions can be as fatty as some cuts of beef and pork. You want the breast only, either roasted or smoked.

WATCH OUT FOR POTATO, PASTA, AND CHICKEN SALADS. A skimpy half cup of a typical potato salad adds 180 calories. (It's all that mayonnaise.) If you want something starchy, ask for a whole wheat roll or slice of bread.

DRESS LIGHTLY. Many salad bars offer low-fat or nonfat versions of ranch, honey mustard, italian, and even caesar dressings. Plain oil and vinegar is a fine choice, too, if you bear in mind that a tablespoon of olive oil has 120 calories. —LISË STERN

colored bold orange by beta-carotene—was bred in Holland.

And this root clearly packs a punch. In the Iowa Women's Health Study, researchers found that the more carrots women ate, the lower their odds of getting lung cancer. Another study concluded that women who ate carrots more than twice a week were only half as likely to get breast cancer as women who avoided them.

In winter Tamara Murphy likes to brighten her table with carrot soup. Chop a bunch of carrots, simmer them in chicken stock until they're soft, season with salt and pepper, then puree. Try adding a bit of orange juice or freshly grated ginger, she suggests, to complement the soup's natural sweetness. Carrots sold with their tops on tend to be freshest—if the greens aren't wilted.

cabbage

"HE HAD FOUND HIMSELF, IN THE A & P, ravished by the glory of the pyramided cabbages," writes John Updike in one of his stories, "the pure sphericity, the shy cellar odor, the solid heft." Heft indeed. Cabbage, along with its kin broccoli and brussels sprouts, probably has more—and more potent—cancer-fighting substances than anything else in the market.

Cabbages come in green, red, purple, and white, with smooth or crinkly leaves. Lightly sauté cabbage slices to make a savory bed for grilled chicken breast with a teriyaki glaze. Or wrap salmon fillets and lemon slices in microwaved cabbage leaves, secure the bundles with toothpicks, and cook 10 minutes in a steamer.

table talk

the green party

Women who have more than one alcoholic drink a day should make sure to load up on foods rich in folate. The B vitamin appears to lower the risk of breast cancer in heavy drinkers. (The more you drink, the higher your risk.) Spinach, asparagus, beans, and orange juice are good sources.

spinach

TOTAL UP THE VIRTUES of Popeye's favorite green. Start with potent antioxidants that squelch free radicals before they have the chance to tear into healthy cells. Then add folic acid, which may shield cells from genetic damage. It all affects your cancer risk.

A study at the University of Minnesota found that women who frequently ate spinach and other green leafy vegetables showed comparatively low rates of lung cancer. And scientists at the National Institute of Environmental Health Sciences uncovered evidence that eating two or more servings of spinach a week might lower women's breast cancer risk, too.

"What I love to do at home is sauté spinach very lightly in a flavorful olive oil with a little bit of lemon juice," Murphy says. "The lemon adds just the right brightness." For a seductive side dish, warm a citrusy vinaigrette and drizzle it on torn spinach leaves. Toss until the greens wilt slightly, then top with sautéed shiitake mushroom slices and a little crumbled feta or goat cheese.

beans

THEY MAY COME LAST, but they're definitely not least—not by a long shot. Beans of all kinds are loaded with protease inhibitors, compounds that may make it harder for cancer cells to invade nearby tissue. Fava beans contain quercetin, which blocks carcinogens in the gastrointestinal tract. Soybeans are rich in isoflavones, which may reduce breast cancer risk by counteracting the tumor-promoting influence of estrogen.

The easiest legumes to love are lentils. They come in several shades, cook quickly, and meld beautifully with many kinds of foods. And even if you don't much care for beans, you can sneak many varieties into your favorite meals: Spoon drained and rinsed canned black beans seasoned with cumin into tacos and wraps. Add garbanzos to a tomatoey pasta sauce. Or simply toss kidney beans into a crisp green salad.

can't live without it? here's
the skinny on meat

Easy steps make today's lean cuts luscious.
And when summer arrives, nothing
matches flavor from the barbecue grill.

By Timothy Gower

photographs

by jeff ohiro

There once was a time when admitting to a lust for juicy steaks was like revealing a dietary death wish. The suicide-by-sirloin notion began to evolve more than a generation ago, as heart experts learned that foods rich in saturated fat can raise the levels of cholesterol in your blood, making you a prime candidate for a heart attack. When studies also suggested higher risks of cancer and osteoporosis, experts steered us away from the butcher counter.

But there's good reason to believe that the branding of meat as murderous is misguided and even inaccurate. First of all, many cuts are quite low in fat: Broiled top round steak has half the saturated fat of a chicken thigh; roasted pork tenderloin has only a bit more than skinless chicken breast. The data on osteoporosis is mixed; in fact, a recent study found that women who ate the most meat had the *fewest* bone fractures. And cooking meat properly can help keep the carcinogens produced by high heat at bay.

Cardiologist Lynn Smaha, president of the American Heart Association, hasn't eaten so much as a hamburger in ten years. But he tells his patients it's fine to eat modest portions of meat a couple of times a week. "If I told them to eat a diet devoid of red meat," he says, "they probably wouldn't listen to anything I said."

On the downside, "modest portions" means servings of three or four ounces, which amounts to steaks and pork chops the size of a deck of cards. To most palates, lower-fat cuts don't taste as good because fat helps carry the meat's flavor and adds to its juiciness. And lean meat is laced with more connective tissue than fatty meat is, so it tends to be less tender.

Sound like a catch-22—you can eat red meat, but only if you don't enjoy it? Not so. You simply have to learn a few tricks.

pick the best cuts

IT MAY BE HEARTENING to know that virtually all beef and pork sold today has less fat than meat products did a generation ago. According to animal nutritionist Gary Cowman (yes, that's his real name) of the National Cattlemen's Beef Association, livestock

are bred leaner than ever to meet the demands of to-day's health-conscious consumers. Cuts that include the words *loin* and *round,* in particular, qualify as lean.

The cuts of beef top and bottom round are probably best cooked with moist heat, using methods such as braising and stewing. But when summer comes around and you're ready to pull out the barbecue grill,

TEST YOURSELF
how safe is
YOUR FOOD?

Come summer, don't let the heat spoil your fun—or your food. Take this quiz to see if you'll know when to shoo guests from the congealed coleslaw.

1 If the power goes out or the fridge fails, which of these is safe to keep?
   a) butter   b) hard cheeses
   c) jam   d) mayonnaise
   e) all of the above

2 Food poisoning from sliced fruit isn't a worry. TRUE OR FALSE

3 At a picnic, your potato salad and cold cuts are safe to eat for up to
   a) one hour   b) two hours
   c) three hours   d) all day

4 After marinating meat, it's okay to use some of the marinade as a sauce.
   TRUE OR FALSE

5 Most food poisonings occur when cooked food cools. TRUE OR FALSE

   ANSWERS

   1 E. If they smell fine, they are fine. Kept cool, these staples can last for days.

   2 False. While fruit left out is generally safe, people have gotten sick from bacteria on melons, which are less acidic. Play it safe: Serve slices on ice.

   3 A. Never leave a meal in the heat for more than an hour—and include the time it was in the car.

   4 False. If raw meat has soaked in it, the marinade is suspect. Set aside some sauce before you begin, and apply it with a clean brush when the meat is done.

   5 True. A dish must go from the oven to the dinner table to the fridge in less than four hours. Otherwise, bacteria will have a chance to thrive in the danger zone—temperatures between 41° and 140°.

the cuts to reach for are sirloin tip, top loin, and tenderloin—and flank steak, too. Look for labels that say *select,* a term that means the meat has less fat than cuts dubbed *choice* or *prime.* If the label doesn't specify, you can safely assume it's select.

marinate for taste and safety

YES, THOSE UNADORNED LOIN STEAKS may beg for a little something. That's where marinades and dry rubs come in. "They won't give meat the same flavor that fat would give it," says Bruce Aidells, coauthor (with Denis Kelly) of *The Complete Meat Cookbook* (Houghton Mifflin, 1998). "But spice rubs and marinades give meat another flavor that's still tasty." The book includes dozens of recipes for rubs and marinades. Both add zip to lean cuts, but marinades also protect against cancer-causing agents.

Here's why: Cooking meat or poultry at high temperatures, in the broiler or on the grill, produces compounds known as heterocyclic amines, or HCAs. The longer you cook the meat, the more HCAs form—which is risky since HCAs have caused cancer in lab animals, and evidence suggests they can cause tumors in humans.

Marinating meat and poultry before high-heat cooking appears to fend off the HCAs, though, says molecular biologist James Felton of Lawrence Livermore National Laboratory, in Livermore, California. Felton and his colleagues have been able to cut HCAs with a variety of marinades. They think moisture helps keep the meats cooler, squelching the carcinogens.

sear, then grill lightly

WHEN SUMMERTIME ROLLS AROUND, many of us will be whipping out the barbecue grill. Aidells offers a tip especially for outdoor cooks that makes good health sense. When you barbecue any red meat, he suggests, start by quickly searing both sides. After a minute or two, step in with your tongs before any dripping fat can ignite flare-ups. Leaping flames not only produce smoke that smothers your dinner in carcinogens, but they also char the meat, giving it a bitter taste. So proceed with cooking by moving the meat to a part of the grill near, but not directly over, the coals or flame.

Then keep a close watch. "The more you cook a lean piece of meat, the drier it gets," Aidells says. Beef tastes best cooked medium or rare. Even pork can be served with traces of pink in the center. To hit just the right degree of doneness, remove the meat a teeny bit early; it'll continue to cook for the next several minutes before you serve it. Letting it settle for five to ten minutes also allows the juices to permeate the cut.

And the next time you're invited to eat at the home of some health-nut friends—the ones who always seem to offer only chicken or fish—feel free to pipe up and ask, "Hey, where's the beef?"

table talk

cooked to perfection To grill lean cuts, you need a digital instant-read food thermometer, which lets you cook meats to a safe internal temperature without losing flavor. Barbecue lovers like theirs cooked to medium at most (140° to 150° for beef and lamb, 145° to 150° for pork); the U.S. Department of Agriculture suggests grilling to well-done (160°) for extra safety. Ground meats should always be well-done.

great flavors **on the grill**

SURE, YOU CAN USE AN electric grill during cold weather, but in the summer you'll want to bring out the best flavor of meat with an old-fashioned outdoor barbecue. And forget hamburgers and hot dogs: Just a little imagination turns your humble backyard cookout into a gourmet's dream.

Need some help lighting the creative flame? These two easy recipes from Robin Vitetta-Miller should get you going: Pecan-raisin bread stuffing and a honey-mustard glaze add a touch of sweetness to savory pork tenderloin, and a marinade of yogurt and spices keeps lamb kebabs tender, moist, and flavorful as they're roasting over the coals.

grilled pork tenderloin with pecan-raisin bread stuffing

SERVES 4

PREPARATION AND MARINATING: 30 MINUTES

COOKING: 20 MINUTES

¼ cup honey
1 tablespoon dijon mustard
½ teaspoon allspice
1 1-pound pork tenderloin (or 2 8-ounce tenderloins)
2 cups cubed pecan-raisin bread or rolls
2 teaspoons olive oil
1 tablespoon chopped fresh rosemary

■ In a shallow dish, whisk together honey, mustard, and allspice. Add pork, and turn to coat. Cover with plastic, and refrigerate at least 20 minutes, up to 1 hour.
■ Preheat grill.
■ In a large bowl, combine bread, oil, and rosemary; toss to coat. Using a sharp knife, slice down center of tenderloin almost to bottom, to make a deep pocket. Flatten sides with your hands, then fill pork with bread mixture. Pull pork up and around to close pocket, and secure opening with toothpicks.
■ Grill pork 8 to 10 minutes per side or until a thermometer inserted deep in the meat reads about 150°. Transfer pork to a cutting board, and let stand 5 minutes. Slice crosswise into rounds.

Per serving: Calories 360 (27% from fat), Fat 11 g (2 g saturated), Protein 27 g, Carbohydrate 39 g, Fiber 2 g, Cholesterol 67 mg, Iron 3 mg, Sodium 197 mg, Calcium 40 mg

tandoori lamb kebabs
with yogurt dip & couscous

SERVES 4
PREPARATION AND MARINATING: 40 MINUTES
COOKING: 10 MINUTES

1 8-ounce container nonfat plain yogurt, divided
2 teaspoons ground cumin
1 teaspoon coriander
1/2 teaspoon ground ginger
1/4 teaspoon cayenne pepper
1 pound lamb leg meat cut into 2-inch cubes
2 small zucchini, cut into 2-inch cubes
3/4 cup red seedless grapes
1 1/2 cups uncooked couscous
1/2 cup minced, peeled cucumber
1/4 teaspoon freshly ground black pepper

■ In a shallow bowl, combine 2 tablespoons of the yogurt, cumin, coriander, ginger, and cayenne. Mix well, add lamb, and stir to coat. Cover with plastic, and refrigerate at least 20 minutes, up to 6 hours (longer marinating will overtenderize the meat).

■ Preheat grill.

■ Skewer lamb, zucchini, and grapes on metal or wooden skewers, alternating ingredients. Grill 8 to 10 minutes or until lamb is cooked through, turning frequently.

■ Meanwhile, to prepare couscous, bring 2 cups water to a boil. Add couscous, stir, cover, and remove from heat. Let stand 5 minutes.

■ To make the yogurt dip, combine remaining yogurt, cucumber, and pepper in a small bowl. Mix well, and refrigerate until ready to serve.

■ When kebabs are done, spoon couscous onto 4 individual plates. Arrange 2 lamb kebabs on top of couscous. Offer yogurt dip on the side.

Per serving: Calories 496 (14% from fat), Fat 8 g (3 g saturated), Protein 38 g, Carbohydrate 68 g, Fiber 5 g, Cholesterol 76 mg, Iron 3 mg, Sodium 117 mg, Calcium 155 mg

drink to your health
wondrous water

It's more than a thirst quencher. It may be the simplest, coolest way to shed pounds, ease headaches, and even fight off cancer.

By Michael Tennesen

We cannot live without water. Fereydoon Batmanghelidj is on a deeply personal if not slightly bizarre crusade to make sure you never forget it. This Virginia-based physician—known by friends as Dr. Batman—is serious about water and its potential to improve our health. He frequently takes to the nation's airwaves to share his message of hope and hydration.

You may want a drink before you hear this message. First of all, the author of *Your Body's Many Cries for Water* (Global Health Solutions, 1997) declares that America is suffering from an epidemic of chronic dehydration. But in his view, that's not our only problem. "Heartburn, headache, joint and back pain, and fatigue are not true diseases," says Dr. Batman. "They're dehydration-induced disorders. I tell people, 'You're not sick—you're thirsty.'"

Over lunch, Dr. Batman shares the odd story of how he became the nation's most visible champion of water. It all began after the fall of the Shah of Iran in 1979, when he was sent to jail as a political prisoner. While he was imprisoned, an inmate with an excruciating ulcer came to him for relief. The Iranian-trained physician dispensed the only "medicine" he had at the time: water. And he says it worked. Just two glasses later, he swears, the man was cured. So Dr. Batman, wondering whether this cure would benefit others, launched a prison-based study to explore the subject.

Here's where the story gets really weird. When his jailers offered him freedom, Dr. Batman declined. Instead, he spent four more months behind bars so that he could complete his research. That's what I'd call a dedicated professional.

The experience helped convince him that your kitchen sink is dispensing a regular wonder drug, one that has the power to cure asthma, allergies, high blood pressure, and more. "The cholesterol buildup on blood vessel walls is the body's natural defense against water loss," says Dr. Batman.

Frankly, it all seems off-the-wall to me. And I'm not alone: When I run his theories by a few experts, the reactions range from ridicule to anger. Ann Bolger, a cardiologist with the University of California at San Francisco, laughs at Dr. Batman's rationale for

should you HIT THE BOTTLE?

If you crave purity, bottled water is your best bet—right? Maybe not. Even if your thirst quencher of choice is a pristine-sounding purified, mineral, spring, or artesian well water that costs a bucket, you'd probably be just as safe or safer saving your money and getting your fill at the faucet.

That's because bottled water isn't subjected to the stringent standards for removing bacteria, parasites, and chemicals required of municipal water. Studies show that around a quarter of all bottled water exceeds state health limits for acceptable levels of contaminants. And most brands can't match tap for optimal levels of fluoride, an additive that fights tooth decay.

What's more, there's a good chance your bottled water is tap water. One recent study found that at least 25 percent of what's promoted as pure is just municipal water that's been refiltered and repackaged with slick labeling.

If you still plan to go with bottled water, first visit the Web site of the National Sanitation Foundation (www.nsf.org), which rates bottled water for purity. Among the group's top picks: Dannon, Evian, Volvic, and Mountain Valley.   —NINA WILLDORF

cholesterol buildup. "Hmm," she says. "I know a guy who thinks we should eat more fat to keep the blood slippery."

But while the line between Dr. Batman's science and pure speculation may seem a bit slippery, there is evidence that he's on to something. Just ask Susan M. Kleiner. This is a woman you would never confuse with Fereydoon Batmanghelidj. The 42-year-old fitness fanatic is an affiliate assistant professor with the Nutritional Sciences Program at the University of Washington in Seattle and a nutrition consultant for pro basketball's Seattle SuperSonics. She does, however, share one thing with Dr. Batman—a fascination with the medical potential of water.

So she went hunting: at the library, on the Internet, hounding fellow scientists. Her goal was to chart the consequences of chronic mild dehydration, which she defines as a 1 to 2 percent loss of body weight through fluid loss. In the end, she assembled and published the first comprehensive survey of the medical literature on water.

Now Kleiner is convinced, too. "More than half of the nation is walking around chronically mildly dehydrated," she says. And, she believes, the consequences are real. Physicians have long recommended drinking lots of water to prevent some problems—kidney stones and constipation, for instance. But Kleiner says there's surprising evidence that a minor water shortage in your body can cause some major health problems.

So break out the glassware. Kleiner, for one, says the cure may be as simple as drinking eight to ten 8-ounce glasses of water a day. Here's a look at the science on water's healing powers.

a cancer fighter on tap?

IT SOUNDS TOO GOOD TO BE TRUE. And it's certainly too soon to tell. But a number of recent studies have suggested that water's cancer-fighting powers are for real.

Consider colon cancer. In a study conducted at the Fred Hutchinson Cancer Research Center in Seattle, researchers concluded that women who drank more than four glasses of water a day lowered their risk of getting the disease to about half that of women who imbibed two glasses or less. That reduction was almost comparable to the cancer-fighting benefits of eating five servings of fruits and vegetables a day. And though only a few participants emptied eight glasses or more a day, the ones who did enjoyed an even greater protective effect. Other beverages just couldn't match this power: Subjects who drank lots of coffee, soda, or juice didn't budge their chances of trouble.

How could water work that magic? Ann Shattuck, an epidemiologist who coauthored the study, thinks water can turn your intestinal tract into an express train in which troublemakers have no chance to stop and loiter. Water makes waste move through the system more quickly, which, she says, means carcinogens have less time to come in contact with colon walls.

table talk
the winning waters
Judges at the annual Berkeley Springs water tasting named Halstead Spring, Kentwood Artesian, McKenzie Mist, Le-Nature's, Calistoga Mineral, and Mountain Valley Sparkling the nation's tastiest bottled waters. The yummiest tap water flows in Yucca Valley, California.

A similar effect may keep cancer from taking hold in the urinary tract—home to your bladder, kidney, ureter, and other friends. One study at the Cancer Research Center of Hawaii, for example, found that women who reported drinking the most tap water every day were a whopping 80 percent less likely to develop bladder cancer than those who drank the least. A few studies done earlier reported no such dramatic result, perhaps because they were conducted in areas where tap water is chlorinated more than the average. But epidemiologist Lynne Wilkens, who led the trial, says the data showed the power of naturally purified water. "It was clear," says Wilkens. "The more they drank, the higher the reduction of risk."

There's even evidence that taking more trips to the tap might fight off breast cancer. In a case study, British researchers reported that women who defined themselves as water drinkers ran a much smaller risk of getting the disease than women who didn't. How much? In premenopausal participants, the odds were reduced by a third, and postmenopausal women enjoyed an even greater benefit. The authors concluded that the findings were impressive enough to warrant further study.

control your weight

GOT THE MUNCHIES? You may want to pour yourself a glass of water to fight the urge. And don't laugh—it might work.

The strange thing is, there's a chance you're just hungry for the wet stuff. "We have a poor thirst mechanism," Kleiner says.

one down
SEVEN TO GO

Drinking water may not be rocket science, but figuring out how to slurp down eight 8-ounce glasses without gagging can present a challenge to the best of us. Here are some tips from the experts, including Susan Kleiner, affiliate assistant professor with the Nutritional Sciences Program at the University of Washington in Seattle, on how to get your fill.

HOW MUCH IS ENOUGH? The average woman needs about 2.3 quarts of water a day. Solid foods contribute a quart at best, so you have to drink the rest. But if you work out, you need to guzzle more. You should also pour it on when the mercury rises—an extra ounce of water for every degree over 64.

START THE DAY RIGHT Drink 16 ounces of water first thing, before you down your coffee. Take your vitamins with a glass of water. Chase toothbrushing with another.

WORK OUT WITH WATER To avoid a sky-high body temperature or heart rate, drink extra fluids during the 24 hours preceding exercise, then down about 16 ounces of water a couple of hours before you start.

TOSS THE SODA Beverages with caffeine and alcohol are diuretics—a term that means they draw extra fluids out of your body to produce more urine. A German study revealed that adults who drank six cups of coffee a day lost 2.7 percent of their total body water, enough to cause chronic mild dehydration.

STAY CLOSE TO WATER Keep a filled-up water bottle within reach all day.

DRINK WHILE YOU DRINK Toss back a glass of water for every cocktail, beer, or caffeinated beverage you consume.

BLOATED TRUTH Water retention is a common symptom of PMS. But drinking water won't make it worse. In fact, the opposite is true, says Kleiner. "If the body perceives it isn't getting enough fluid, it will hold on to the fluid it has."

THIRSTY LIES You've got to drink before the word *parched* comes to mind. That's because our thirst mechanism can be a poor indicator of water needs, says Kleiner. In the German study above, most of the dehydrated java junkies never felt thirsty. —M.T.

"Sometimes we don't recognize the difference between thirst and hunger."

But there's more to water's weight-control powers than that. Multiple studies have shown that people who boost their fluid intake over the long haul drop the pounds. In one case study, an obese woman lost 42 pounds in 18 months by following a program that stressed a big increase in water consumption.

The explanation may be simple: Water can take the edge off hunger. "If you drink water with your meal, you are more likely to feel full," says Kelly Brownell, a professor of psychology at Yale and the developer of a weight-loss program called LEARN.

Not everyone thinks it's so simple. Barbara Rolls is a professor of nutrition at Pennsylvania State University and coauthor with Robert A. Barnett of the diet book *Volumetrics* (HarperCollins, 2000). She believes our hunger mechanism is crafty enough to tell that water isn't food. To fool the brain, she says, you need to *cook* water into your diet through foods such as hot cereal, pasta, and soup. And in fact, researchers confirmed that dieters who sipped soup four times a week took in 100 fewer calories a day than did soup skippers.

At least everyone can agree on one thing: Water quenches your thirst with nary a calorie. But juice, iced tea, and soda only add needless calories to your diet; Rolls says studies have proved that sugar-laden soft drinks will not decrease your daily calorie intake one bit.

table talk
check your water
Find out which contaminants are flowing through your pipes with the WaterSafe Home Drinking Water Test. The single-use kit costs $17 and measures levels of lead, nitrites, nitrates, chlorine, and certain pesticides; a chart tells you if they exceed standard levels. To order, call 888/438-1942.

heal your headaches

HAVE YOU EVER SPENT A LONG morning rubbing your temples and otherwise cursing a nasty hangover? Then you're sobering proof that a little water shortage can cause a lot of discomfort. After all, morning-after misery is little more than alcohol-induced dehydration. And *dehydration* is a word you don't want to see in the same sentence as *brain*, an organ that's mostly water. Studies show that headaches are one of the most frequently reported symptoms of both mild and more severe dehydration.

Jerome Goldstein, director of the San Francisco Headache Clinic, has seen the evidence. He firmly believes that dehydration can send you running to the medicine cabinet—both because it upsets the balance of sodium and potassium in your noggin and because it may urge the brain to get stingy with its water supply, increasing pressure on the organ. The theories sound fancy, but the solution, says Goldstein, may be simple: Drink more water.

Other beverages are no substitute. Goldstein thinks some kinds of drinks can actually turn *up* the volume on pain. "Headache sufferers tend to drink beverages with lots of caffeine and artificial sweeteners," says Goldstein. "And unlike water, these seem to cause discomfort."

glad you asked

Answers to your questions about eating right

I eat seven to ten servings of vegetables every day but don't really like fruit. Am I missing out on anything important?

Most of the vitamins, minerals, and disease-fighting antioxidants in fruit are also plentiful in vegetables. Peppers and broccoli, for example, are loaded with vitamin C, and the beta-carotene in cantaloupe and mangoes is even more abundant in carrots and yams. One nutrient you might lack is limonene, a cancer fighter found in citrus peel. A bit of lemon or lime zest on your salad or steamed vegetables will meet your daily quota.

Veggie haters, on the other hand, are missing essentials that fruit and even vitamin supplements can't replace. Try tempting these picky eaters with succulent, fresh-picked produce from the garden or farmers' market.

Are sun-dried tomatoes as nutritious as those fresh from the vine?

Almost, though if it's a healthy dose of vitamin C you're after, you may want to go back to the garden.

A whopping 17 pounds of tomatoes are needed to make just 1 pound of sun-dried. The vine-ripened fruits are first sliced and then either placed outside to dry or put into special tunnels; unfortunately, exposure to oxygen inactivates the fruit's vitamin C.

The other nutrients are far hardier. Fiber and the cancer-fighting pigments lycopene and beta-carotene are not only preserved but also concentrated in a sun-dried tomato, so don't pass up the pungent flavor of the wrinkled version for health reasons. A few slices can add depth and pizzazz to almost any sauce or sandwich.

If you usually skip the oil-packed variety to save calories, don't—or at least add a little olive oil; it will help your body absorb the lycopene.

Many cereals list the additives BHA and BHT among their ingredients. Are these bad for me or my children?

Not according to the FDA. The chemicals that you mention are actually antioxidants. They're added in trace amounts to many processed foods such as margarine and potato chips to keep the fat in those foods from going bad. (Rancid fat won't make you sick, but it sure smells and tastes lousy!)

If you're worried because studies in the 1980s linked high doses of BHA and BHT with cancer in lab mice, keep in mind that the rodents were fed huge doses. Once the FDA took a hard look at the data, it ruled that the tiny amounts in our food are harmless.

Still nervous? You can sidestep the issue by eating and serving only locally made baked goods and fresh produce. But there's no reason any of us should fret about noshing on the occasional Cheeto.

I'm trying to reduce my salt intake, but I'm having a hard time doing it. I love salt! Do you have any advice on cutting down without losing the flavor?

Most of us need to trim only 1,000 milligrams of salt from our diets. Here are five easy ways to do it that won't disappoint your taste buds. **Check the labels.** Two versions of the same food can have dramatically different sodium levels. Pick the right loaf of bread, and you can save about 225 mg of sodium per slice. **Don't scoff at low-sodium foods.** Yes, some taste pretty blah, but many are essentially the same as the originals. A serving of low-sodium crackers saves you 100 mg; a cup of low-sodium chicken broth more than 1,000.

Favor fresh vegetables. Most canned veggies are heavy on salt. Sauté a half cup of fresh mushrooms for your pasta instead of using canned, and you save 300 mg. **Go easy on fast foods.** Have a turkey sandwich from the deli instead of a Taco Bell chicken fajita, and you save 1,500 mg. Ask for less mayo, though; it packs a lot of sodium. **Add salt at the table.** When you cook with salt, you often use more than you need. But the salt we add from the shaker makes up only about 10 percent of our sodium intake.

I eat little beef and fall short of the 50 grams of protein I should get daily. Although I eat beans often, I hear they're an "incomplete" protein. How can I get everything I need?

R elax. It's true that meat easily provides all nine of the protein building blocks (amino acids) that our bodies need, and that most plants, in contrast, don't deliver a full set. Beans are missing one of those amino acids, and rice is missing two. When eaten together, the two foods fill in each other's blanks to form the "complete protein" you've heard about.

Nutritionists used to think it was crucial to get a full set of amino acids in every meal, but recent studies have shown that whether eaten at the same time or on consecutive days, amino acids tend to loiter in the body for 24 hours or so—plenty long enough to find each other and make a complete protein. So if you're eating a varied diet, you're probably fine. Perhaps better than fine: Most of us get too *much* of our protein from meat, especially from fatty cuts.

I've heard conflicting information about the amount of fat that is acceptable in my diet. How much do you recommend? And does the kind of fat matter?

The U.S. government recently released a revised draft of its official dietary guidelines, which contain the usual exhortations: Eat plenty of fruits and vegetables, munch more grains, blah, blah, blah. But instead of urging you to avoid fat, officials suggest that you should eat moderate amounts of polyunsaturated and monounsaturated fats, such as those found in vegetable and olive oils.

Although the guidelines still recommend that you get no more than 30 percent of your calories from fat, experts concede that a little more is probably okay—as long as it isn't the artery-clogging saturated variety.

abdominal pain

Abdominal pain is most often a sign of a mild ailment such as indigestion or stomach flu. But severe pain can signal an emergency, and long-lasting pain may indicate a serious illness that needs medical attention.

SYMPTOMS	WHAT IT MIGHT BE	WHAT YOU CAN DO
Sharp, ongoing pain in abdomen that radiates to back and chest; fever; nausea; vomiting; swollen abdomen; sweaty skin.	Pancreatitis—inflamed pancreas. ■ Cholecystitis—inflamed gallbladder.	Call 911 or go to emergency room **right away**. Acute pancreatitis can cause shock, which can be fatal if not treated quickly.
Sharp abdominal pain, perhaps with other acute symptoms.	Intestinal blockage. ■ Appendicitis. ■ Pelvic inflammatory disease (see page 209). ■ Heart attack. ■ Perforated stomach ulcer (see page 218). ■ Shock from allergy. ■ Diabetic emergency (see diabetes, page 181). ■ Poisoning.	Call 911 or go to emergency room **right away**.
Severe, cramping pain in middle abdomen that radiates to right side or back and often disturbs sleep; nausea; vomiting; gas.	Gallstones (see page 189).	In a first attack, call doctor for emergency advice. If you can't reach one, call 911 or go to emergency room. Do not eat or drink anything.
Severe pain in lower side of back that moves toward groin or abdomen; urge to urinate often, or painful or stopped-up urination; murky, smelly, or bloody urine; nausea and vomiting; sweating.	Kidney stones. ■ Kidney infection.	Call doctor for prompt appointment. Then drink lots of water to help stone pass, and take a nonaspirin pain reliever if you need to (see pain relief box, page 207).
Cramping or pain in abdomen, nausea, diarrhea, vomiting, fever, fatigue, weakness, gas.	Stomach flu (see nausea and vomiting, page 202). ■ Food poisoning.	If, with vomiting and pain, you have blurred or double vision, muscle weakness, or trouble speaking or swallowing, call 911 or go to emergency room **right away**; these may be signs of botulism, a sometimes fatal bacterial food poisoning.

abdominal pain

SYMPTOMS	WHAT IT MIGHT BE	WHAT YOU CAN DO
Pain in upper right abdomen increasing over days, fever, fatigue, nausea and vomiting. Sometimes dark urine, pale stools, yellowed eyes and skin.	Hepatitis (see page 196). ■ Pancreatic cancer.	Call doctor for prompt appointment.
Pain or cramps in abdomen, diarrhea, bloody stool, pus in stool, fever, fatigue, weight loss.	Crohn's disease. ■ Ulcerative colitis. ■ Bacterial dysentery, particularly if you have been overseas.	Be careful not to become dehydrated (see diarrhea, page 183). Call doctor right away if you have bloody stools or if you think you have bacterial dysentery.
Pain that is worse when sore spot on abdomen is touched; severe abdominal cramping, often more painful on the left; nausea; fever; chills; diarrhea, constipation, or thin stools.	Diverticulitis—inflamed pouches in colon.	Call doctor for prompt appointment if you have blood in your stools.
Ache or pain in abdomen or groin when lifting or bending over, swelling or bulge under skin in abdomen or groin.	Hernia.	Call doctor for appointment. Some hernias need care right away.
Ache or pain in abdomen with diarrhea, constipation, or bouts of both; mucus strands in stool; extreme gas or bloating; nausea, usually after meals; fatigue.	Irritable bowel syndrome.	See irritable bowel syndrome, page 200. (For self-care, also see diarrhea, page 183.)
Pain in upper abdomen, nausea, vomiting, diarrhea, loss of appetite, burping or gas, heartburn.	Stomach ulcer. ■ Gastritis.	See ulcers and gastritis, page 218.
Pain and cramps after drinking milk or eating other dairy foods, gas and bloating, diarrhea, nausea, rumbling sounds from abdomen.	Lactose intolerance—trouble digesting cow's milk, cheese, butter, ice cream, and other dairy foods.	Eat fewer dairy foods or none. Try soy milk, lactose-free dairy products, and acidophilus yogurt. Lactase enzyme supplements also may help.

breast pain or lumps

Breasts change with puberty, the menstrual cycle, pregnancy, and age. Starting at puberty, women should examine their breasts every month so that they know the breasts' structure and can detect any masses or lumps (see breast self-exam box, facing page). Most changes in breasts are normal, but some require medical care.

SYMPTOMS	WHAT IT MIGHT BE	WHAT YOU CAN DO
Lump (usually painless) in breast or underarm area; flat area or indentation on breast; change in contour, texture, size, or symmetry of breast; change in nipple (such as indrawn or dimpled look, itching or burning feeling, or discharge that may be dark or bloody).	Noncancerous cyst. ▪ Noncancerous tumor. ▪ Breast cancer (if breast is painful, could signal advanced stage).	Call doctor for prompt appointment. Most lumps are not cancerous, but it is very important to have an exam. Biopsy may be needed to diagnose or rule out breast cancer.
After having just given birth: pain and tenderness in breast, hard or swollen breast, fever, area with pain and redness.	Infection of breast (mastitis), caused by bacteria. Pain and redness can mean an abscess.	Call doctor for advice and appointment. Keep on breast-feeding. If you get an abscess, use a breast pump on infected side and feed on uninfected side. If you have a fever, rest in bed and drink plenty of fluids.
Pain, tenderness, or swelling in breasts; missed period; fatigue; nausea.	Pregnancy.	Call doctor for advice and appointment for pregnancy test. Wear support bra.
Breast pain while taking estrogen.	Drug side effect.	Call doctor for advice.
Lumpy or swollen breasts; pain or discomfort, chiefly in the week before menstrual period.	Fibrocystic breasts. More than half of all women develop this harmless condition, most often between the ages of 25 and 50.	Call doctor for advice if you notice lumps for first time; if you notice a new lump; or if a lump becomes larger, harder, or more painful. Limit intake of caffeine. Wear support bra.
Pain or tenderness in breasts before menstrual period.	Premenstrual syndrome. ▪ Irregular periods.	See premenstrual syndrome, page 210, and menstrual irregularities chart, page 156.

how to do a breast self-exam

A regular breast self-exam is one of the best ways to find a cancerous tumor when it is small, before the cancer has a chance to spread. Check yourself at the same time every month, 2 to 3 days after your period. (Remember, self-examination is not a substitute for regular exams by a doctor.)

1 Stand facing a mirror with your arms at your sides. Look for anything unusual on your breasts: dimples, scaly patches, puckers, or discharge coming from a nipple.

2 Check for changes in the contours of your breasts. Watch in the mirror as you lift your hands behind your head, clasp your hands, and press them against the back of your head.

3 Check again with your hands on your hips and your elbows pulled forward.

4 Squeeze your nipples gently to check for discharge.

5 With one arm raised, use the fingertips of your other hand to feel your breast for any lumps under the skin. Start in your armpit and move toward your breast, pressing in small areas about the size of a quarter. (Try this in the shower; your fingers will slide more easily over soapy skin.)

Use a definite pattern—a spiral, line, or wedge. Cover the entire breast, as well as the upper chest and underarm. Repeat on other side.

   spiral Start at the outer edges of the breast and slowly work your way around it in smaller and smaller circles.

   line Start under your arm and slowly stroke up and down, progressing across the breast.

   wedge Start at the outer edge of the breast and move slowly toward the middle, then back to the edge.

6 Repeat step 5 lying on your back, with one arm over your head and a pillow under your shoulder. Use one of the patterns above to check each breast.

If you find a lump, unusual firmness, a change in shape, or any discharge from a nipple, call your doctor.

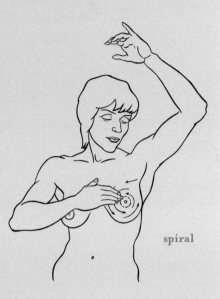

spiral

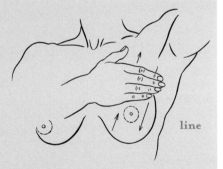

line

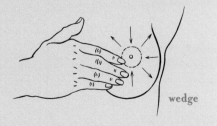

wedge

chest pain

Never ignore chest pain, especially in an adult. It's hard to tell one kind of chest pain from another, so if it is severe or lasts more than a few minutes, call 911.

SYMPTOMS	WHAT IT MIGHT BE	WHAT YOU CAN DO
Mild to severe pain, pressure, or squeezing in center of chest that may spread to jaw, neck, back, or arms (often left arm); sweating, nausea, or shortness of breath; anxiety.	Heart attack.	Call 911 **right away.** If you have aspirin, take a half tablet. (Don't do this if you're already taking a daily aspirin.)
Pain or chest tightness with breathing. In adults: sudden, sharp chest pain with shortness of breath that gets worse. In young people: possibly vague or minor pain that spreads to neck or back with some trouble breathing.	Collapsed lung. Sometimes occurs in young people for no apparent reason, or in adults who have asthma or chronic bronchitis. May follow a recent chest injury.	Call 911 **right away.**
Severe, stubborn, ripping chest pain that may spread to abdomen and upper back; dizziness and fainting.	Aortic aneurysm—weak spot with tear in main artery from heart. Most often caused by coronary artery disease (see heart disease, page 192) or high blood pressure (see page 199).	Call 911 **right away.** Surgery may be needed to repair aorta.
Sharp chest pain, worse when breathing in; shortness of breath; possibly fever.	Pleurisy—inflamed sac around lungs; often a complication of pneumonia or tuberculosis.	Call 911 or go to emergency room **right away.**
Dull pain, pressure, or squeezing in center of chest that may feel like stomach upset or heartburn; may spread to jaw, neck, back, or arms (usually left arm); brought on or made worse by stress or activity, easing with rest in 30 seconds to 5 minutes.	Angina. ■ Coronary artery disease (see heart disease, page 192).	Call doctor for prompt appointment, but if symptoms persist 10 minutes or longer, call 911 **right away.**

chest pain

SYMPTOMS	WHAT IT MIGHT BE	WHAT YOU CAN DO
Chest pain, trouble breathing, easy fatigue, uneven heartbeat (palpitations), fainting (sometimes).	Problem with heart rhythm. ■ Mitral valve prolapse—heart valve allows blood to leak backward. Affects more women than men; may run in families.	Call doctor for prompt appointment. For mitral valve prolapse, beta-blockers may ease palpitations and chest pain. Antibiotics should be taken before dental work or surgery to prevent infection of heart's lining. **For more help:** American Heart Association, 800-242-8721, hours vary.
Pain or tightening in chest; rapid heartbeat; shortness of breath; numbness or tingling in hands; fear.	Anxiety. ■ Panic attack. ■ Hyperventilation—rapid breathing that lowers level of carbon dioxide in blood.	If you can't function as usual, call doctor for advice.
Burning or pressure in chest or upper abdomen, worse on bending over or lying down, especially when stomach is full; belching. Symptoms can resemble those of heart attack.	Heartburn. ■ Esophageal reflux—stomach acid backs up into esophagus when muscle that prevents this becomes weak. ■ Ulcer. ■ Gastritis.	See ulcers and gastritis, page 218. If you're not sure about the symptoms, call your doctor **right away;** you may need to be checked for a heart problem.
Severe burning or aching pain on one side of chest that may spread to back and is not affected by breathing; followed a few days later by blisters and itchy rash.	Shingles—painful blisters or a rash caused by the same herpes virus as chicken pox. Most common in adults over age 50.	Ease pain with ice packs or painkillers. Use calamine lotion to relieve itching. Call doctor for emergency advice if you have eye pain or blisters on your face. Call for prompt appointment if you have a fever over 101 degrees.
Sharp pain that gets worse with movement or deep breathing, or when area is pressed; may follow severe coughing or sneezing, or chest injury.	Pulled muscle. ■ Inflamed cartilage. ■ Injured rib.	Rest; apply an ice pack (a bag of frozen peas wrapped in a dishcloth works well) several times a day, 10–15 minutes at a time. Take a painkiller—aspirin, ibuprofen, or acetaminophen (see box, page 207).

eye & vision problems

Here are some of the most common eye and vision problems, as well as some of the most serious. If you have concerns about your vision, call your doctor for advice.

SYMPTOMS	WHAT IT MIGHT BE	WHAT YOU CAN DO
Sudden vision changes, such as blindness, double vision, blurring, flashes of light, floating dark shapes, loss of peripheral (side) vision; acute, sustained pain.	Stroke. ■ Transient ischemic attack—temporary blockage of artery, with symptoms like stroke. ■ Optic neuritis—inflammation of optic nerve.	Call 911 or go to emergency room **right away** if you have sudden blindness or loss of part of visual field.
Redness, watering, pain, or a feeling of having something in the eye.	Foreign body in eye.	Go to emergency room if something is in colored part of eye or if you can't get particle out of white of eye.
Blurred vision; slow loss of peripheral (side) vision; sudden, severe eye pain; halos around lights; teary, aching eyes; headache; nausea; vomiting.	Glaucoma—buildup of pressure inside the eye; can damage optic nerve.	Call doctor for prompt appointment. Prescription drugs may help.
Blurred vision, sensitivity to light, ache or pain in eye, headache, redness (no discharge).	Iritis/uveitis—inflammation inside eye.	Call doctor for prompt appointment. Prescription drugs may help.
Rapid or gradual vision loss; dim or distorted vision, especially when reading; dark, empty area in center of visual field; straight lines look wavy.	Macular degeneration—the macula, a tiny spot at center of retina, begins to break down or scar. Symptoms usually appear after age 55.	Call doctor for prompt appointment. Some forms can be slowed with laser treatment. **For more help:** Association for Macular Diseases, 212-605-3719, M–F 11–3 EST; *www.macula.org.*
Flashes of light, floating dark shapes, loss of peripheral (side) vision.	Retinal detachment—hole in retina. Risk increases with age, with severe myopia, and after cataract surgery.	Call doctor for prompt appointment. In early stages, vision can be restored with surgery.
Small, painful red bump at base of eyelash.	Stye.	Apply a soft, clean washcloth soaked in warm water. Hold for 10–15 minutes. Repeat 2–4 times a day.

eye & vision problems

SYMPTOMS	WHAT IT MIGHT BE	WHAT YOU CAN DO
Red and itchy eyelids.	Blepharitis—inflammation and scaling of eyelids.	Wash eyelids with warm water containing a few drops of baby shampoo, or with over-the-counter eyelid wash. Call doctor for advice and appointment if ailment doesn't clear up with home treatment.
Hazy vision, blurriness around lights, frequent changes in eyeglass prescriptions, white area visible in pupil.	Cataracts—fogging of the eye's clear lens.	If you think you have a cataract, call doctor for advice.
White of eye is bloodshot, sticky or watery discharge, itching.	Conjunctivitis—inflammation of membrane that covers inside of eyelid and white of eye.	Wash away discharge with warm water. Call doctor for prompt appointment if vision is affected or if you have lots of pain or discharge; you may have a staph or strep infection.
Blurred vision when looking at nearby objects, eyestrain, headaches.	Presbyopia—inability to focus for near vision. Occurs with age as lens loses elasticity.	Call doctor for advice and appointment. Eyeglasses or contact lenses can help.
Blurred vision when looking at distant objects.	Myopia, or nearsightedness. May run in families.	Call doctor for advice and appointment. Eyeglasses or contact lenses can correct it.
Red spot covering all or part of white of eye.	Subconjunctival hemorrhage—bleeding from small blood vessels in membrane over eyeball.	Harmless, though can look alarming. Usually no apparent cause; may follow injury, coughing, or sneezing. Should clear up in 2–3 days. Call doctor for advice if painful or if bleeding recurs.
Dry, hot, or scratchy eyes.	Lack of moisture due to aging, medications, or air pollution.	Moisten eyes with over-the-counter "artificial tears." Apply cold compresses.
Spots or "threads" that float across field of vision.	Floaters—collagen fragments floating in the jellylike liquid that fills the eye.	Usually harmless. Call doctor for advice the first time you see them.

fever

The average body temperature is 98.6 degrees, but some people have higher or lower normal levels. Temperatures also tend to rise as the day goes on. In adults, a fever is a temperature of 100 or higher. A reading of 100.4 in infants under 3 months, 102 in children, or 103 in adults is reason to call your doctor for advice. Many of us feel our foreheads to detect a fever, but that isn't reliable. Use a glass or digital thermometer.

SYMPTOMS	WHAT IT MIGHT BE	WHAT YOU CAN DO
Fever after some hours in a hot place, no sweating, rapid heartbeat, confusion, loss of consciousness.	Heatstroke.	Call 911 or go to emergency room **right away.**
Fever with very painful headache, stiff neck, nausea, aversion to light, drowsiness, confusion, red or purple rash (sometimes).	Meningitis—inflammation of the membranes that cover the spinal cord and brain.	Call 911 or go to emergency room **right away.**
Fever and stiff jaw, muscle spasms and pain, sweating, trouble swallowing.	Tetanus (sometimes called lockjaw)—bacterial infection from a wound.	Call 911 or go to emergency room **right away.**
Sudden, high fever; vomiting and diarrhea; red rash; fatigue; headache, confusion, and dizziness.	Toxic shock syndrome.	Call 911 or go to emergency room **right away.**
In children: fever, sudden seizures; turning blue in face (maybe).	Fever seizure.	If seizure is severe or lasts more than a few minutes, call 911 or go to emergency room **right away.** Otherwise, lay child on side or stomach, away from sharp objects. Most often harmless.
Rapid onset of fever, chills, pounding heart, confusion, signs of infection.	Blood poisoning.	Call doctor **right away;** if you can't reach one, call 911 or go to emergency room.
Low fever, pain in lower right part of abdomen, nausea and vomiting.	Appendicitis.	Call doctor for prompt appointment. Meanwhile, don't eat or take laxatives; surgery may be needed.

fever

SYMPTOMS	WHAT IT MIGHT BE	WHAT YOU CAN DO
Low fever at first, higher 1–3 weeks later; pain in lower pelvis; foul discharge from vagina; painful urination.	Pelvic inflammatory disease (see page 209).	Call doctor for prompt appointment.
Fever and cough, with or without sputum; chest pain; shortness of breath.	Pneumonia.	Call doctor for prompt appointment.
Sudden onset of fever and sore throat with white coating on tonsils; bright red rash about 24 hours later.	Scarlet fever.	Call doctor for prompt appointment.
Fevers, night sweats, swollen lymph nodes, repeat infections, weight loss, fatigue, diarrhea, sores.	HIV infection. ■ AIDS.	Call doctor for advice and testing appointment.
Low fever, nausea or loss of appetite, yellowish skin or eyes (jaundice), dark urine, light-colored stools, fatigue.	Hepatitis (see page 196).	Call doctor for advice and appointment.
Fatigue lasting weeks or months, bad sore throat, fever, swollen lymph glands.	Mononucleosis—viral illness spread by close contact such as kissing; attacks breathing system, liver, spleen, and lymph glands; most common in teens and young adults.	Call doctor for advice and appointment. Getting well takes 10 days to 6 months. Go back to normal activities over time.
Persistent low fever; coughing, sometimes with bloody sputum; chest pain; weight loss; heavy night sweats.	Tuberculosis.	Call doctor for advice and appointment.
High fever (over 103), weakness, headache, chills, raw throat, dry cough, runny nose, aching muscles.	Flu (see page 186).	Call doctor for advice. In children, fever of 102 or higher may be risky.
In children: fever with dry cough, loud breathing, runny nose, red eyes, blisters, swelling, or rash.	Any of many childhood diseases.	Call doctor for advice.

headaches

Most people have an occasional harmless headache, but many Americans—some 50 million—have intense, chronic head pain. Symptoms vary from person to person; you may have all or only some of them. Headaches can also be a sign of serious illness.

SYMPTOMS	WHAT IT MIGHT BE	WHAT YOU CAN DO
Sudden, severe headache; paralysis, weakness, or numbness on one side of body; nausea, vomiting; delirium; often seizures or loss of consciousness; trouble speaking, moving, or seeing; dizziness and confusion; possibly fever.	Stroke.	Call 911 **right away.**
Fever, headache, nausea and vomiting, stiff neck, aversion to light, red rash (sometimes), confusion.	Meningitis—inflammation of the membranes that cover the spinal cord and brain.	Call 911 or go to emergency room **right away.**
Headache on waking that gets worse when you lie down, nausea and vomiting, double vision, dizziness, loss of memory, personality changes. Head pain comes on slowly but persists and grows worse over time (often months).	Brain tumor.	Call doctor for prompt appointment.
Intense eye pain, headache, nausea and vomiting, vision problems.	Glaucoma—buildup of pressure inside the eye; can damage optic nerve.	Call doctor for prompt appointment.
Sudden, intense headache; dry mouth; sticky saliva; fatigue; thirst (sometimes).	Dehydration—particularly if headache follows nausea and vomiting (see page 202) or diarrhea (see page 183).	Call doctor for prompt appointment if symptoms are severe. Drink small amounts of liquids often.
Severe, throbbing pain, often on one side of head; vision problems; aversion to light and noise; dizziness; nausea; vomiting.	Migraine headache.	Use over-the-counter pain-killers. Rest in dark room. Apply ice packs. See doctor about stronger medication or other help if pain persists or recurs.

knee pain

The knee is a hinge meant to swing one way—forward and back—within limits. Twisting to the side or bending too far back can cause injury. Most knee trouble can be prevented. When things do go wrong, treatment often brings good results.

SYMPTOMS	WHAT IT MIGHT BE	WHAT YOU CAN DO
Pain and perhaps a "pop" at moment of injury; swelling, stiffness, a "wobbly" knee, trouble walking.	Ligament sprain or rupture, and/or cartilage damage.	Call doctor for prompt appointment. Use RICE treatment for pain and swelling (see box, page 208).
In teens: pain and swelling about 2 inches below kneecap; may cause limping or prevent running.	Osgood-Schlatter disease— inflamed tendon and bone.	Call doctor for advice and appointment. Use RICE treatment (see box, page 208).
Pain, swelling, and stiffness in knee joint.	Arthritis (see page 165).	Call doctor for advice and appointment.
Tender, stiff, and swollen knee; pain when bending knee; possibly fever or redness.	Bursitis—inflammation where bones, tendons, and ligaments meet.	Call doctor for advice and appointment.
Pain just below kneecap, may be worse when sitting or straightening leg; may be felt after running or jumping; knee pain and tightness that worsen with movement.	Patellar tendinitis, "runner's knee" or "jumper's knee" (see overuse injuries, page 205).	Call doctor for advice and appointment. Use RICE treatment for pain and swelling (see box, page 208).

menstrual irregularities

All women should have pelvic exams as often as once a year if they are sexually active, so that any problems can be found and treated early. Be sure to tell your doctor about any changes in your menstrual cycle.

SYMPTOMS	WHAT IT MIGHT BE	WHAT YOU CAN DO
Missed or very heavy, painful menstrual periods; cramps, pain, or pressure in lower abdomen; vaginal spotting or bleeding. Sometimes no symptoms.	Ectopic pregnancy— pregnancy outside uterus, usually in fallopian tube.	Call doctor for prompt appointment. If bleeding or abdominal pain is severe, call 911 or go to emergency room **right away.**
Bleeding or spotting during pregnancy.	Common, but may signal a problem.	Call a doctor for prompt advice. If you can't reach one, call 911 or go to emergency room **right away.**
Very heavy or painful periods, chiefly toward the end; pain in lower abdomen, vagina, or lower back that may begin just before period and worsen just after; pain during intercourse; blood in urine or stool while menstruating; nausea and vomiting just before period begins.	Endometriosis—disorder in which tissue that lines uterus grows outside uterus and becomes attached to other organs.	If you have symptoms for the first time or if pain is severe, call doctor for prompt appointment.
Very heavy, irregular, or missed menstrual periods; pain in lower abdomen or back; foul-smelling vaginal discharge; pain during intercourse; fever and sometimes chills.	Pelvic inflammatory disease (see page 209)—infection of reproductive organs, often caused by sexually transmitted diseases (see chart on page 158).	Call doctor for prompt appointment.
Changes in heaviness of flow, length of periods, or time between periods; aches or pain in abdomen; feeling of fullness, swelling, or pressure in abdomen; frequent urination.	Noncancerous ovarian cyst. ▪ Noncancerous ovarian tumor. ▪ Ovarian cancer.	Call doctor for prompt appointment. It's vital to diagnose cancer right away.

menstrual irregularities

SYMPTOMS	WHAT IT MIGHT BE	WHAT YOU CAN DO
Very heavy or painful menstrual period that begins a week or more late.	Early pregnancy and miscarriage.	If you think you may be pregnant and you are bleeding, call doctor for advice and appointment.
No menstrual period for several months.	Amenorrhea (absence of menstruation), which can be caused by emotional distress, hormone imbalance, dieting or eating disorders (see eating disorders, page 185), or strenuous athletic training. ■ Pregnancy. ■ Breast-feeding. ■ Menopause. ■ Abnormality of reproductive organs. ■ Use of certain drugs. ■ Stopping use of birth control pills.	Call doctor for advice. Note: If a young woman is over 16 and has never had a menstrual period, schedule appointment with doctor.
Very heavy periods; bleeding between periods; pain or discomfort in lower back or abdomen; frequent urination; constipation; possibly sudden, sharp pain in lower abdomen. Sometimes no symptoms.	Uterine fibroid tumors—common, noncancerous masses in uterus. Sometimes tumor becomes twisted, cutting off its blood supply and causing severe pain.	Call doctor for advice and appointment. Write down dates you are bleeding and how many pads or tampons you use each day.
Very heavy or painful menstrual periods while using IUD or after you stop taking birth control pills.	Common side effect of IUDs. ■ Hormonal changes caused by going off the Pill.	Call doctor for advice about your birth control method.
Very heavy menstrual period soon after childbirth.	Normal.	If you have more than 2 heavy periods after giving birth, call doctor for advice.
Menstrual flow that is always heavy; periods that last more than 7 days; large clots of blood.	Probably no problem, but heavy bleeding can result in anemia (see page 164).	If bleeding is very heavy (you use more than 1 pad or tampon in an hour), call doctor for advice.

sexually transmitted diseases

Sexually transmitted diseases (STDs) may produce no symptoms at first. When symptoms do show up, they may be confused with those of other diseases. If you are infected but don't have symptoms, you can still pass on an STD. Note, too, that an open sore or irritated skin from an STD puts you at greater risk of catching HIV. So if you have sex with more than one person, testing and checkups are vital, as is safe sex.

SYMPTOMS	WHAT IT MIGHT BE	WHAT YOU CAN DO
Early to later: sore throat; fever; swollen glands in the neck, underarms, and groin. Fatigue, fever chills, and night sweats. Frequent colds, cold sores, oral fungal or yeast infections. Sudden weight loss, chronic diarrhea, dry cough, breathing problems, sores, vision loss. Confusion, memory loss.	AIDS—Caused by HIV (human immunodeficiency virus), found in blood, semen, and vaginal fluids, and sometimes in saliva and breast milk. HIV is spread mostly through sexual contact or by sharing needles. An infected woman can pass it to her child during childbirth or breast-feeding.	Call your doctor for a prompt appointment. Get an HIV test right away. In most cities, you can get the test without giving your name. If you are infected, the sooner you know it the better, so that you can start treatment to slow the onset of AIDS.
Watery mucus from vagina, burning with urination, mild lower abdominal pain 1–3 weeks after infection. Some people (mostly women) may have no symptoms.	Chlamydia—bacterial disease. Can result in pelvic inflammatory disease in women (see page 209) or sterility. In newborns exposed during childbirth, can cause pneumonia, eye infections, and blindness.	Call doctor for prompt appointment. You and your partner(s) should be treated with antibiotics.
Itching or burning pain in genital area, then red bumps in or on genitals that may turn into blisters or open sores 2–10 days after infection. These go away within 3 weeks. Later attacks (with same symptoms) heal faster.	Genital herpes—viral infection spread through sex, from cold sores, or, rarely, by hands that have herpes blisters or sores. Most contagious when symptoms are present. Baby can catch from mother during childbirth.	Call doctor for prompt appointment. Medications shorten outbreaks and make them less severe. Don't have sex until sores heal. **For more help:** National Herpes Hotline, 919-361-8488, M–F 9–7 EST.
Small, round, red, flat, itchy bumps on genitals, around anus, or inside vagina; can also appear in mouth of someone who has had oral contact with genitals of infected person.	Genital warts—infection by human papillomavirus (HPV). Some strains of HPV raise risk of cervical cancer. After warts are removed, virus remains and can cause future outbreaks.	Call doctor for prompt appointment. Treatment can include drugs or laser surgery. Don't use over-the-counter wart treatments. Women who've had warts should get a Pap smear every 6 months.

sexually transmitted diseases

SYMPTOMS	WHAT IT MIGHT BE	WHAT YOU CAN DO
Thick yellowish discharge from vagina, burning and itching with urination, maybe discharge from rectum 2–10 days after infection. In later stages in women: abdominal pain, bleeding between periods.	Gonorrhea—bacterial infection. If left untreated, may spread to joints, tendons, or heart. May also cause pelvic inflammatory disease in women (see page 209). Infants exposed during birth can become blind.	Call doctor for prompt appointment. Treatment consists of antibiotics and painkillers. Don't have sex until doctor says it's safe. Your partner(s) should be tested and treated even if they have no symptoms.
Painless sores on or in genitals, rectal area, or mouth, and enlarged lymph nodes near sores 10 days to 3 months after infection. If untreated, in second stage (3 weeks to several months later): mild fever, rash, patchy hair loss, sore throat.	Syphilis—bacterial infection. Can damage brain, nervous system, and heart; can be fatal. Highly contagious in first 2 stages but not in third stage. Infected mothers may pass infection to infants during childbirth.	Call doctor for prompt appointment. Antibiotics can cure syphilis, although in later stages some damage cannot be reversed. Don't have sex during treatment. Your partner(s) should be tested and treated.
In women, heavy greenish-yellow or gray discharge from vagina, pain during intercourse, vaginal odor, painful urination 4–20 days after infection. Men may have no symptoms.	Trichomoniasis—infection caused by parasite. May increase risk that baby born to infected mother will be premature or underweight.	Call doctor for prompt appointment. You and your partner(s) will be treated with antibiotics. A man may have no symptoms but can infect others if not treated. Don't have sex until treatment is finished.

for more help

organizations   National HIV/AIDS Hotline, Centers for Disease Control and Prevention, English: 800-342-2437, 24-hour line; Spanish: 800-344-7432, 8AM–2AM EST. Calls are confidential. Staff answers questions and refers callers to experts on health and other issues.

■ National Institute of Allergy and Infectious Diseases, Office of Communications, Bldg. 31, Room 7A-50, 31 Center Dr., MSC 2520, Bethesda, MD 20892-2520. *www.niaid.nih.gov.* For fact sheet on STD: *www.niaid.nih.gov/factsheets/stdinfo.htm.*

■ National STD Hotline, Centers for Disease Control and Prevention, 800-227-8922, 24-hour line. Staff answers questions and gives lists of public clinics and testing sites.

web sites   Go Ask Alice, *www.goaskalice.columbia.edu.* Columbia University's health question-and-answer service. Covers a wide range of topics, including sexual health.

■ The Safer Sex Institute, *www.safersex.org.* Offers tips on safer sex and facts about STD prevention.

book   *Sexually Transmitted Diseases: A Physician Tells You What You Need to Know,* by Lisa Marr, M.D. Gives basic anatomy information and describes symptoms and treatments for 22 STDs. Johns Hopkins Press, 1999, $16.95.

problems & solutions

allergies

signs and symptoms

Hay fever (allergic rhinitis):

- Frequent sneezing.
- Itchy or teary eyes.
- Runny or stuffy nose.
- Itching in back of throat or on roof of mouth.

Allergic asthma:

- Sneezing, wheezing, and coughing.
- In some cases, trouble breathing.

Food allergies:

- Outbreaks of itchy, red, or bumpy skin.
- Upset stomach.

Drug allergies:

- Outbreaks of itchy, red, or bumpy skin, sometimes with flulike symptoms such as headache, low fever, and joint pain.

You have an allergy when your body over-reacts to things that don't bother other people. To fight what it mistakes as a threat, your immune system unleashes a compound called histamine that can provoke the sneezing, itching, and other symptoms of allergies.

Hay fever is one of the most common allergies—nearly 1 in 5 Americans has it. Pollen, bits of animal skin called dander, household dust, dust mites, and molds can set it off.

Food allergies—which are rare—occur more often in children than adults; children tend to outgrow them by the age of 3. The foods that most often cause allergies include nuts, eggs, and milk. Seafood and peanuts tend to produce the strongest reactions, even shock or death in rare cases; the treatment is a shot of epinephrine. People seldom outgrow seafood and peanut allergies. Reactions to drugs such as penicillin or to insect stings can be just as deadly.

Many allergies can be handled with minor changes at home. If yours are severe, though, your doctor might prescribe antihistamines, steroid nasal sprays, or shots to relieve your symptoms. Some people with allergies find a measure of relief in complementary treatments such as homeopathy, acupuncture, or herbs.

what you can do now

- If you're allergic to pollen, try to stay indoors with the windows closed when pollen levels are likely to be high, especially if it's windy. To keep cool, use your air conditioner if you have one, or open a window and put a clean ordinary furnace filter across it.
- To relieve hay fever symptoms, try an over-the-counter antihistamine or decongestant. Antihistamines block the action of histamine, so they help relieve itchy eyes, sneezing, and runny nose; they can also cause drowsiness, though some prescription versions don't. Decongestants reduce stuffiness. They aren't always as effective as antihistamines, but they can bring relief without the sleepiness. Check with your doctor or pharmacist before using any of these drugs if you are already taking other over-the-counter or prescription medicines.
- If you're allergic to insect stings or have severe reactions to some foods, ask your doctor for an emergency kit with an antihistamine and an epinephrine shot. Always carry the kit with you.

- If you often have itchy or teary eyes, try over-the-counter eyedrops, or ask your doctor about eyedrops that contain antihistamines or cromolyn sodium.

when to call the doctor

Call 911 **right away:**
- If you get a rapid heartbeat and skin welts along with flushing, itching, dizziness, and trouble breathing. You could be having a potentially fatal reaction called anaphylactic shock.

Call 911 or go to an emergency room **right away:**
- If it becomes very difficult or painful to breathe. You may be having an attack of **asthma** (see page 167).
- If you have severe stomach cramps, vomiting, bloating, or diarrhea. This could signal a reaction to a food.

Call for advice:
- If you have recurring allergies. Your doctor may refer you to an allergy specialist, who can test you to find out what causes your attacks.

how to prevent it

- Try to figure out what you're allergic to so that you can avoid it. (If you're allergic to a common drug such as penicillin, be sure to wear a medical alert tag.)
- If you're allergic to cats or dogs, stay away from them—or at least see that your pets are bathed often, and keep them out of your bedroom.
- If you're allergic to molds, keep your house clean and dry. Key trouble spots are bathrooms (chiefly shower stalls), refrigerator drip trays, basements, and closets. Use a dehumidifier in muggy weather or if your basement is damp.
- If you sneeze and cough year-round, you may be among the millions of people who are allergic to dust mites (tiny bugs that live in house dust). Try to keep your house—your bedroom most of all—free of dust. Encase mattresses in nonallergenic covers. Wash your bedding weekly in hot water (at least 130 degrees); if you keep your water heater set lower to protect your children from scalding, try a Laundromat. Leave your floors bare or use washable area rugs instead of carpets. Avoid upholstered furniture and other dust-catchers. Vacuum often (use a nonporous bag), or better yet, have someone else do it.
- If you have a severe food allergy, read package labels. When dining out, ask what's in dishes before you order.
- Don't smoke, and avoid smoky places, dust, and insect sprays.

for more help

Organizations: American Academy of Allergy, Asthma and Immunology, 611 E. Wells St., Milwaukee, WI 53202. 800-822-2762, 24-hour recording, or 414-272-6071, M–F 8–5 CST, for questions and information about allergies; *www.aaaai.org*. Staff sends brochures. At Web site, click on *Patient/Public Resource Center* and choose a topic.
- American Academy of Otolaryngology–Head and Neck Surgery, 1 Prince St., Alexandria, VA 22314. 703-836-4444, M–F 8:30–5 EST; *www.entnet.org*. Send a business-size self-addressed stamped envelope and request a brochure on allergies. At Web site, click on *Patient Info,* then *Allergy.*
- Asthma and Allergy Foundation of America, 1233 20th St. NW, Suite 402, Washington, DC 20036. 800-727-8462, M–F 8–7 EST; *www.aafa.org*. Web site lists local support groups.
- National Jewish Medical and Research Center, 1400 Jackson St., Denver, CO 80206. 800-222-5864 (Lung Line Information Service), M–F 8–5 MST, or 800-552-5864 (Lung Facts), 24-hour recording that offers information on breathing problems; *www.nationaljewish.org*. Nurses send brochures, answer questions, and make referrals. At Web site, click on *Diseases We Treat,* then *Allergy Programs.*

Web sites: The Allergy Learning Lab, *www.allergylearninglab.com*. Addresses allergy symptoms, treatments, and triggers.
- National Pollen Network's Allernet, *www.allernet.com*. Answers questions and offers a directory of allergy specialists.

Books: *Allergies: The Complete Guide to Diagnosis, Treatment, and Daily Management,* by Stuart H. Young, M.D., Bruce S. Dobozin, M.D., and Margaret Miner. Covers advances in treatment. Plume, 1999, $13.95.
- *The Complete Allergy Book,* by June Engel, Ph.D. Explains causes of allergies and gives tips on avoiding triggers and treating symptoms. Firefly, 1998, $14.95.

anemia

signs and symptoms

Main symptoms:

- Feeling tired and weak.
- Pasty skin; pale gums, nail beds, and eyelid linings.
- Shortness of breath, dizziness, and fainting.
- Headaches and trouble focusing.

Iron deficiency anemia:

Main symptoms, plus:
- Brittle nails.
- Black or bloody stools from bleeding in the intestines.

Folic acid deficiency anemia:

Main symptoms, plus:
- Sore mouth and tongue.
- Loss of appetite.
- Swollen abdomen.
- Nausea and diarrhea.

Vitamin B12 deficiency anemia:

Main symptoms, plus:
- Sore mouth and tongue.
- Problems with walking and balance.
- Tingling in hands and feet.
- Memory loss and confusion.

If you are anemic, your blood has trouble carrying oxygen to your tissues and taking away carbon dioxide. You become anemic either because you don't have enough red blood cells or because your red blood cells lack a protein that lets them carry oxygen. There are many kinds of anemia.

Women who have heavy menstrual flow, or who are pregnant or nursing, may get **iron deficiency anemia.** It is most often handled with iron supplements. But if the anemia stems from ailments that cause blood loss, such as **ulcers** (see page 218) or stomach or colon cancer, the problem behind it needs to be treated.

Lack of folic acid, a vitamin needed to make red blood cells, can cause **folic acid deficiency anemia.** Teens, pregnant women, smokers, alcoholics, and people who don't eat well are at risk.

Vitamin B12 deficiency anemia (the most common type is called pernicious anemia) may affect the brain, spinal cord, and mental functions for life. In the United States, B12 anemia is rarely caused by a lack of B12 in the diet. Instead, it most often comes on if you're unable to absorb the vitamin from food—a problem that can be genetic. Conditions such as inflammatory bowel disease also can reduce absorption of B12.

A rare form, **aplastic anemia,** isn't related to diet; it can be caused by a virus or by radiation, powerful medicines, or toxins such as benzene.

Anemia can sometimes be a sign of leukemia, lymphoma (cancer of the lymph system), chronic kidney disease, or other chronic ailments.

what you can do now

If you think you have anemia, call your doctor. **Note:** Don't take over-the-counter iron pills. Too much iron can cause symptoms like those of anemia and make you feel worse, and may make it hard to tell what's really wrong.

when to call the doctor

Call 911 or go to an emergency room **right away:**
- If, after taking iron pills, you get bloody diarrhea, fever, fatigue, vomiting, or seizures. Too much iron in your system can be fatal.

Call for advice:

- If you have symptoms of anemia.
- If you are being treated for diet-related anemia and don't get better in 2 weeks.

how to prevent it

To get enough iron:

- Eat plenty of iron-rich foods, such as potatoes, broccoli, raisins, beans, oatmeal, and blackstrap molasses.
- Include lean red meat, liver, and shellfish in your diet.
- Don't drink coffee or tea with meals. They contain a substance that makes it hard for your body to absorb iron.

To get enough folic acid:

- Eat plenty of citrus fruits (grapefruit, oranges), beans, and green vegetables.
- Include liver, eggs, and milk in your diet.
- If you drink alcohol, drink moderately—no more than 1 drink a day for women, 2 for men. (A drink is a 12-ounce beer, a 5-ounce glass of wine, or a 1.5-ounce shot of hard liquor.) Alcohol can affect how well your body absorbs folic acid.
- If you're pregnant or nursing, or if you have very heavy periods, discuss your diet with your doctor.

To get enough vitamin B12:

- Include meat, chicken, fish, and dairy products in your diet. Buy cereals with added B12.

for more help

Organization: National Heart, Lung, and Blood Institute Information Center, P.O. Box 30105, Bethesda, MD 20824-0105. 301-592-8573, M–F 8:30–5 EST; *www.nhlbi.nih. gov.* Staff answers questions and sends brochures about anemia.

arthritis

signs and symptoms

Osteoarthritis:

- Joint pain that is made worse by movement.
- Stiffness in the morning.
- Knobby growths on finger joints.

Rheumatoid arthritis:

- Painful, swollen joints that may feel warm.
- Low fever, loss of weight and appetite, feeling "sick all over."
- Morning stiffness.
- Skin lumps, often on the elbows, fingers, or buttocks.
- Dry, itching eyes and dry mouth.

Gout:

- Severe, sudden pain in a joint, often the wrist, big toe, or knee.
- Redness, swelling around joint.
- Fever.

Arthritis is a name given to more than 100 kinds of mild to crippling joint problems that cause swelling, pain, and stiffness. Three types are most common:

Osteoarthritis is caused by chips and cracks in the smooth cartilage that cushions the joints. When bone surfaces have too little cushioning, they rub together and may grow bumps, called spurs, that irritate nearby tissue. Osteoarthritis is the most common form of arthritis, affecting more than 23 million Americans. More than half of those older than 65 have osteoarthritis. It most often occurs in the hands or in weight-bearing joints such as the knee and hip.

Rheumatoid arthritis results when the lining of the capsule around a joint becomes inflamed and thickened, causing swelling, pain, and stiffness. Rheumatoid arthritis can also inflame the eyes and lungs. Some experts think it's the result of a problem with the body's immune system—the body attacks its own tissues as if they were foreign invaders. It may also be hereditary. Rheumatoid arthritis most often affects people between 20 and 50, and more women than men, some 2.5 million Americans.

Gout usually affects men over 40 and is caused by high blood levels of uric acid, one of the body's waste products, which forms crystals in the joints. The immune system tries to defend the body against these crystals, and the joint becomes inflamed and painful. Symptoms of each attack go away in about a week.

Treatment of arthritis depends on the type and how bad it is. Most cases can be treated with gentle exercise to keep the bones and muscles strong and supple. Drugs also reduce pain, swelling, and stiffness. New painkillers called COX-2 inhibitors offer relief with less risk of the stomach ulcers and bleeding caused by common arthritis drugs. For rheumatoid arthritis, two new types of drugs help ease pain by actually slowing the disease's progression; there's even a new device that filters inflammation-causing antibodies from the blood in advanced cases. Gout can be treated with drugs to reduce uric acid in the blood. And in some severe cases of osteoarthritis and rheumatoid arthritis, surgery may be used to smooth rough joint surfaces or replace a damaged joint.

what you can do now

- For rheumatoid arthritis, take aspirin or the anti-inflammatory painkiller recommended by your doctor. If these upset your stomach, try an "enteric-coated" brand that delays release of the drug until it has passed through your stomach. Or ask your doctor about other drugs aimed at reducing the risk of ulcers.
- For osteoarthritis, use acetaminophen. If you have gout, don't take aspirin, which inhibits the body's ability to excrete uric acid. Take aspirin, ibuprofen, or naproxen separately; never combine them (see **pain relief** box, page 207).
- Apply cold packs to swollen, painful joints, or warm packs for stiffness without other symptoms, for 10 minutes every hour.
- For pain relief, apply an over-the-counter cream that contains methyl salicylate or

capsaicin, a substance in hot peppers.
- Twice a day, put each joint gently through a full range of motion to prevent stiffness.
- Take a warm shower or bath in the morning to relieve stiffness.
- Enroll in an arthritis self-help program or join a support group with other people going through the same things you are.
- To ease the strain on painful hand joints, use electric can openers and large rubber grips for pens or tools.
- Don't grip objects tightly for a long time.
- Eat more than 2 servings a week of fish rich in omega-3 polyunsaturated fatty acids (salmon, mackerel, or sardines) or take capsules of omega-3 to help reduce inflammation.
- Get lots of rest.

when to call the doctor

- If you have joint pain or stiffness that gets in the way of normal activities.
- If you have fever or chills along with other arthritis symptoms. You may have infectious arthritis, caused by bacteria, which can be treated with antibiotics.
- If you get the painful symptoms of gout.
- If your arthritis doesn't get better.

how to prevent it

Osteoarthritis:
- Exercise gently and often to keep your bones and muscles strong. Swimming, biking, yoga, and low-impact or water aerobics are ideal.
- If you weigh more than you should, lose those extra pounds. Too much weight puts added pressure on the joints.
- Try not to do the same movements over and over—for instance, typing.
- Stand up straight to ease strain on joints.

Rheumatoid arthritis:
There's no known way to prevent rheumatoid arthritis.

Gout:
- Control your weight, but don't fast; fasting can raise levels of uric acid.
- If you drink, drink moderately—women should have no more than 1 drink a day,

men no more than 2. (A drink is a 1.5-ounce shot of hard liquor, a 5-ounce glass of wine, or a 12-ounce beer.)

- Avoid protein-rich foods such as organ meats, shellfish, and beans.
- Drink plenty of water—at least 10 big glasses a day to help flush out uric acid.

complementary choices

- Acupuncture may help. Studies by the National Institutes of Health and others have found it relieves chronic arthritis pain.
- Some people with arthritis find that stress reduction such as yoga or meditation eases their pain. Massage also may help.
- Supplements of two natural substances, glucosamine and chondroitin, appear to help maintain cartilage and even repair damage from arthritis.

for more help

Organizations: Arthritis Foundation, 1330 W. Peachtree St., Atlanta, GA 30309. 800-283-7800, 24-hour recording, or 404-872-7100, M–F 9–5 EST; *www.arthritis.org.* Provides tips on exercise and pain control, and lists support groups near you. Membership, starting at $20, includes a subscription to *Arthritis Today* magazine.

- National Institute of Arthritis and Musculoskeletal and Skin Diseases Information Clearinghouse, 1 AMS Circle, Bethesda, MD 20892-3675. 877-226-4267, M–F 8:30–5 EST; *www.nih.gov/niams.* Click on *Health Information* and then on *NIAMS Brochures and Other Publications.*

Web site: Intelihealth, *www.intelihealth.com.* Click on *Arthritis* for facts and articles on the disorder.

Books: *The Arthritis Foundation's Guide to Alternative Therapies,* by Judith Horstman. Advice on nontraditional arthritis treatment. Longstreet Press, 1999, $24.95.

- *Mayo Clinic on Arthritis,* edited by Gene G. Hunder, M.D. Kensington, 1999, $14.95.
- *250 Tips for Making Life With Arthritis Easier,* by Shelley Peterman Schwarz. Longstreet Press, 1997, $9.95.

asthma

signs and symptoms

Mild or moderate attack:

- Coughing.
- Feeling of tightness in the chest.
- Noisy breathing (wheezing).
- Trouble catching your breath.

Severe attack:

- Rapid, shallow breathing.
- Trouble talking because of rapid breathing.
- Racing pulse.
- Panic.

About 1 person in every 15 has asthma. If you have it, your bronchial tubes—the tiny airways in your lungs—are inflamed and supersensitive. Most of the time you can breathe normally, but not during an asthma attack. During such an episode, the airways swell and fill with mucus, and muscles around them tighten. When that happens, you may cough, wheeze, and feel short of breath. Episodes can come on fast and last from a few minutes to a day or longer.

No one knows why some people have asthma and others don't; we do know, though, that most asthma episodes are triggered by things you inhale. Dust, pollen, pet dander (bits of skin), germs, molds, smoke, and chemical fumes can spark an attack. So can exercise, cold air, certain foods—seafood or peanuts, for instance—emotional peaks and dips, a common cold, and pregnancy. About a third of women with asthma find that it gets worse when they're pregnant. For a small number of people, aspirin and some other painkillers can start an attack.

Asthma is a chronic disease. That means you may have it for the rest of your life, with symptoms that come and go. It often starts during childhood, and it's more common and more serious among African American children. Many youngsters seem to outgrow it, but it can return when they're adults.

Without prompt medical help, severe asthma can be fatal. Once you know how to manage it, though, chances are you can control it by taking medications and by staying away from things that trigger an attack.

what you can do now

- Monitor your breathing regularly with a peak flow meter if your doctor recommends it. A peak flow meter measures how well air moves in and out of your lungs. A dip in your meter's reading may warn you—hours ahead—that an episode is coming. Taking medicine may prevent or ease the attack.
- Recognize the signs of an oncoming episode. Many people with asthma learn to detect an episode quickly, so they can take steps to keep it from becoming severe. Typical warning signs include:
  - Tightness in the chest.
  - Scratchy throat and coughing.
  - Feeling very tired.
- Keep all your medicines in one place. They may include a bronchodilator—a spray drug to open your airways—in an inhaler that controls the dose. Rinse your mouth with water each time you use it to prevent thrush, a yeast infection (see **fungal infections,** page 187).

During an episode:

- Remain calm and quiet. Staying relaxed will help you breathe more easily.
- Don't lie down. You can breathe better when you sit upright and lean forward slightly, resting your elbows on a table.
- Use your medication exactly as instructed. Write down each dose and the time you took it; overdoses can be dangerous.
- Ask a friend, coworker, teacher, or family member to stay with you.

when to call the doctor

Call 911 or go to an emergency room **right away** if you notice any of these signs of troubled breathing:

- Difficulty talking because you feel you're suffocating.
- Nostrils flaring with the extra effort needed to pull in air.

- Skin between the ribs looking sucked-in as you inhale.
- Lips and nails tinged blue.

Call for a prompt appointment:

- The first time you have long-lasting trouble breathing, with or without coughing and wheezing.
- If the medicine your doctor prescribes fails to work as quickly as it's supposed to.
- If you cough up green, yellow, or bloody mucus.
- If you feel strange new symptoms. These may be side effects of your drugs or may mean your asthma is getting worse.

how to prevent it

Anyone with asthma should be under a doctor's care. New approaches to treatment and new medicines can help prevent or ease episodes, with fewer side effects than before. Also:

- Track your attacks by keeping a diary: How frequent? How severe? What happened just before? Notice whether certain foods, drugs, or actions seem to bring on an attack. You can't avoid everything that might bring on an attack. Still, keep an eye on:
  - Pollen and dirty air. When you know that pollution levels are high, keep windows closed and use air conditioning if you can.
  - Dust. Vacuum often, wearing a dust mask. Or, if you can, ask someone else to do it.
  - Humidity. Dust mites and molds (common allergy triggers) love damp air, so use a dehumidifier to control them. Clean the tank often.
  - Cockroaches. These insects are one of the leading causes of asthma attacks in children. Ward off cockroaches by storing food in airtight containers and wiping up crumbs right away.
  - Dust-catchers in the bedroom, such as large shelves of books. Move them out.
  - Pillows. Doctors often recommend foam-rubber pillows. But recent research suggests that the densely woven covers on down pillows may repel dust mites and pet dander better than foam does. If you can, try both to see which you prefer.
  - Bedding. Avoid wool blankets and down comforters; use washable cotton blankets

instead. Wash blankets every week. Wash sheets and pillowcases more often if you can. The wash water should be 130 degrees or hotter to kill mites. (If you keep your water heater set lower to protect children from scalding, try a Laundromat.) Use a dryer; pollen sticks to anything that's hung outside.

- Pets. If being around cats or dogs causes attacks, don't keep pets with hair or fur. If you can't bear to part with Kitty or Fido, try to bathe your pet every week and keep it out of the bedroom.
- Don't smoke, and stay out of smoky rooms and away from people who are smoking.
- Exercise regularly, but don't overdo it. Swimming is good—unless chlorine in pools bothers you—since the damp air helps ease breathing. If a certain exercise triggers your asthma, try others.
- Ward off colds and flu by washing your hands often and getting a yearly flu shot.
- Learn ways to relax such as yoga, meditation, or deep breathing; easing stress can reduce the number and strength of attacks.

for more help

Organizations: Allergy and Asthma Network/Mothers of Asthmatics, 2751 Prosperity Ave., Suite 150, Fairfax, VA 22031. 800-878-4403, M–F 9–5 EST; *www.aanma.org.* Offers information and brochures.

- American Lung Association, 1740 Broadway, New York, NY 10019. 800-586-4872, M–F 9–5 your time; *www.lungusa.org.* Refers you to a local ALA chapter and gives information. At Web site, click on *Diseases A to Z,* then *A–Z Listing of Lung Diseases,* then *Asthma.*
- Asthma and Allergy Foundation of America, 1233 20th St. NW, Suite 402, Washington, DC 20036. 800-727-8462, M–F 8–7 EST; *www.aafa.org.*
- National Jewish Medical and Research Center, 1400 Jackson St., Denver, CO 80206. 800-222-5864 (Lung Line Information Service), M–F 8–5 MST; 800-552-5864 (Lung Facts), 24-hour recording that offers information on breathing problems; *www. nationaljewish.org.* Nurses answer questions,

make referrals, and send brochures. At Web site, click on *Diseases We Treat,* then *Asthma Programs.*

Web sites: Asthma Information Center, *www. mdnet.de/asthma.* Patients and professionals share the latest information on treatments.

- Journal of the American Medical Association's Asthma Information Center, *www. ama-assn.org/special/asthma.* Offers in-depth news, literature, and clinical guidelines.

Books: *Essential Guide to Asthma,* by the American Medical Association. Pocket Books, 2000, $6.99.

- *The American Lung Association Family Guide to Asthma and Allergies: How You and Your Children Can Breathe Easier,* by the American Lung Association Asthma Advisory Group, with Norman H. Edelman, M.D. Little, Brown, 1998, $13.95.

back pain

signs and symptoms

- Pain low in the back; may be severe. It can come on quickly or slowly; it may be constant or occur only at certain times or when you are in a certain posture; it may be confined to one place or move to other parts of your back.
- Numbness, tingling, or a shooting pain in your legs or buttocks, often on one side.
- Pain made worse by coughing, sneezing, twisting.
- Stiffness.

Call a doctor **right away** if you also have these symptoms of nerve damage:

- Numbness or weakness, especially numbness around your groin or rectal area.
- Bladder or bowel control trouble.
- Weakness in one or both legs.

Most of us get back pain now and then, often in the lower back. In fact every year half the working people in the United States are bothered by low back pain at some time.

The spinal column, also called the backbone, is a series of bones (vertebrae) cushioned by small shock absorbers (disks) and held up by muscles and ligaments. Most low back pain comes from muscle or ligament strain, disk problems, stress, or sometimes all of these. The pain often goes away on its own, but it may return later.

Disks break down somewhat with age or from a lot of bending and twisting. In some cases, a swollen disk may press on a nerve in the lower back and send pain down the buttocks or legs. Most disk problems will clear up with proper care. In severe cases, surgery to remove the disk or part of it may help stem the pain and let the back be more functional.

what you can do now

- When your back starts hurting, apply an ice pack to reduce pain and swelling. Leave it there 10 to 15 minutes every hour. After 2 days, apply a heating pad or hot towel, or take hot showers. The heat will increase blood flow, bringing healing white cells to the sore spot.
- When pain is bad, lie flat on the floor with your knees bent and your lower legs on a chair or pile of pillows. This helps flatten the lower back and ease the strain.
- Sitting may be hard on a sore back. Stay away from soft chairs. Instead, try a straight-backed chair and don't sit down for a long time. Don't sit up in bed.
- Walk as much as you can, but only if walking doesn't make your pain worse.
- If pain disturbs your sleep, put pillows under your knees when lying on your back.
- If you sleep on your side, bend your knees and put a pillow between them. Don't lie on your stomach.
- Take acetaminophen, aspirin, or ibuprofen for the pain (see **pain relief** box, page 207). Don't bother with prescription drugs for relaxing muscles; they work no better and often have side effects.

exercise to strengthen back & stomach muscles

for your back
- Lie on your back on the floor. Straighten your back by pulling in your stomach muscles. Bend one knee and pull it against your chest, clasp your hands behind it, and straighten your leg. Repeat several times with each leg.
- Stand with your back against a wall with your heels about 4 inches from the wall. Pull in your stomach and roll your pelvis so your lower back lies flat against the wall. Repeat several times.

for your stomach
- Lie down with your back straight, your legs bent at the knees, and your feet flat on the floor. Fold your arms in front of your chest. Curl your head and shoulders off the floor without bending your neck forward. Hold for 5 seconds, then curl back down. Repeat several times. As you get stronger, increase the number of repetitions.

when to call the doctor
Call for advice **right away** (if your doctor is not in, call 911 or go to an emergency room):
- If you have back pain with symptoms of nerve damage, especially loss of bladder or bowel control.

Call for advice and an appointment:
- If back pain is severe or disrupts your normal activities.
- If the pain doesn't go away within a few days or keeps coming back.

how to prevent it
- Exercise as often as you can. Avoid twisting or wrenching your body, or doing anything that seems to make your back pain worse. Walking, swimming, and even walking in a swimming pool are ideal.
- Do exercises to strengthen the abdominal muscles (always do abdominal crunches with your knees bent). Also, stretch the muscles that run parallel to your spine (lie flat on

your back; pull one knee, then the other, toward your chest until both knees are tucked).

- Try yoga. Doctors and people with back pain like it for building strength and flexibility. It also helps you relax.
- Wear comfortable, low-heeled shoes.
- If you sit for long periods, make sure your work surface is at the right height for comfort and that your chair provides good lower back support. Walk around for a few minutes every half hour or so. If sitting is painful, try changing your work space so that you can stand with one foot on a low block.
- Don't lift and twist at the same time. Lift by bending your legs, not your back, and lift as little weight each time as possible.
- Lose weight if you need to. A big belly puts strain on the lower spine.

complementary choices

- Studies by the National Institutes of Health and others have found that acupuncture can be used to relieve pain from many conditions, including migraines, bladder infections, and chronic musculoskeletal problems.
- Chiropractic or osteopathic treatment may help. Some back pain is caused by misaligned spinal vertebrae, which affect surrounding muscles and may pinch nerves. Realignment of the spine through chiropractic, or gentle manipulation of other areas of the body through osteopathy, often relieves pain.
- Massage can loosen tight, painful muscles. Swedish massage, shiatsu, and rolfing are common types. Techniques vary, so you may need to try several to find a type that works for you.
- If you think stress could be the cause, learn to spot—and avoid—situations that make you tense. Many people don't realize that stress is making them tighten their back muscles (see **stress,** page 215).
- Learning some relaxation methods may help ease the pain. Practice deep breathing or meditation.

- Biofeedback—using electronic devices to monitor and control signals from your body —can help relieve pain. Biofeedback also may reduce stress.

for more help

Organizations: American Chronic Pain Association, P.O. Box 850, Rocklin, CA 95677. 916-632-0922, M–F 8:30–5 PST; *www.the acpa.org.* Offers pain management skills, advice, and recommended reading.
- National Chronic Pain Outreach Association, P.O. Box 274, Millboro, VA 24460. 540-862-9437, M–F 10–3 EST.
- Texas Back Institute, 6300 W. Parker Rd., Plano, TX 75093. 800-247-2225, M–F 8–5 CST; *www.texasback.com.*

Web site: Spine Universe, *spineuniverse.com.* Thorough site covering new technology and diagnostic tools and how to find a specialist.

Books: *Back Pain: How to Relieve Low Back Pain and Sciatica,* by Loren Fishman, M.D., and Carol Ardman. Discusses back pain sources and cures. W. W. Norton, 1999, $13.95.
- *The Back Pain Helpbook,* by James E. Moore, Ph.D., and Kate Lorig, R.N., Dr. P.H. Perseus Books, 1999, $15.

carpal tunnel syndrome

signs and symptoms

- Numbness and tingling in the first 3 fingers.
- Shooting pain in the hand, wrist, and sometimes forearm.
- Pain that may be worse at night, causing trouble sleeping.
- Weakness in the hands and fingers (in severe cases).

The pain and numbness of carpal tunnel syndrome (CTS) come from repeated use of the wrists in the workplace, often for typing, or in sports. Also known as a repetitive strain injury (RSI), it happens when a nerve that runs through a narrow channel covered by ligaments below the surface of the wrist is squeezed by fluid or inflamed tissue in the carpal (wrist) tunnel.

CTS is also common in women when pregnancy or menopause causes fluid buildup. **Arthritis** (see page 165), **diabetes** (see page 181), and hypothyroidism may also cause it.

CTS is easy to treat if it's caught early; left untreated, it can damage nerves and muscles. Injections in the wrist may help reduce the worst pain and swelling. As a last resort, pressure on the nerve can sometimes be eased by surgery in the doctor's office.

what you can do now

- Stretch and exercise your wrists every day (see box on facing page).
- Rest the hand and wrist when possible.
- If you have trouble sleeping, wear a wrist splint at night to reduce pressure on the nerve. Most drugstores carry splints.
- At work, wear a wrist splint if it helps, and change movements that cause pain.
- If you do much typing, try using a variable-position keyboard. Also put a pad in front of the keyboard to support your wrists.
- Cut salt from your diet; this may help reduce swelling.
- Drink plenty of water—at least 8 large glasses a day.
- Take ibuprofen, naproxen, or aspirin to reduce pain and swelling (see **pain relief** box, page 207).
- Apply a cold pack, 10 minutes on, 10 minutes off, for an hour. A bag of frozen peas wrapped in a washcloth works well.

when to call the doctor

- If pain and other symptoms persist or get worse despite a month of home care.

how to prevent it

- Change your hand position often when typing. Take 5-to-10-minute breaks hourly.
- As you work, make sure your hands are in line with your forearms, not cocked backward. Pause every few minutes and rest your wrist on a pad; office supply stores carry them.
- Some people find that vitamin B6 helps. Take no more than the recommended daily amount; high doses can be harmful.
- Ask your employer to check with an expert in workplace design about ways to ease wrist strain on the job.

complementary choices

- Seek some kind of physical therapy such as massage, hydrotherapy, low-level electrical

---

other hand & wrist pain

fracture
Pain that worsens with pressure; swelling, bleeding, or bone showing. Call your doctor for prompt advice. If he or she isn't available, call 911 or go to an emergency room **right away.**

dislocation
Swelling in a joint, pain, trouble moving the joint. Apply an ice pack for swelling, and use a splint to prevent movement. Call your doctor for a prompt appointment.

ganglion
A round, soft or hard cyst under the skin, often on the wrist, sometimes painful. It's harmless, but call your doctor if it hurts or swells. He or she can drain or remove it.

osteoarthritis
Cartilage worn away in one or more joints. Causes pain, may limit movement (see **arthritis**, page 165).

rheumatoid arthritis
Pain in a joint, with swelling, redness, and stiffness (see **arthritis**, page 165).

stretches to help your wrists

try these exercises 3 times a day.

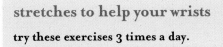

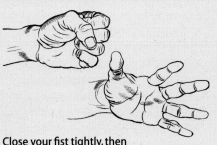

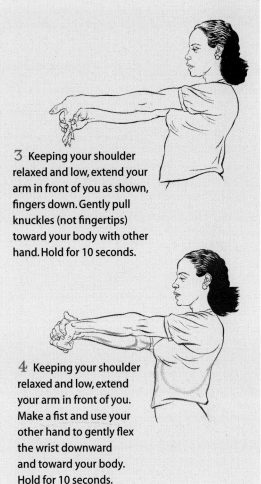

1 Close your fist tightly, then release, spreading fingers wide. Repeat 5 times.

2 Keeping your shoulder relaxed and low, extend your arm in front of you, palm out, fingers up. Use your other hand to pull back on your knuckles (not fingertips). Hold for 10 seconds.

3 Keeping your shoulder relaxed and low, extend your arm in front of you as shown, fingers down. Gently pull knuckles (not fingertips) toward your body with other hand. Hold for 10 seconds.

4 Keeping your shoulder relaxed and low, extend your arm in front of you. Make a fist and use your other hand to gently flex the wrist downward and toward your body. Hold for 10 seconds.

JEFFREY SMITH

stimulation, or ultrasound to reduce inflammation and swelling.

- A soothing compress made with grated ginger and hot water may offer relief.

for more help

Organizations: American Academy of Orthopaedic Surgeons, 6300 N. River Rd., Rosemont, IL 60018. 800-346-2267, M–F 8–5 CST; *www.aaos.org.* At Web site, click on *Patient Education,* then *Hand,* then *Carpal Tunnel Syndrome.*

- Arthritis Foundation, 1330 W. Peachtree St., Atlanta, GA 30309. 800-283-7800, 24-hour recording, or 404-872-7100, M–F 9–5 EST; *www.arthritis.org.*

Web site: RSI Page, *www.engr.unl.edu/ee/eeshop/rsi.html.* This site about repetitive strain injury gives thorough information, advice, and other online help.

Books: *The Repetitive Strain Injury Handbook,* by Robert Simon, M.D., and Ruth Aleskovsky. Describes an 8-step recovery program and includes tips on prevention. Owl Books, 2000, $15.

- *The Repetitive Strain Injury Recovery Book,* by Deborah Quilter. Offers tips on how to heal from repetitive strain injuries. Walker, 1998, $14.95.

chronic fatigue syndrome

signs and symptoms

- Flulike symptoms; severe fatigue that lasts longer than 6 months and is not caused by work or exercise.
- Weakness and fatigue that last for more than 24 hours after mild exercise (sometimes fatigue occurs 1 or 2 days later).
- Sore throat.
- Low fever (temperature as high as 101 degrees) or chills.
- Painful lymph nodes.
- Headaches of a new type, pattern, or severity.
- Pains that spread to joints without causing redness or swelling.
- Short-term blind spots and trouble looking at light.
- Trouble thinking or staying focused; forgetting things; being moody and confused.
- Trouble sleeping.

Little is known about chronic fatigue syndrome (CFS). Its causes are unclear, and it is diagnosed by ruling out other diseases. But researchers are beginning to untangle some aspects of it. CFS strikes people of all ages and races and of both sexes, though most people diagnosed with it are women. There's no proof that you can catch it from other people.

The pain, fatigue, and problems with thinking that mark the ailment often keep people out of work or school. This can lead to depression. Symptoms often ease up or go away after a number of months or years, but they may come and go indefinitely.

Treatment stresses plenty of rest, gentle exercise, and a healthful diet. Drugs such as antidepressants and over-the-counter pain relievers can help ease some symptoms. Also, medicines that target some of the underlying problems are being tested.

fibromyalgia

Fibromyalgia may accompany chronic fatigue syndrome and is sometimes confused with it. Symptoms include pain in muscles, tendons, and ligaments (though not in joints), fatigue, and sleep problems. Unlike chronic fatigue syndrome, fibromyalgia can be spotted with the "18 Tender Points" test, which applies pressure to 18 body parts. Tenderness in at least 11 often means fibromyalgia.

Fibromyalgia tends to affect women between the ages of 20 and 50, although people of both sexes and all ages get it. It may be present all the time or it may run in 3- or 4-day cycles. Symptoms are treated with antidepressants, painkillers, and muscle relaxants. Frequent exercise also may help.

for more help
Fibromyalgia Network, 800-853-2929, M–F 8–4 PST. Call for names of doctors, a list of support groups in your area, and a newsletter.

what you can do now

- Take over-the-counter painkillers, such as ibuprofen, for muscle aches and headaches (see **pain relief** box, page 207).
- Stay active, but don't become overtired.
- Join a support group for people with chronic pain or depression.

when to call the doctor

- If you have fatigue that won't go away and other symptoms of CFS.
- If you feel new symptoms after you have been diagnosed.

how to prevent it

There is no known way to prevent chronic fatigue syndrome.

for more help

Organizations: American Chronic Pain Association, P.O. Box 850, Rocklin, CA 95677. 916-632-0922, 8:30–5 PST; *www.theacpa.org*.

Call for information and a list of support groups for people with chronic pain.

- Centers for Disease Control and Prevention, 1600 Clifton Rd., Atlanta, GA 30333. Voice Information System, 888-232-3228, 24-hour recording; *www.cdc.gov/ncidod/diseases/cfs/cfshome.htm*. Offers data on current research and treatments.
- Chronic Fatigue and Immune Dysfunction Syndrome Association of America, P.O. Box 220398, Charlotte, NC 28222. 800-442-3437, 24-hour recording, or 704-365-2343, M–Th 9–5, F 9–1 EST; *www.cfids.org*. Sends information, a newsletter, notices of forums for patients, and a list of local support groups.
- National Institute of Allergy and Infectious Diseases Communications Department, National Institutes of Health, 301-496-5717, M–F 8:30–5 EST; *www.niaid.nih.gov/publications*. Staff members answer questions by phone. At Web site, click on *Chronic Fatigue Syndrome*.

Books: *Alternative Medicine Guide: Chronic Fatigue, Fibromyalgia & Environmental Illness*, by Burton Goldberg. Physicians discuss the techniques that helped their patients. Future Medicine, 1998, $18.95.

- *Chronic Fatigue Syndrome: A Comprehensive Guide to Symptoms, Treatments, and Solving the Practical Problems of CFS*, by Gregg Charles Fisher. Warner Books, 1997, $16.99.

colds

signs and symptoms

- Runny nose.
- Sore throat and hoarseness.
- Watery eyes.
- Coughing.
- Low fever, usually below 100 degrees.

If you have a scratchy throat, runny nose, and cough, you've most likely caught a viral infection of the head and throat known as the common cold. Colds are caused by more than 200 viruses that get into the body chiefly through the nose and tear ducts.

You can't catch a cold from getting your feet wet or sitting in a drafty room—you get it from a virus. But simple safety measures can help protect you from this contagious ailment.

what you can do now

Nobody has found a cure yet for the common cold, but there are things you can do to feel less sick. They start with staying home from work or school for the first 3 or 4 days—not only to rest and recover, but to prevent your cold from spreading to other people as well. Also:

- Drink lots of fluids to avoid dehydration.
- Take a painkiller for aches and fever. (Never give aspirin to a child or teenager who has a cold, chicken pox, the flu, or any other illness you suspect of being caused by a virus; see **pain relief** box, page 207.)
- If you have a sore throat, try gargling with salt water a few times a day. (Mix 1 teaspoon salt in 8 ounces warm water. Don't swallow.) Sucking on plain hard candy may also help.
- To clear up a stuffy nose, try over-the-counter saline drops or sprays. You can also make your own (mix one-half teaspoon salt in 8 ounces lukewarm water). Use a dropper or a bulb syringe to squirt it into your nose 2 to 4 times a day. Or you can put the solution in the palm of your hand and sniff it in, a nostril at a time. Wait a few minutes and then blow your nose gently.
- Don't smoke, and avoid smoky places.
- Try taking a 500-milligram tablet of vitamin C 4 times a day; some researchers say it may shorten the duration of your cold and make it milder. But taking too much vitamin C can cause diarrhea.
- Use a cool-mist humidifier or a vaporizer or take hot, steamy showers to keep your nasal passages from drying out.

when to call the doctor

Call for a prompt appointment:
- If you have a fever of 100 degrees or higher and facial swelling or severe pain in the ears. You may have an ear infection.

what to look for in cold & cough medicines

Cold medicines are a $3.1 billion-a-year industry. Many combine far more ingredients than you need, and some may even make you feel worse.

Doctors suggest that you buy generic drugs with only 1 ingredient—such as aspirin, a cough suppressant, or an oral decongestant—rather than brand-name "mega" formulas, which try to tackle many symptoms at once. Here are some drugs that don't do much to relieve cold symptoms:

- **Antihistamines.** Although they help clear up runny noses and sneezing, they can also dry out the nasal passages too much. Also, in older men, they may cause urination problems.
- **Expectorants.** There is no proof that these loosen mucus.
- **Nasal decongestant sprays.** Although they help shrink swollen nasal passages, they often have a "rebound effect," meaning that the tissues in the nose may swell back up, sometimes even worse than before, after a few days of use.

Cough suppressants (antitussives) also have pros and cons. Some coughs are "productive"—that is, they help bring up mucus from the lungs—so it's better not to suppress them. Dry, hacking coughs, though, are best treated with an antitussive syrup or lozenge. The medicine may make you sleepy, so don't drive if you take it.

Also, don't take decongestants with certain antidepressants.

- If you have severe throat pain and your throat or tonsils have a white or yellow coating. You may have tonsillitis or strep throat (see **sore throat,** page 214).
- If you have a severe cough with thick, colored mucus; a cough that lasts more than 10 days; or bluish lips or nails. You may have pneumonia.

Call for advice:

- If you have a headache with pain around the face, a sore upper jaw, or yellow or green mucus coming from your nose or throat; these are signs of a sinus infection.
- If a fever lasts longer than 4 days or goes higher than 102 degrees.
- If your cold hasn't improved after 10 days or has gotten worse.

how to prevent it

- Most colds are spread by touch. To help prevent a cold:
  - Keep your hands away from your eyes, nose, and mouth.
  - Wash your hands often.
  - Clean doorknobs, counters, phones, and hard children's toys with a disinfectant such as Lysol.
  - Blow your nose on paper tissues, not cloth handkerchiefs (cold germs can linger on cloth until you wash it).
  - Try to stay away from people who are sneezing and coughing.
- Since stress, allergies, and menstrual periods may make you more vulnerable to illness, try to get extra sleep—it helps your immune system—and take especially good care of yourself when you're feeling under the weather.

complementary choices

- Echinacea appears to help boost the immune system to fend off colds. Take the herb at the first signs of symptoms. Use echinacea only now and then; its effect on the body seems to fade after about 8 weeks of steady use. It comes as capsules and as a tincture.
- Chicken soup really does seem to help. It contains an amino acid that helps clear the lungs. Make your soup as hot, spicy, and garlicky as you can stand.
- Try to look on the bright side. Studies show that a positive attitude helps your immune system fight disease.

for more help

Organization: American Lung Association, 1740 Broadway, New York, NY 10019.

800-586-4872, M–F 9–5 your time; *www.lungusa.org.* Refers you to a local ALA chapter and gives information. At Web site, click on *Diseases A to Z,* then on *Guidelines for the Prevention and Treatment of Influenza and the Common Cold.*

Books: *Finally . . . The Common Cold Cure,* by Ray Sahelian, M.D., and Victoria Dolby Toews, M.P.H. Gives all-natural remedies for the common cold. Avery, 1999, $9.95.

■ *77 Ways to Beat Colds and Flu: A People's Medical Society Book,* by Charles B. Inlander and Cynthia K. Moran. Bantam, 1996, $4.99.

depression

signs and symptoms

■ Constant feelings of pessimism or sadness.

■ Feelings of worthlessness, hopelessness, guilt, or despair.

■ Lack of interest or pleasure in life—work, relationships, food, and sex.

■ Lack of energy; fatigue.

■ Sleep problems: insomnia, oversleeping, or waking too early frequently.

■ Trouble focusing, remembering, making decisions, and doing simple tasks; a feeling of moving in slow motion.

■ Unusual weight loss or gain.

■ Frequent thoughts of death.

■ Nagging ailments—such as headaches or stomach pain—that don't get better with treatment.

Feeling blue is normal—up to a point. When people are so unhappy they can't work, enjoy life, or even function normally, they have an ailment called depression.

The causes—and treatments—of depression are hotly debated, but clearly your genes, surroundings, brain chemistry, and life experiences all play a part. Depression can strike at any age, even in childhood, though its severe forms most often affect adults. Women are twice as likely as men to receive a diagnosis of depression.

Depression can take many forms. Feelings such as sadness, pessimism, or self-pity in response to painful events are sometimes called **depressive reactions.** These feelings, which are normal, can be quite severe but most often go away in a short time without treatment.

There's also a form of chronic, low-level depression called **dysthymia.** People who have it aren't severely depressed or suicidal, but they have little joy in life and feel downcast about the future. Some suffer from fatigue, sleep problems, and low self-esteem, and tend to heap blame on themselves. They have a hard time making choices or shaking their gloomy mood, and they sometimes fall into major depression.

A woman may feel a letdown after childbirth. Postpartum "blues" may begin 3 to 10 days after delivery, last around 2 weeks, and require only emotional support from family and friends. **Postpartum depression** begins about 3 weeks after delivery and can last at least a month. If it is severe or lasts longer than that, it may need treatment.

People who suffer from **major depression** feel so miserable that they have trouble living day to day. They are often in despair and are troubled by guilt, sleep problems, fatigue, crushing sadness, and feelings of emptiness and worthlessness. They may be suicidal or obsessed with death.

In rare cases, they may lose touch with the real world and have delusions and hallucinations. Their depression—which may have started with a major loss and can last for months—may lift, only to return later. Research suggests that this kind of depression is linked to the brain chemicals that affect mood and behavior, and that it may run in families.

When depression comes in fall or winter and then fades in the spring or summer, it is called **seasonal affective disorder** (SAD). People with SAD are affected by the lack of sunlight and often go through major mood shifts between the seasons.

Mood swings are even more extreme for people with **manic depression,** also known as **bipolar affective disorder.** They go back and forth from being very active or "high" (though they may also be moody, unfocused, and paranoid) to feeling sluggish and beaten down by despair, with periods of normalcy in between. Episodes usually occur once or twice a year.

what you can do now

- Get help. See your family doctor to rule out illness. Sometimes depression is a symptom of disease.
- Ask your doctor or pharmacist if any medicine you are taking could be causing your depression.
- Ask your doctor about counselors who work with depressed people, and about medication for depression.
- Get some physical exercise every day—join a class or group. Research shows that people who exercise regularly are less likely to be depressed or stressed.
- Try a support group. Many are peer-led groups for people who had traumas in childhood (for instance, alcoholic parents or abuse) or who have had major losses. It's important to get support from people who treat you with respect and understanding.
- Find out as much as you can about depression from self-help and professional organizations. You can find many online.
- Don't use alcohol or street drugs to feel better: Alcohol is a depressant.
- If you have SAD, ask an expert about indoor lighting that mimics sunlight. Get out in the sun when you can, or take a trip to a sunny place.

when to call the doctor

Call your doctor or a mental health professional for advice:

- If you, your child, or someone close to you has suicidal thoughts or depression that doesn't seem to lift. (Check your phone book: Many cities have suicide hotlines.)
- If depression seriously disrupts work, school, or relationships. Psychologists, psychiatrists, social workers, and peer counselors all work with people who are depressed. They take varied approaches to treatment, from psychotherapy ("talk therapy") to medication.

how to prevent it

- Don't isolate yourself.
- When you're feeling blue, find a friend or someone to talk with about your troubles.
- Stay active. Research shows that regular exercise can improve your mood.
- Be sure to get enough sleep (see **sleep disorders,** page 212).
- Eat balanced meals.
- Take a break from watching, listening to, or reading the news.

complementary choices

- Some people find that taking an extract of the herb Saint-John's-wort each day helps ease depression. You may not feel an effect until you've taken it for a week or two. Don't combine the herb with prescribed antidepressants, and be aware that your skin may become more sensitive to sun exposure.
- Acupuncture may help. Studies show that it triggers the release of certain brain chemicals that relieve depression and anxiety.
- Kava, an herbal remedy made from a Polynesian root, which is effective in treating anxiety, may also relieve depression in some people. You can find it as tea, capsules, or tinctures at your local health food store.

for more help

Organizations: National Empowerment Center, 599 Canal St., Lawrence, MA 01840. 800-769-3728, M–F 9–4 EST; *www. power2u.org*. Mental health consumers' group lists support groups and drop-in centers and offers print and audio items.
- National Institute of Mental Health, Public Inquiries, 6001 Executive Blvd., Room 8184, MSC 9663, Bethesda, MD 20892. 301-443-4513, M–F 8:30–5 EST; *www.nimh.nih.gov*. Offers brochures on depression. At Web site, click on *For the Public,* then on *Depression*.
- National Mental Health Association, 1021 Prince St., Alexandria, VA 22314-2971. 800-969-6642, 24-hour recording, or 703-684-7722, M–F 9–5 EST; *www.nmha.org*. Sends pamphlets on depression, provides

counseling, and suggests services and support groups.

Book: *Overcoming Depression,* 3rd edition, by Dimitri F. Papolos, M.D. A thorough guide to depression. Revised and updated. HarperCollins, 1997, $15.

dermatitis

signs and symptoms

One or more of these:

- Thick, itchy, dry red patches of skin on any part of the body.
- A pink or red rash anywhere, caused by something such as a chemical.
- Blistered, crusty, or scaly skin in round patches, often on the legs, buttocks, hands, or arms.
- Oily yellow scales on or near the face (nose, eyebrows, ears, scalp).
- Scaly, reddened skin, sometimes with craterlike sores, on lower legs.

Dermatitis is another name for a skin irritation or rash. There are many types. They vary by the kind of rash and where it is on your body.

Contact dermatitis (red bumps and blisters that often weep and crust over) can appear anywhere on the body. It's most often caused by an irritation or allergy to a skin-care product or a plant such as poison ivy or poison oak (see **poison oak and ivy** box, page 180). You may get this type of dermatitis when your skin reacts to certain soaps (including bubble-bath soap) and detergents, chlorine, and some man-made fibers. Condoms, latex or rubber gloves, and nickel-plated jewelry can cause contact dermatitis. So can leather and new clothing. Be sure to wash new clothes before wearing them for the first time. Perfumes and other items in makeup may also bring it on (see **choosing skin-care products** box at right).

Another type, **nummular dermatitis,** is marked by round, red, oozing places, most often on the arms and legs. Stress and other skin problems can bring it on. Older people with dry skin or who live in dry climates often get it. It gets worse if you bathe in very hot water. It usually clears up by itself.

Seborrheic dermatitis appears most often on the scalp (in the form of dandruff) and face. In infants, a yellow, scaly rash is known as cradle cap. Some experts think dandruff comes from a fungus; it may be made worse by plugged oil glands or by stress. People with immune disorders such as AIDS are prone to it.

Stasis dermatitis is a scaly, dry, reddish rash, usually on the lower legs and ankles. Poor circulation can bring it on.

Extreme, constant itchiness anywhere on the body may be eczema, also known as **atopic dermatitis.**

what you can do now

- For contact dermatitis, seek out the cause and get rid of it. If you find, for example, that nickel-plated jewelry or some type of makeup is the problem, you can simply stop wearing it.

choosing skin-care products

If you see a rash on your scalp, neck, or face, something you're using for skin care or makeup could be the culprit. Perfume, makeup, antiperspirant, sunblock, suntan lotion, and shampoo all can upset the skin.

A scent or preservative is most often to blame, but items labeled "unscented" can cause trouble, too. They still may contain irritating fragrances or other chemicals. "Fragrance-free" is a better choice.

Even if a product says it's organic, natural, nonallergenic, or hypoallergenic, your skin may react to it. If you have sensitive skin, choose your skin-care products with caution. Start with a fragrance-free product and apply it to a small area to see how your skin responds. Switch brands until you find one that doesn't cause a rash.

- Test yourself if you think your skin reacts to makeup. Apply a small bit of the product to your arm, and cover the spot with a bandage (if you're allergic to these, use gauze and paper tape). If you get a red, itchy rash within 48 hours, the product is the cause, and you'll know to avoid it.
- To ease swelling and itching, toss a half-cup of cornstarch or oatmeal bath powder (sold in drugstores) into a warm (not hot) bath. Soak your skin—but only for a half hour so that you don't lose too many of the oils your skin needs. Use a fragrance-free, mild soap or cleanser. Or use the oatmeal as a compress.
- For dry or flaky skin, try petroleum jelly or scent-free body lotion. For an oozing rash, use calamine lotion.

poison oak & ivy

Poison oak, poison ivy, and poison sumac grow as shrubs or vines throughout the United States except in Hawaii, Alaska, and some Nevada deserts. If you're outdoors just about anywhere else, your skin and the clear, oily sap in these plants' leaves, stems, and roots may meet—with nasty results.

The rash you get is a form of contact dermatitis (see **dermatitis**, page 179). Symptoms differ from person to person, but they often include a line or streak on the skin that may look like insect bites within 12 to 48 hours after exposure. Redness and swelling follow, then blisters and severe itching. In a few days, the blisters begin to dry. The rash can take from 10 days to 3 weeks to go away.

You can't pass the rash to another person, or spread the rash to another part of your body. But if the oily poison remains on your clothes or gets in your home and touches your skin, the rash may return.

to prevent exposure:
- Learn what poison oak, ivy, and sumac look like in all seasons, and stay away. Be warned, though, that the plants come in many shapes and sizes, and all varieties can get you even when they've lost their leaves. Even in dead plants, the oil can remain active for years.
- Cover up as much as possible and use a barrier lotion on exposed skin. These clay-based compounds keep the oil from attaching to your skin. Ivy Block was the first of them to be approved as a preventive; other products containing the same active ingredient—5 percent bentoquatam—work as well.

- Beware of pets that have run in the woods. The oil can cling to their fur and rub off on you. Hose them down when they return from an adventure.

if you've been exposed:
- Clean the oil off exposed skin as soon as you can. If you have rubbing alcohol handy, splash it on, straight from the bottle. It will remove the oil as it runs off. Rinse with plenty of running water. Air dry your skin or pat dry—don't rub—with a towel.
- If you don't have alcohol, get to a cold running stream, a lake, or a garden hose quickly. Rinse well. Don't use soap; rubbing the lather can spread the poison.
- Or try gently covering exposed skin with sand or even dirt (make sure there aren't any poison oak or ivy leaves in it). This will help absorb the oil. Rinse off with plenty of water.
- At the end of a day in the woods, throw your clothes in the washing machine and use a garden hose to rinse your tools, shoes, gear, and pets. Then give yourself a thorough shower.

if you have a rash from poison oak or ivy:
- Don't scratch the rash or blisters. To ease itching, calamine lotion is your best bet. Cortisone creams and other over-the-counter anti-itch products are no match for the plants' oils.
- Soak often in cool or lukewarm water with a half cup of baking soda or oatmeal bath powder (sold in drugstores).
- If your symptoms are severe or if you're getting new outbreaks after 10 days, call your doctor.

- Shampoo your hair with a tar shampoo if you have dermatitis on the scalp. Your scalp may sunburn more easily for a few hours after using the shampoo, so stay out of the sun. (Never use this shampoo on children—it's too harsh. Use a baby shampoo instead, and wash your child's hair every day.)
- If you have red, oozing sores, apply washcloths that have been soaked in warm, salty water and wrung out. Don't use over-the-counter hydrocortisone cream; it raises your risk of infection.
- For stasis dermatitis on the legs and ankles, sit or lie with your legs raised above your hips many times a day. Try wearing support stockings.
- Don't scratch. Cut nails short to keep from breaking the skin.
- Try hydrocortisone cream on unbroken skin.

when to call the doctor

- If your skin hasn't improved after 2 or 3 weeks of home care, medicated shampoos, or over-the-counter creams.
- If you have signs of an infection, such as sores with pus.

how to prevent it

- If you've been exposed to a chemical agent, wash your skin with a mild cleanser and water as soon as you can.
- To keep the air around you moist, use a humidifier at home and work.
- If your skin is prone to dermatitis, choose untreated cotton or other natural-fiber fabrics for clothing. Make sure clothing isn't too tight.
- Don't wear nickel-plated earrings or other nickel-plated jewelry. Choose jewelry made with surgical stainless steel, sterling silver, or gold instead.
- When washing dishes or handling chemicals, wear cotton-lined rubber gloves to protect your hands.
- After washing your hands or bathing, apply a lotion that has no preservatives or scents while your skin is still damp.

for more help

Organization: American Academy of Dermatology, 930 N. Meacham Rd., Schaumburg, IL 60173-4975. 888-462-3376, 24-hour recording, or 847-330-0230, M–F 8:30–5 CST; *www.aad.org*. Call or send a business-size self-addressed stamped envelope for a pamphlet on dermatitis. Also lists doctors near you. At Web site, click on *Patient Information* and then on *Patient Education*, and choose from listed topics.

diabetes

signs and symptoms

- Extreme thirst and hunger.
- Need to urinate often, sometimes every hour.
- Weight loss for no known reason.
- Blurred vision.
- Lasting tiredness.
- In women: frequent yeast and bladder infections, sometimes missed menstrual periods.

Diabetes mellitus affects about 16 million people in the United States, yet perhaps only 2 out of 3 of them know they have it. *Mellitus*, from the Latin for "sweetened with honey," refers to having too much unused sugar in the blood.

People who have the most common type, which tends to show up in older adults, often think their symptoms are a result of aging or being overweight. As a result, they don't get the treatment they need. Untreated diabetes can cause severe problems, including stroke and heart attack, blindness, kidney trouble, nerve damage, and loss of limbs due to circulatory problems.

The two main types of diabetes are type 1 and type 2. Type 1 most often starts in childhood when the pancreas fails to make insulin, a hormone that converts sugar in the muscles to energy. People with type 1 diabetes need daily insulin shots.

About 90 percent of diabetes is type 2: The muscles can't use insulin even though the body may be making enough of it. People with type 2 may not need insulin shots.

Type 2 used to be called adult-onset diabetes because it mostly comes on after age 40. You're at risk if someone else in your family has type 2 diabetes. A high-fat diet, lack of exercise, and being overweight also raise the risk.

Some women get a kind of high blood sugar called gestational diabetes when they are pregnant. In most cases, it goes away once the baby is born.

While neither type 1 nor type 2 diabetes can be cured, you can manage either one quite well by watching your blood sugar levels and combining medicine, exercise, and a healthful diet.

what you can do now

- If you know you have diabetes, follow your doctor's advice about diet, exercise, and tracking your blood sugar levels.
- Keep a log to help manage your diabetes. For a month, record your blood sugar level many times each day, always at the same times (use a home glucose monitor). Also record when and what you eat at each meal; the type of exercise you do and for how long; and your times of low and high energy. Take this record to your doctor.
- Practice good foot care. Check your feet often for cuts and sores. Call your doctor if you think you have an infection.
- Get eye exams often.
- Eat a low-fat, low-cholesterol diet to keep your blood sugar and weight in check.
- Exercise often to help balance your blood sugar, control your weight, and cut your risk of heart disease. Ask your doctor how that works, and about the right way to balance your blood sugar with medicines.
- Wear a medical alert tag. Make sure the tag includes the type of diabetes you have.
- Stay in touch with your doctor and schedule visits with him or her often.
- If your blood sugar level drops too low, you may notice symptoms of hypoglycemia:

confusion, dizziness, or weakness; sweating; shaking; hunger; headache; and blurred vision. As soon as you can, drink or eat one of these: 4 ounces of fruit juice or a sugared drink; some candy, such as 6 or 7 jelly beans or 3 large marshmallows; 1 cup of skim milk; or half a tube of Glucose (80-gram size). If you don't feel better in a few minutes, have one more portion. (Don't eat chocolate for quick sugar—the fat in it slows the rate at which sugar gets into your bloodstream.)

- If your blood sugar level rises too high, you may have hyperglycemia. Symptoms include blurred vision, thirst, hunger, and the need to urinate. Test your blood sugar level with your monitor. If it is much higher than normal, call your doctor promptly.

when to call the doctor

Call 911 or go to an emergency room **right away:**

- If your stomach hurts, you are breathing quickly and urinating very often, you are tired and nauseated, and your breath is very sweet. You may have ketoacidosis, a sometimes fatal ailment.
- If you are extremely thirsty, tired, weak, and confused. You may have very high blood sugar levels that could lead to coma.
- If you are with a person known to have diabetes who loses consciousness.

Call for a prompt appointment:

- If you have symptoms of diabetes, or if your child does.
- If you have diabetes and you get the flu. Flu and some other illnesses can make your blood sugar levels go out of control.
- If you have any problems with your vision.
- If you notice swelling that is not normal, particularly in the legs.
- If you have painful urination or feel the urge to urinate often.

how to prevent it

There is no way to prevent type 1 diabetes. To prevent type 2 diabetes:

- Keep your weight within the healthy range for your age, height, and build.

Some drugs can affect blood sugar levels, which people with diabetes need to track very closely.

- Aspirin can lower blood sugar if taken in large amounts over a long period of time.
- Phenylephrine, epinephrine, and ephedrine—found in some asthma and cold medicines and even herbal teas—can raise blood sugar and blood pressure.
- Fish oil, which some people take to lower their cholesterol, may raise blood sugar.
- Caffeine, found in coffee, sodas, appetite suppressants, some headache drugs, "pep" pills, and diuretics, may also raise blood sugar.

- Exercise often. This is vital to prevent diabetes and to manage it once it occurs.
- Eat a high-fiber, low-fat diet, and don't eat large meals or skip meals.
- If you are over 40 and overweight, or have a family history of diabetes, get screened for diabetes every 1 to 3 years.

for more help

Organizations: American Diabetes Association, 1701 N. Beauregard St., Alexandria, VA 22311. 800-342-2383, 8:30–8 EST; *www.diabetes.org*. Offers facts on how to manage diabetes and other brochures, and helps you find local diabetes groups.

- Juvenile Diabetes Foundation, 120 Wall St., 19th Floor, New York, NY 10005-4001. 800-533-2873, M–F 9–5 EST; *www.jdf.org*. Lists local chapters that have free materials, and gives names of doctors near you.
- National Diabetes Information Clearinghouse, 1 Information Way, Bethesda, MD 20892-3560. 301-654-3327, M–F 8:30–5 EST; *www.niddk.nih.gov/health/diabetes/diabetes.htm* for an online brochure on diabetes. Offers free printed information.

Books: *American Diabetes Association Complete Guide to Diabetes: The Ultimate Home Reference,* 2nd edition. Offers a wide range of in-

formation on how to manage diabetes, in an easy-to-read format. American Diabetes Association, 2000, $23.95.

- *101 Nutrition Tips for People With Diabetes,* by Patti B. Geil, M.S., R.D. Gives advice on nutrition, weight loss, meal planning, and medication. American Diabetes Association, 1999, $14.95.
- *The Type 2 Diabetic Woman,* by M. Sara Rosenthal. Focuses on how to work with your doctor, make lifestyle changes, and prevent long-term complications. Lowell House, 1999, $17.95.

diarrhea

signs and symptoms

- Loose, watery stools.
- Frequent bowel movements.
- Abdominal pain or cramping.

Diarrhea occurs when stools move faster than usual through the intestines, before the body can take out the water they contain. Its causes include viruses, a reaction to food, food poisoning, **stress** (see page 215), too much alcohol, and some drugs, especially antibiotics. Diarrhea can also result from drinking untreated water that contains giardia, a parasite that attacks the intestines, or from other parasites and amoebas.

In some cases, diarrhea may indicate a more serious disease such as **irritable bowel syndrome** (see page 200), inflammatory bowel disease, diverticulitis, or colon cancer.

what you can do now

- Don't eat solid food at first. This will let your digestive tract rest.
- Don't take over-the-counter antidiarrhea products for the first few hours; let your system get rid of whatever is causing the problem. If you do use such products, don't take them for more than a day or two without asking your doctor.

- Sip clear, warm liquids (water, tea, or broth), sports drinks, or flat sodas (ginger ale, cola, or other sodas that have been left open to lose their fizz). Drink only small amounts for the first few hours, then as much as your stomach can handle.
- If your stomach takes the fluids, try eating bland, bulk-adding foods such as bananas, white rice, or toast.
- While you are recovering, don't eat dairy products or fiber-rich foods such as salads and fruit, and don't drink alcohol. Avoid milk for several days: With acute diarrhea, you can temporarily lose the lactase enzymes that help you digest milk, so drinking it will make the problem worse.
- If your diarrhea is severe, watch out for dehydration. Signs include dry mouth, sticky saliva, and dark yellow urine in smaller amounts than usual. You can buy rehydration drinks such as sports drinks (or Pedialyte or Infalyte for infants) to help replace lost fluids and minerals—or you can make your own (see box at right).

when to call the doctor

Call for emergency advice (if you can't get any, call 911 or go to an emergency room):
- If the diarrhea comes with severe cramping, light-headedness, chills, vomiting, or fever higher than 101 degrees.
- If you notice signs of severe dehydration— dry mouth, sticky saliva, dizziness or weakness, and dark yellow urine. Dehydration can be dangerous for older people and for young children.

Call for a prompt appointment:
- If stools are bloody or tarry, or contain mucus or worms. (Some medicines and iron may make the stools look black, which isn't anything to worry about.)

Call for advice and an appointment:
- If you have diarrhea often, or if you get it while you are taking a medication.
- If diarrhea lasts for more than 2 days (1 day for a child under 3, or 8 hours for an infant under 6 months).
- If you have been traveling and may have been drinking untreated water.

rehydration recipe

To make a rehydration drink at home for anyone older than 12, mix 1 quart water with 1 teaspoon table salt, one-half teaspoon baking soda, 4 teaspoons cream of tartar, and 3 to 4 tablespoons sugar. NOTE: Don't give to children 12 and under. Use only a store-bought drink such as Pedialyte or Infalyte.

- If diarrhea and constipation come and go in turn for more than a few weeks. You may have **irritable bowel syndrome** (see page 202) or—though less likely—colon cancer.

how to prevent it

- Avoid foods you know your body can't handle well.
- When traveling in foreign countries, drink only bottled or boiled water or canned drinks. Don't use ice in drinks. Peel fruits and vegetables. Don't eat foods that have been sitting out.
- Take *Lactobacillus acidophilus* in liquid or capsules or *Lactobacillus GG* capsules (Culturelle) before meals, especially when you travel to developing countries or have finished a course of antibiotics. These "good" bacteria help fight toxic germs in your gut. Wash capsules down with bottled water; acids in some fruit juices may destroy the beneficial bacteria.
- See **nausea and vomiting** (page 202) for tips about food-related diarrhea.

for more help

Organizations: International Foundation for Functional Gastrointestinal Disorders, P.O. Box 17864, Milwaukee, WI 53217. 888-964-2001 or 414-964-1799, M–F 8:30–5 CST; *www.iffgd.org*. Provides support and printed advice on bowel problems.
- National Digestive Diseases Information Clearinghouse, 2 Information Way, Bethesda, MD 20892-3570. 301-654-3810, M–F

8:30–5 EST; *www.niddk.nih.gov/health/digest/pubs/diarrhea/diarrhea.htm* for facts on diarrhea and how to treat it.

Web site: Centers for Disease Control and Prevention's online brochure on chronic diarrhea, *www.cdc.gov/ncidod/dpd/parasites/diarrhea/factsht_chronic_diarrhea.htm*.

eating disorders

signs and symptoms

Anorexia:

- Eating very little food and dieting even while losing a lot of weight.
- Feeling fat even when far below normal weight.
- Compulsive exercising.
- Irregular or no menstrual periods.
- In women, increase in facial and body hair.
- Dry, yellow, or sallow skin.
- Depression, moodiness, impatience, social withdrawal.
- Constant use of over-the-counter diet pills or laxatives.

Bulimia:

- Frequent periods of overeating, followed by vomiting in secret.
- Spending long times in the bathroom, especially after meals, and signs of frequent vomiting (such as bloodshot eyes) or laxative or diuretic use (dizziness).
- Cavities, damage to tooth enamel, and gum disease caused by stomach acids from frequent vomiting.
- Compulsive exercising.

As many as 8 million people in the United States are thought to have eating disorders: mental illnesses in which the person becomes obsessed with food and body image. Anorexia nervosa (self-starvation) and bulimia nervosa (binge eating and/or purging) are the most common. Both can be fatal, and they require prompt professional care.

Anorexia is most common in young women, but it can affect anyone. It often looks at first like a normal concern about weight. But it grows out of control as the person becomes locked into a vicious cycle of frantic dieting and overexercise. The person with anorexia views herself or himself as fat even when emaciated. A person with bulimia, in contrast, goes on eating binges—sometimes eating up to 20,000 calories at one sitting.

About one-fourth of people with bulimia have also had anorexia. The causes may involve low self-esteem, troubled family life, worries about body changes during adolescence, and social pressure to look thin. Both conditions seem to run in families.

Treatment may include nutrition counseling, individual or family therapy, and support groups. Antidepressant drugs can help with bulimia, even in people who aren't depressed. A serious eating disorder may need to be treated in a hospital.

what you can do now

- Get help from a doctor specializing in eating disorders as soon as you can. The longer an eating disorder goes untreated, the harder it is to reverse. Your family doctor may be able to refer you.
- Treat yourself or anyone who has the problem with love and understanding—be aware that this is a mental illness.
- Avoid diet pills, laxatives, and diuretics. Overuse of diet pills can result in stroke; taking too many laxatives and diuretics can cause heart failure.

when to call the doctor

- If you see symptoms of anorexia or bulimia, especially with depression or talk of suicide.
- If you find that you or a member of your family is constantly worrying about weight and appearance.

how to prevent it

- Give your children healthy attitudes toward food and body image. Handle issues of eating and weight with sensitivity. Don't criticize or joke about your child's looks.

- As a parent, be willing to admit your mistakes and to accept those of your children. Anorexia and bulimia are more common in families that emphasize high achievement. Try to keep the pressure down.

for more help

Organizations: Eating Disorders Awareness and Prevention, 603 Stewart St., Suite 803, Seattle, WA 98101. 800-931-2237, M–F 8–12 and 1–5 PST; *www.edap.org.* Promotes and creates prevention programs, distributes materials, and gives referrals to therapists.
- National Association of Anorexia Nervosa and Associated Disorders, P.O. Box 7, Highland Park, IL 60035. 847-831-3438, M–F 9–5 CST; *www.anad.org.* Answers questions and refers callers to lists of experts and support groups.
- Overeaters Anonymous, *www.overeaters anonymous.org.* A 12-step program with chapters around the world. Check the white pages for the chapter nearest you. If you don't find one, write OA's Worldwide Service Office, 6075 Zenith Ct. NE, Rio Rancho, NM 87124, or call 505-891-2664, M–F 8–5 MST, for a list of chapters.

Book: *The Eating Disorder Sourcebook: A Comprehensive Guide to the Causes, Treatments, and Prevention of Eating Disorders,* by Carolyn Costin. Lowell, 1999, $16.95.

flu

signs and symptoms

- Fever over 103 degrees.
- Chills and muscle aches.
- Fatigue and weakness.
- Headache and eye pain.
- Sore throat.
- Dry cough.

Flu (influenza) is a contagious disease caused by a virus that enters the body through the nose or mouth and often invades the lungs. Flu shows up mainly in winter and early spring, making the rounds of homes, schools, and offices. The virus changes from year to year; some varieties lead to more severe outbreaks than others. Children are more likely than adults to get the flu, but it's most often mild. Older adults and people with lung disease or other chronic illness have a high risk as well; for them the disease is often more severe.

Flus and colds are much alike, but flus are more severe, with higher fevers and aches and pains. A bad case of the flu may send an otherwise healthy person to bed for 3 to 5 days, but he or she will most likely be well within 1 or 2 weeks.

what you can do now

The more rest you get, the sooner you'll get well. And staying home keeps you from spreading the virus at school or work: Flu is contagious for 3 or 4 days after symptoms appear. To get well quickly:
- Drink as many fluids—water, juice, hot tea—as you can. Try some frozen juice bars for variety.
- Have chicken soup and bouillon; the heat may relieve the stuffed-up feeling.
- Take a painkiller for aches and fever. (Never give aspirin to a child or teenager who has a cold, the flu, chicken pox, or any other illness you suspect of being caused by a virus; see **pain relief** box, page 207.)
- Avoid over-the-counter medicines aimed at treating more than 1 symptom (see box on **cold medicines,** page 176).
- Ask your doctor about virus-fighting drugs that can reduce the length and strength of flu. By taking one of them, you may also help family members avoid catching your flu.

when to call the doctor

Flu is a special danger for people with chronic illness such as respiratory, heart, or kidney disease; cancer; cystic fibrosis; recurring anemia; or diabetes. If you have one of these—or if you are HIV positive—call your doctor at the first sign of flu symptoms.

Call for a prompt appointment:
- If you have a fever or chest pain that keeps

coming back, or if you cough up mucus that is thick, colored, or bloody; you may have pneumonia or bronchitis.

- If you have an earache, facial swelling, drainage from your ear, or severe pain in your face or forehead. These may indicate another illness, such as sinusitis or an ear infection.

Call for advice:

- If you have a fever higher than 102 degrees, or one higher than 100 degrees for more than 3 to 4 days.

how to prevent it

The flu virus changes every year, so you can't become immune. Also, a flu vaccine might not work if it's designed for a virus different from the one that comes to your area. But if you are over 65 or have a chronic illness, a flu shot every fall is a good idea. Also, consider getting a flu shot if you work in a health care institution, or if you simply can't spare time off to recover from the flu.

- If you are pregnant, ask your doctor if you should get a flu shot.
- If you are allergic to eggs, or if you think you are, check with your doctor before getting a flu shot.
- Ask your doctor about the new oral vaccines that may help keep you from getting the flu.

The flu virus is spread in the spray from coughs and sneezes, so avoiding people who have the flu may lessen your chances of getting it. Also:

- Wash your hands often to reduce your risk of catching a cold or the flu.
- Don't smoke, and avoid smoky places.
- Keep your immune system healthy by eating well, getting enough sleep, keeping stress levels low, and drinking plenty of water.

for more help

Organizations: American Lung Association, 1740 Broadway, New York, NY 10019. 800-586-4872, M–F 9–5 your time; *www. lungusa.org*. At Web site, click on *Diseases A to Z*, then go to *Guidelines for the Prevention and Treatment of Influenza and the Common Cold.*

- Centers for Disease Control and Prevention, 1600 Clifton Rd., Atlanta, GA 30333. 888-232-3228 (Voice Information System), 24-hour automated line; *www. cdc.gov.* Choose from several topics about the flu and flu shots. At Web site, click on *Health Topics A–Z* and then *Flu.*

Book: *The Natural Way to Beat the Common Cold and Flu: A Holistic Approach for Prevention and Relief,* by Richard Trubo. Berkley Publishing Group, 1998, $6.50.

fungal infections

signs and symptoms

Athlete's foot:

- Itching, scaling, and redness that often starts between the toes.
- Dryness, flaking, or blisters on the toes or soles of the feet.
- Toenails that thicken and become layered or scaly and yellowish.
- Odor, in severe cases.

Yeast infection:

- Thick, white, cheesy discharge from the vagina.
- Itching, pain, or tenderness around the genitals (men or women). In men, the head of the penis may be inflamed.
- Pain or soreness during sex.
- Urge to urinate often. Urine may sting or burn.
- Creamy yellow or white coating in the mouth or throat or on the tongue that can be easily scraped off and may be painful (thrush).
- A red, itching rash with flaky white patches on moist skin areas, such as around the genitals, between the buttocks, or under the breasts.

More people get **athlete's foot** (tinea pedis) than any other fungal infection. It can be vexing, but it's easy to control if treated right away.

The fungus that causes athlete's foot is like those that cause jock itch and yeast infections. It breeds in closed, damp places and feeds on dead skin cells. Walking barefoot in the shower at a gym and around pools may increase your chance of getting athlete's foot. Moisture, sweating, and shoes that don't let your feet breathe can make it worse.

Many women get yeast infections, which occur when a fungus that's already in the body displaces the helpful bacteria that keep it under control. The infection begins in the vagina and may spread if left untreated. If you are pregnant or taking oral antibiotics or birth control pills, you are more likely to get the infection. Men, too, can get yeast infections, which irritate the penis.

Thrush is a yeast infection in the mouth. It makes a white or yellow coating that may look like milk and is easy to scrape away, exposing raw, red skin. Babies frequently get thrush. So do people with AIDS and others with weak immune systems, such as people being treated with chemotherapy. Taking large doses of antibiotics may bring on thrush. So can the steroid inhalers many people use for asthma.

People who perspire a lot or who are overweight and likely to have folds of skin that rub together also are prone to fungal infections.

Athlete's foot and yeast infections can usually be cured quickly.

what you can do now

Athlete's foot:
- Wash twice a day, and dry well between the toes after showering or swimming.
- Apply an over-the-counter antifungal powder or cream to your feet, and sprinkle some powder in your shoes every day.
- Wash sports shoes at least once a week.
- Wear clean cotton socks, and don't wear the same shoes each day.
- Take your shoes and socks off at home to give your feet plenty of air.

Yeast infection:
- Use condoms or stop having intercourse until you get treatment if you have a yeast infection in the vagina (it can be passed on to others).

- If you're sure it's yeast, use an over-the-counter yeast medicine. Read the label and follow the steps.
- Wear clean cotton underwear, and avoid panty hose and tight jeans and pants.
- Eat plain yogurt containing active cultures if you get a yeast infection after taking antibiotics for another ailment. The bacteria in the yogurt will help control the yeast.
- For thrush, try a gentle mouthwash to loosen the white coating.

when to call the doctor

Athlete's foot:
- If your foot has an odor that doesn't go away after treatment at home—a sign that you have a severe case.
- If your rash starts to spread or isn't better after 2 weeks of self-care. Once athlete's foot spreads, it is hard to get rid of and often returns.
- If the infection has reached your nails. This is hard to clear up. It also makes your nails more prone to bacterial infection because moisture gets trapped in the cracks.

Yeast infection:
- If you suspect you have one and you aren't better after using an over-the-counter medicine. Your doctor can prescribe antifungal suppositories, creams, or tablets for you (and maybe for your sexual partner).
- If you see signs of thrush. Your doctor may prescribe antifungal creams, pills, or suppositories.

how to prevent it

- Bathe daily and dry your body well.
- Avoid tight shoes and underwear, especially in hot weather.

Athlete's foot:
- Expose your feet to the air as much as possible. Wear plastic sandals in public dressing rooms and showers.

Yeast infection:
- Don't use feminine hygiene sprays or douches, which may kill the helpful bacteria in the vagina that can ward off a fungus.

- Wear underwear and workout clothes made of cotton or another "breathable" fabric. Nylon doesn't let air near the skin and gives fungi a chance to grow.
- Wash your workout clothes in hot water after each use.
- If you have repeated bouts of the infection and you take the Pill, ask your doctor about trying a different method of birth control.
- If you use a steroid inhaler for asthma, rinse your mouth after each use to help prevent thrush (see **asthma,** page 167).

for more help

Organizations: American Academy of Dermatology, 930 N. Meacham Rd., Schaumburg, IL 60173-4975. 888-462-3376, 24-hour recording, or 847-330-0230, M–F 8:30–5 CST; *www.aad.org.* At Web site, click on *Patient Information* and then on *Patient Education,* and choose from listed topics.

- American Podiatric Medical Association 800-366-8227, 24-hour recording that takes request for pamphlets on athlete's foot; *www.apma.org.*
- National Women's Health Network, 514 Tenth St. NW, Suite 400, Washington, DC 20004. 202-628-7814, T & Th 9–5:30 EST; *www.womenshealthnetwork.org.* Call for a brochure on yeast infections.

gallstones

signs and symptoms

- Intense pain in the center of the abdomen that radiates to right side or upper right back.
- Nausea and vomiting.
- Gas and indigestion.
- Fever and chills.
- Yellow-tinged skin and eyes (jaundice).
- Light-colored stools or dark urine.

Gallstones are hard lumps of cholesterol or bile salts that collect in the gallbladder. This small pear-shaped organ holds bile, a digestive juice. The stones can be as little as a grain of salt or as large as a lime. Most cause no harm and no symptoms.

A gallstone attack occurs when a stone gets trapped in one of the bile ducts (the tubes that carry bile from the gallbladder to the small intestine). You may have an attack a few hours after a big meal or during the night. Attacks can last several hours. Gallstones may cause jaundice if bile backs up into the liver.

Gallstones may run in families. They are found most often among American Indians and Mexican Americans. You're more likely to have them if you're overweight or obese, eat a lot of fatty foods, or lose a lot of weight quickly. Women are at higher risk than men, especially pregnant women and women who use birth control pills or are on estrogen replacement therapy. For everyone, risk rises with age.

Treatment for repeated, painful attacks is often surgery to remove the gallbladder. This procedure is simpler now for the patient than it used to be, with less pain and a quicker recovery.

what you can do now

- If you have symptoms of a gallstone attack, get medical help right away. In the meantime, do not eat or drink.

how you'll know you have gallstones

The most common diagnostic tool doctors use to locate gallstones is ultrasound. Pulses of sound waves beamed into your body create images of organs such as your gallbladder. If stones are present, the sound waves will bounce off them, revealing their location.

Gallstones often show up during an abdominal ultrasound or X-ray being done for some other problem. Ultrasound has several advantages: It is noninvasive, which means nothing is injected or inserted into the body. It is painless, it has no known side effects, and it does not involve radiation.

when to call the doctor

Call 911 **right away:**

- If you have sudden, squeezing pain in the upper abdomen and are also nauseated, sweating, and short of breath. You may be having a heart attack.

Call for emergency advice (if you can't get any, call 911 or go to an emergency room):

- If you think you are having your first gallstone attack or if you have fever along with the pain.

Call for a prompt appointment:

- If you notice a yellow cast to the skin and eyes (jaundice).
- If you have been told that you have gallstones, and you have sharp abdominal pain that lasts more than 2 hours.

how to prevent it

- Keep to your ideal body weight.
- Ask your doctor before trying to lose weight, and diet with common sense.
- Some experts say you can cut the risk of gallstones with a diet that is high in fiber and low in fat and cholesterol.

for more help

Organizations: American Gastroenterological Association, 7910 Woodmont Ave., Suite 700, Bethesda, MD 20814. 301-654-2055, M–F 8:30–5 EST; *www.gastro.org/digestinfo. html*. Visit the online Digestive Health Resource Center.

- National Digestive Diseases Information Clearinghouse, 2 Information Way, Bethesda, MD 20892-3570. 301-654-3810, M–F 8:30–5 EST; *www.niddk.nih.gov/health/digest/pubs/gallstns/gallstns.htm* for an online brochure on gallstones.

headaches

signs and symptoms

- Throbbing or steady dull pain in the head, sometimes on just one side. Often with other symptoms, such as nausea or dizziness (see **headaches** chart, page 154).

Most headaches are mild and harmless, and go away with rest and a dose of an over-the-counter pain reliever. But others are more severe, and some can signal a serious problem such as stroke or glaucoma. Some headaches are chronic, meaning they occur almost daily for months or even years. The most common types of headache are tension, migraine, cluster, and sinus.

Ninety percent of headaches are **tension headaches**—a steady, dull pain in the scalp, temples, or back of the head. They are often the result of muscles getting tight because of stress, fatigue, or poor posture.

Migraine pain can be severe, and may come with nausea and vision problems such as light flashes or partial blindness. No one knows exactly what causes a migraine, but the pain is most likely a result of changes in the blood flow to and from the brain. A migraine can be triggered by any number of factors, including stress, certain foods and medications, and hormonal changes. Migraines are more common in women than in men and tend to run in families.

Cluster headaches can be even more agonizing than migraines, with pain that starts around one eye and spreads to that side of the head. Men are more likely than women to suffer from cluster headaches, which strike suddenly 1 to 3 times a day for days or weeks—the "cluster"—before fading, often for months or years. Then they may return.

Sinus headaches are caused by sinus infections or congestion.

The past few years have brought stunning advances in headache care; for example, a new family of drugs called triptans is proving to be effective in the treatment of migraines. If you repeatedly get headaches but haven't consulted a doctor lately—or ever—now is the time to do so. An expert who's up on current ways to diagnose and treat headaches can help you keep the pain from ruling your life.

what you can do now

- Try an over-the-counter painkiller such as acetaminophen, ibuprofen, or aspirin. (Never give aspirin to a child or teenager who has chicken pox, the flu, a cold, or any other illness you suspect of being caused by a virus; see **pain relief** box, page 207.) Be aware that in some people, daily use of these pain relievers over the course of several weeks may actually perpetuate headaches.
- Rest in a dark room, but don't lie down if you have a cluster headache. Lying down can make a cluster headache worse. Put an ice pack or a cold, wet cloth on your forehead, or a warm one if that feels better.
- Massage your forehead and temples for 10 minutes. Place 2 fingers at the middle of your forehead at the hairline. Using gentle pressure, work them slowly down the sides of the forehead to your temples.
- Stretch your neck by rolling your head, gently pressing forward at the base of your skull, and shrugging your shoulders. A self-massage of your neck can also ease the pain for a while. Starting where the neck muscles meet your skull, work your way down, across your shoulders, and up again to the base of the skull.

when to call the doctor

Call 911 or have someone take you to an emergency room **right away:**
- If your headache is sudden and severe, and you have other symptoms such as dizziness, visual changes, numbness, or weakness of a limb.
- If you also have a fever and a stiff neck.
- If your headache comes on after a head injury.

Call for an appointment right away:
- If the headache is more painful or unlike any you've had before.

- If your headaches are severe and you have other symptoms such as nausea, flashes of light, runny nose, or a stuffed-up nostril. These are signs of migraines or cluster headaches.

Call for an appointment:
- If your headaches occur as often as once a week—or last longer than 24 hours.
- If your headaches often seem to be caused by allergies, sinus infection, or depression. Treatment for these ailments can ease pain.
- Keep a headache diary. Note the time and date of each headache and its symptoms. Write down all you can remember about what you ate and drank and what you did in the 6 to 8 hours before it came on. Look for "triggers" for the headaches, and do what you can to avoid them.
- Avoid foods that contain the substance tyramine if they seem to cause your headaches. Such foods include ripe cheeses, nuts, peanut butter, pizza, and red wine.
- Practice correct posture. Sit up straight and don't keep your neck bent for long.
- Take rest breaks every hour if you're doing hard work such as moving furniture or digging in your garden.
- When you're reading or writing, make sure you have enough light, but not so much that it glares off the page; squinting can tighten muscles. Take 10-minute breaks every hour.
- If your headaches seem to be caused by allergies, make sure your house is free of dust and mold. Don't go outside when pollen is high (see **allergies,** page 162, for other ways to prevent allergy attacks).
- Don't skip meals, sleep too little, or sleep too much on weekends. These can all produce headaches.
- Some drugs, such as birth control pills, can provoke migraines. If your headaches seem to be caused by a drug, talk to your doctor.
- Don't smoke, and avoid smoky places such as bars. Smoke can cause migraines.
- Some people find that acupuncture and acupressure can relieve the pain of tension and migraine headaches.

- Biofeedback, a technique through which you learn to control processes such as heart rate and body temperature, may help ease head pain and relieve the stress that sometimes causes it. Your doctor can recommend a clinic where you can learn the basics.
- A massage therapist can help relieve head pain by loosening tight muscles and relieving tension.
- Reduce stress. Try regular exercise, a meditation class, and taking breaks during a hectic day.
- Both vitamin B2 (riboflavin) and magnesium have reduced the frequency of migraines in study subjects. Try taking 400 milligrams of vitamin B2 or 20 millimoles of magnesium every day.

for more help

Organizations: The American Council for Headache Education, 19 Mantua Rd., Mt. Royal, NJ 08061. 800-255-2243, 24-hour recording; *www.achenet.org.* For a $20 member's fee you get a quarterly newsletter, pamphlets, and a list of doctors.

- National Headache Foundation, 428 W. St. James Pl., 2nd Floor, Chicago, IL 60614-2750. 888-643-5552, M–F 8–6 CST; *www.headaches.org.* Staff members answer questions about headache types, causes, and treatment; also send free brochures on headaches and a list of doctors who are members. For a $20 member's fee you get a bimonthly newsletter, handbooks on headaches, and discounts on books.

Book: *Headache Help: A Complete Guide to Understanding Headaches and the Medications That Relieve Them,* by Lawrence Robbins, M.D., and Susan Lang. Houghton Mifflin, 2000, $15.99.

heart disease

signs and symptoms

To protect your heart, it's vital to prevent artery disease (atherosclerosis), which can damage your health before you have any symptoms. Watch for the following indications of heart disease:

- Dull chest pain (angina) or simply a feeling of tightness or heavy pressure. It's most often in the center of the chest but can spread into the arms and jaw. With rest, angina goes away in 30 seconds to 5 minutes.
- If the pain lasts, gets worse, comes more often, or comes during rest; this could mean you're having a heart attack. (Women are less likely than men to have severe chest pain.) Call 911 **right away.**

Heart disease is not the only result of damaged arteries. Atherosclerosis can also cause stroke.

- If you lose your balance, speech, or vision; have trouble moving; or have a sudden tingling, numbness, or loss of movement in a limb, you may be having a stroke. Call 911 **right away.**

Another risk is peripheral vascular disease, which is marked by:

- Muscle fatigue, weakness, or pain in the buttocks or legs, most often in the calves when you walk.
- Cold feet.
- Discolored skin, sores that won't heal, and sudden sharp pains in the legs or feet when you rest.

Heart disease, also called cardiovascular disease, is far and away the leading cause of death in the United States. It occurs when the arteries that supply blood to the heart muscle become narrowed. If these coronary arteries can't supply enough blood to the heart during exertion or strong emotions, your heart complains and you feel chest pain (angina). A heart attack happens when a blood clot forms in a coronary artery and blocks blood flow to a part of the heart. This most often happens where plaque has built up and damaged the artery's walls.

The walls of a healthy artery are smooth and elastic, so blood flows freely. But sometimes a substance known as plaque builds up inside an artery; the process is called atherosclerosis. The walls of the vessel thicken and grow rough and stiff, narrowing the artery.

Plaque deposits build up when a person has high levels of cholesterol in the blood. The problem runs in some families. Lack of exercise, a high-fat diet, smoking, and untreated **high blood pressure** (see page 199) or **diabetes** (see page 181) also increase your chances of having atherosclerosis.

The risk rises with age; heavy people are at more risk than those who are lean. Men are in more danger than women, up to a point: The risk for women goes up sharply once they reach menopause. Women over 35 who smoke and take birth control pills may also increase their risk.

Most of us are likely to have some narrowed arteries by the time we're in our 50s or 60s. But even before symptoms appear, atherosclerosis can make a person feel tired or generally unwell.

Atherosclerosis not only plays a major role in heart disease, but it can put you at risk for other health problems, including:

Stroke: Some types of strokes occur when clots form in vessels in the brain or leading to it. As in heart disease, this often happens where the vessel is narrowed by plaque. Another type of stroke occurs when a weakened vessel bursts and leaks blood into the brain.

Peripheral vascular disease: This occurs when arteries that go to the arms and legs become narrowed. While it's not always life-threatening, if untreated it can lead to gangrene and the loss of a limb, most often a leg.

If your doctor suspects you have narrowed arteries, he or she may suggest diet and lifestyle changes, and maybe drugs to reduce high cholesterol or control high blood pressure. A technique called balloon angioplasty can sometimes open blocked arteries, or surgery can bypass them.

what you can do now

There is no quick fix. But changes in lifestyle can help you prevent heart disease and cut your risk of stroke and other problems. If your arteries have already begun to narrow, these same changes can slow the process and even reverse it.

- Exercise. Like any muscle, your heart gets stronger with regular work. And a strong heart pumps blood with less effort than a weaker one. Exercise also helps open up clogged arteries, lowers blood pressure, makes clots less likely to form in narrowed arteries, helps keep off extra weight, and helps reduce stress.

The idea of exercising may be a little scary if you haven't been active over the years, or if you've been told you have narrowed arteries, but exercise is extra important then. To make it safer and easier:

- Check with your doctor first if you're at risk for narrowed arteries.
- Start by being just a bit more active each day. Any exercise is better than none, and even brief workouts will lower your blood pressure and cholesterol level. Take the stairs instead of the elevator. Walk your dog for 15 minutes each evening. Your dog and your arteries will thank you.
- When you're used to being more active, add more things that make you breathe harder, sweat a bit, and get your heart pumping. Brisk walking, jogging, biking, cross-country skiing, and swimming are all great for your heart. But find something you like—you'll be more likely to stick with it. Take a couple of months to work up to getting exercise 3 or 4 times a week for 30 minutes at a time.
- Eat right. A low-fat, low-cholesterol diet can help prevent and even reverse narrowing of arteries.

You need some fat and cholesterol to stay healthy. They provide energy and help maintain cell walls. But when you eat extra fat and cholesterol, you store some of it as body fat, and some of that clogs your arteries.

Build your meals around fruits, vegetables, and grains. They have little fat and no cholesterol and are loaded with vitamins, minerals, and fiber. Fiber lowers cholesterol and blood pressure and helps keep your arteries open. Foods rich in fiber include squash, peas, carrots, apples, oranges, soybeans and other beans, oats, and barley.

There are simple things you can do to cut fat and cholesterol:

- Read food labels to know what you're eating. The important things to look for are calories, calories from fat, total fat, saturated fat, and cholesterol. The American Heart Association says to keep your fat intake under 30 percent of your total calories each day. Of this, only about 8 to 10 percent should come from saturated fat (animal fat). Some experts now think your total fat intake can actually be higher than 30 percent, as long as most of it comes from heart-healthy vegetable oils.

- Watch out for trans fats, which are found mostly in solid or semisolid (hydrogenated) vegetable oils such as margarine and shortening. These fats, like saturated fats, raise cholesterol levels. If you use margarine, go for soft spreads. When cooking, use liquid vegetable oils instead of shortening. Check package labels and steer clear of foods containing hydrogenated or partially hydrogenated vegetable oil.

- If you eat red meat, make it a once-in-a-while treat. Eat no more than 6 ounces of meat, poultry, or fish a day. Keep servings to 3 ounces—a cut of meat the size of a deck of cards, half a skinless chicken breast or leg, or three-quarters of a cup of flaked fish.

- Don't fry foods. Bake, broil, steam, or sauté in a nonstick pan.

- If you eat dairy products, choose the low-fat or nonfat versions.

- Go easy on eggs—they have lots of cholesterol. Eat no more than 3 or 4 of them in a week.

- Don't smoke. With the first puff, your risks for narrowed arteries and heart attack go way up. A man who smokes a pack a day doubles his risk; a pack a day increases a woman's risk 5 to 10 times.

  The good news: As soon as you stop smoking, your body begins to recover. Within a year, your risk of heart disease drops to half that of a smoker. Fifteen years after stopping, your risk is the same as that of a person who never smoked.

- If you have **high blood pressure** (see page 199), do what you can to lower it. Your blood pressure is too high if it's above 139/89. Lose weight if you need to, exercise regularly, eat right, and reduce daily stress.

- Have your cholesterol level checked. Best is a total cholesterol reading under 200 milligrams per deciliter of blood. Borderline is 200 to 239. Too high is 240 and over. But total cholesterol tells only part of the story. What's in it also counts. It's good to have a high level of high-density lipoprotein (HDL) and a low level of low-density lipoprotein (LDL). Your HDL should make up at least 25 percent of your total cholesterol (at least 40 milligrams per deciliter). Eating right and exercising will help. If lifestyle changes don't work, your doctor can prescribe medication.

- If you're overweight, take steps to lose the extra pounds.

- Be careful with alcohol. Moderate drinking may help cut the risk of narrowed arteries. But too much can make your heart pump faster and raise blood pressure. It can also damage the heart muscle. What's the definition of "moderate"? No more than 1 drink a day for women, 2 for men. (A drink is a 12-ounce beer, a 5-ounce glass of wine, or a 1.5-ounce shot of hard liquor.)

when to call the doctor

Call 911 **right away:**

- If you feel mild to severe crushing or squeezing pain in your chest. You may also experience nausea, vomiting, sweating, shortness of breath, weakness, or intense feelings of anxiety. You may be having a heart attack.

- If you have aspirin, take a half tablet. If the tablet is enteric-coated, crush it first or chew it. Aspirin taken within 24 hours of a heart attack can reduce its severity. Caution: Don't do this if you're already taking a daily aspirin.

- If you've had chest pain before, but this time it doesn't go away in 5 to 10 minutes.

- If you've had chest pain before, but it's getting worse or you have it while resting.

- If you have any symptoms of a stroke, such as loss of speech or balance, or numbness.

Call for a prompt appointment:

- If you have symptoms of peripheral vascular disease, such as pain in the legs or feet.

how to prevent it

Follow the guidelines in What You Can Do Now, page 193.

- Vitamin E (found in foods such as vegetable oils, wheat germ oil, and almonds) may help prevent heart attack.
- Talk to your doctor about aspirin therapy. He or she may suggest a daily regimen that involves using baby aspirin (81 milligrams), adult-strength aspirin (325 mg), or a combination of both. This over-the-counter medicine helps keep blood from clotting and cuts your risk of a heart attack. Remember: Check with your doctor before starting this routine.
- Enjoy your friends. Friendships can do wonders for your heart. Volunteer, take classes, or join a support group to talk with people who understand.

complementary choices

Studies show that several complementary treatments for artery disease may help.

- Too much stress is hard on the heart. Do what you can to relax: Try deep breathing, meditation, or simply a "time-out" now and then (see **stress,** page 215).
- Rice fermented with red yeast, a spice used in traditional Chinese cooking, contains a natural compound that lowers cholesterol levels. An extract of the substance is sold under the brand name Cholestin.
- Garlic—even half a clove per day—and garlic oil capsules may lower cholesterol.
- Ginkgo biloba seems to help improve blood circulation, especially in the brain and lower legs and feet. This herb comes in capsules, tinctures, and extracts.

Don't use any herbal remedy without checking with your doctor, especially if you're already taking medicine for artery disease.

for more help

Organizations: American Heart Association, 800-242-8721, hours vary; *www.american heart.org.* Staff answers questions and sends brochures.

- National Heart, Lung, and Blood Institute Information Center, Box 30105, Be-thesda, MD 20824-0105. 800-575-9355, 24-hour recording, or 301-592-8573, M–F 8:30–5 EST; *www.nhlbi.nih.gov.*

Web sites: The Franklin Institute Online's The Heart: An Online Exploration, *sln.fi. edu/biosci/heart.html.* A user-friendly tour of the heart and blood system.

- Heart Information Network, *www.heart info.org.* A comprehensive online guide to keeping your heart healthy.

Newsletter: *Heart Advisor,* from the Cleveland Clinic Foundation. Call 800-829-2506, M–F 7AM–midnight EST, to subscribe ($32 a year; 12 issues). Information source for heart health and healing.

Books: *American College of Physicians Home Medical Guide: Coronary Artery Disease,* edited by David R. Goldmann, M.D., and David A. Horowitz, M.D. Dorling Kindersley, 2000, $6.95.

- *Her Healthy Heart: A Woman's Guide to Preventing and Reversing Heart Disease Naturally,* by Linda Ojeda, Ph.D. Hunter House, 1998, $14.95.

hemorrhoids

signs and symptoms

- Stools with red blood, or blood on toilet paper or in toilet bowl.
- Painful bowel movements.
- Lump near the anus, or a swelling that hurts.
- Itching in or near the anus.
- Mucus coming from the anus.

Hemorrhoids are inflamed or swollen veins either inside or outside the anus. Also known as piles, they may result from straining to pass hard stools during bouts of constipation. Other causes may include your genes, aging, pregnancy, chronic diarrhea, and the overuse of laxatives. The pain often lingers for many days and recurs. Still, home treatment can help.

what you can do now

- Try a sitz bath: Sit in warm water for 10 to 15 minutes every few hours. After a bowel movement is a good time.
- Bathe often so your anus stays clean, but be careful when washing the area. Don't scrub the skin. Pat dry.
- Wipe gently. Try cotton balls, alcohol-free baby wipes, or damp toilet paper. Avoid scented or colored toilet paper.
- Many times a day, dab hemorrhoids on the outside of the anus with witch hazel or soothe them with a cold compress.
- To ease painful bowel movements, place a bit of petroleum jelly inside and around the edge of the anus.
- Try an over-the-counter stool softener.
- Use suppositories for pain, but avoid ointments with a local numbing agent (you'll see "-caine" in the name or on the label). These can cause more soreness.
- Don't scratch hemorrhoids. You'll make them worse. Try 0.5 percent hydrocortisone cream to relieve itching.

when to call the doctor

- If bleeding persists for more than a few days. You could have a more serious problem, such as colon cancer.
- If you have lasting or severe pain. You may need outpatient surgery to remove or shrink the hemorrhoids.

how to prevent it

- For softer, more easily passed stools, eat plenty of fruits, vegetables, bran cereals, and whole grain bread. (If you are pregnant, ask your doctor before making any changes in your diet.) Drink lots of liquids (at least 8 big glasses a day) such as water or fruit and vegetable juices.
- Cut back on meat, animal fat, and alcohol.

- Set a regular time for your bowel movements. Also, don't sit on the toilet for more than 5 or 10 minutes.
- If you sit all day at work, take breaks to walk around. Long periods of sitting reduce blood flow around the anus.
- Don't sit on a "doughnut" cushion; these can trap blood in the swollen veins.

for more help

Organizations: American Dietetic Association, 216 W. Jackson Blvd., Chicago, IL 60606-6995. 800-366-1655, M–F 9–4 CST; *www.eatright.org*. Call for a recorded message about nutrition or, for a fee, to speak with a registered dietitian who answers questions about hemorrhoids.

- American Gastroenterological Association, 7910 Woodmont Ave., 7th Floor, Bethesda, MD 20814. 301-654-2055, M–F 8:30–5 EST; *www.gastro.org/digestinfo.html*. At Web site, click on *Hemorrhoids*.
- National Digestive Diseases Information Clearinghouse, 2 Information Way, Bethesda, MD 20892-3570. 301-654-3810, M–F 9–5 EST; *www.niddk.nih.gov/health/digest/pubs/hems/hemords.htm* for an online brochure.

hepatitis

signs and symptoms

Note: Some forms of hepatitis produce no symptoms.

First symptoms are flulike:

- Fever and fatigue.
- Nausea, vomiting, loss of appetite.
- Pain in upper right side of the abdomen.

Other, less common symptoms:

- Dark urine; light-colored stools.
- Jaundice—yellowed eyes and skin.

Hepatitis means "inflammation of the liver." Certain viruses that target the liver are most often the cause. But it can also be brought on—or made worse—by other diseases, poisons, and long-term alcohol abuse or drug abuse.

Viral hepatitis, a worldwide health problem, is highly contagious. Symptoms can be mild or can lead to liver failure and death. It comes in 2 basic forms—oral and blood-borne—with several subtypes:

Oral—hepatitis types A and E. These are spread through feces, tainted food and water, or sex. They are common in places with poor water and toilet facilities. Hepatitis E, rare in the United States, is found mostly in Asia, India, and Africa, but A is common in the United States—1 in 3 Americans has had it.

These types of hepatitis come on quickly and may feel like a mild flu, or they may make you very sick. Nearly everyone with A gets better and is then immune to it. The vaccine for A is advised for anyone who lives or may travel in an area with poor sanitation. Hepatitis E,

for which there is no vaccine, can be fatal to pregnant women.

Blood-borne—hepatitis types B, C, and D. These are spread through body fluids in much the same way as HIV (the human immunodeficiency virus that causes AIDS) is—by intravenous needles, blood, and sexual contact. A person may have few or no symptoms when he or she is first infected, but these types of hepatitis can lead to lifelong problems or death. Most people who have blood-borne hepatitis remain able to pass the illness along for the rest of their lives, even if they have no symptoms.

Hundreds of millions of people worldwide carry hepatitis. Many of them get better, but a large number who get hepatitis B and more than 70 percent who get C have chronic illness. C is the leading reason for liver transplants in the United States. Hepatitis D infects only those who have B and makes it worse.

five kinds of viral hepatitis

TYPE OF HEPATITIS	HOW TRANSMITTED	PEOPLE AT RISK	INCIDENCE IN UNITED STATES	RISKS	VACCINE AVAILABLE
A	Food, water, feces, sex.	Those exposed to poor sanitation.	50% of acute hepatitis cases.	Few long-term effects.	Yes.
B	IV drug use, blood, sex, body fluids.	IV drug users, people with multiple sex partners, health workers.	33% of acute hepatitis cases.	Can be chronic; increases risk of liver cancer.	Yes.
C	IV drug use, blood, sex.	Same as B.	15% of acute hepatitis cases.	High risk of chronic liver disease, cancer.	No.
D	Found only with B.	Same as B.	Not common.	May become chronic.	B vaccine prevents D as well.
E	Food, feces, water.	Travelers to Asia, India, and Africa.	Very rare.	High death rate for pregnant women.	No.

what you can do now

- Don't drink alcohol. Alcohol can damage a healthy liver; it's far worse for a sick one.
- Rest as much as you need to.
- Eat frequent small meals.
- Drink at least 8 glasses of water each day.
- Don't take aspirin or acetaminophen. Ask your doctor about **pain relief** (see box on page 207).
- Urge those close to you to be vaccinated. Tell sex partners you have hepatitis, and practice safe sex.
- If you have chronic B or C, join a support group.

when to call the doctor

- If you have any of the less common symptoms listed on page 196.
- If you have been exposed to hepatitis.
- If you have had hepatitis and you start to have symptoms again.

how to prevent it

- Drink little or no alcohol: for women, that means no more than 1 drink per day; for men, no more than 2. (A drink is a 12-ounce beer, a 5-ounce glass of wine, or a 1.5-ounce shot of hard liquor.)
- If you have a drinking problem or are an alcoholic, get help right away.

Hepatitis A and E:
- Get a vaccination for hepatitis A if you plan to travel to a place where it is widespread or that has poor water or toilet facilities. The vaccine needs 2 to 4 weeks to take effect, but you can get faster-acting short-term shots.
- While in areas with poor sanitation, drink only boiled or bottled fluids. Don't eat unpeeled or uncooked foods or shellfish, and don't use ice cubes.
- Wash your hands with soap and water after using the toilet and before touching food.
- If you are infected with A or E, don't prepare or touch other people's food. Take care to wash hands, clothing, and bedding.

Hepatitis B, C, and D:
- Get a vaccination for B if you have more than 1 sex partner, work in a health field, travel widely, or live with anyone who has B or who is from Asia (where it is widespread). Hepatitis B vaccine is now given at birth. It also protects against type D.
  - Use the same safeguards as for HIV: Practice safe sex. Don't share IV needles, manicuring tools, razors, toothbrushes, or other items that can collect or hold blood.
  - Insist on sterile needles for acupuncture, body or ear piercing, or tattoos.
  - If you are infected, take care not to spread hepatitis to others through your blood or body fluids. Tell sex partners about your illness, and practice safe sex.

for more help

Organizations: American Liver Foundation, 75 Maiden Ln., Suite 603, New York, NY 10038. 800-223-0179, 24-hour line; *www.liverfoundation.org*. Staff answers questions and sends brochures on hepatitis prevention and treatment.
- Hepatitis B Foundation, 700 E. Butler Ave., Doylestown, PA 18901-2697. 215-489-4900, M–F 9–5 EST; *www.hepb.org*. Staff answers questions, suggests support groups, and for a $35 donation sends a quarterly newsletter and directory of liver specialists.
- Hepatitis Foundation International, 30 Sunrise Terr., Cedar Grove, NJ 07009-1423. 800-891-0707 or 973-239-1035 M–F 9–5 EST; *www.hepfi.org*. Counselors answer questions and mail information.

Web site: HepNet, The Hepatitis Information Network, *www.hepnet.com*. Provides online reports on hepatitis, answers to common questions, and links to other Web sites.

high blood pressure

signs and symptoms

High blood pressure, or hypertension, is often called the "silent killer." In most cases, there are no clear warning signs, even as the illness harms your health.

Blood pressure refers to the force of blood pushing against artery walls as it courses through the body. It's normal for your blood pressure to rise and fall through the day with changes in activities and mood. But when it remains high most of the time, it can force the heart to work too hard, which threatens your health. High blood pressure is the most common of all cardiovascular diseases. It is the leading cause of heart attack and stroke.

Blood pressure is measured with a device that records 2 numbers. It's too high if the first number (the peak pressure when your heart beats) is higher than 139 most of the time, or if the second number (the pressure when your heart relaxes between beats) is usually higher than 89. Best is about 110/70.

While the causes of most cases of high blood pressure aren't known, the risk factors are. If high blood pressure runs in your family, your risk is doubled. The risk goes up with age. African Americans have a high risk. If you weigh too much, don't get enough exercise, or are under a lot of stress, you're also at risk. Sometimes high blood pressure can be a sign of other problems, such as **diabetes** (see page 181) or kidney disease.

High blood pressure can be treated with lifestyle changes and, often, with drugs.

what you can do now

- Have your blood pressure checked as often as your doctor advises you to.
- Don't smoke, and avoid smoky places.
- Exercise often—try brisk walking, swimming, or biking. If you're not currently active, check with your doctor before starting an exercise program.
- Eat no more than 2,000 milligrams of salt a day. (A teaspoon of salt equals about 2,100 mg.) Fresh vegetables and fruits are low in salt; fast food and processed foods contain a lot of it.
- Find a healthy outlet for **stress** (see page 215). Try meditation or yoga to relax.

when to call the doctor

Call for emergency advice (if you can't get any, call 911 or go to an emergency room):
- If you have high blood pressure or suspect you do and you have any of these: recurring headaches, chest pain or tightness, frequent nosebleeds, numbness and tingling, confusion, or blurred vision.

Call for advice:
- If you check your blood pressure and it rises and stays high for a number of days.
- If you are pregnant and your blood pressure goes up. High blood pressure can harm both you and your unborn child.
- If you have high blood pressure and lifestyle changes don't help.
- If you're taking drugs to control your high blood pressure and you start to feel dizzy or sleepy, or you become constipated. You may need a different drug. But never stop taking your blood pressure medication without telling your doctor; stopping suddenly can cause problems.

how to prevent it

Follow the suggestions in What You Can Do Now. Also:
- If you're overweight, try to lose the extra pounds.
- If you drink alcohol, drink moderately—no more than 1 drink a day for women, 2 for men. (A drink is a 12-ounce beer, a 5-ounce glass of wine, or a 1.5-ounce shot of hard liquor.)
- If you use birth control pills, give some thought to other methods. The Pill can cause high blood pressure in some women.
- Make sure you get enough potassium (orange juice has a lot), magnesium (leafy greens and whole grains), and calcium

(leafy greens and dairy products). These minerals help control blood pressure.

- Cut fats in your diet—eat less fatty meat, butter, and whole dairy products, and more vegetables, fruits, and grains.

for more help

Organizations: American Heart Association, 800-242-8721, hours vary; *www.american heart.org.* Staff answers questions and sends literature.

- National Heart, Lung, and Blood Institute Information Center, Box 30105, Bethesda, MD 20824-0105. 800-575-9355, 24-hour recording, or 301-592-8573, M–F 8:30–5 EST; *www.nhlbi.nih.gov.* Staff answers questions and sends brochures.

Web site: Heart Information Network, *www. heartinfo.org.* Click on *Hypertension.*

Book: *The American Medical Association's Essential Guide to Hypertension,* edited by Angela Perry. Pocket Books, 1998, $14.99.

irritable bowel syndrome

signs and symptoms

Symptoms of irritable bowel syndrome (IBS) can differ greatly from one person to another but may include:

- Diarrhea, constipation, or both back and forth over a few months.
- Mucus strands in stools.
- Abdominal cramps or pain.
- Lots of gas or bloating.
- Nausea, most often after eating.
- Headaches, fatigue, feeling anxious or depressed.
- A feeling that bowel movements aren't complete.

As you digest your food, your intestinal tract moves it along with waves of muscle contractions. Irritable bowel syndrome occurs when these movements lose their rhythm and upset the process. IBS, also called spastic colon, is the most common digestive ailment, affecting at least 10 to 15 percent of adults at some time. It does not lead to any fatal bowel diseases. It can be hard to treat, though, because no one is sure what causes it. Some experts think it is brought on—or made worse—by **stress** (see page 215) or by a poor diet. It also may be linked to panic disorder.

what you can do now

If you have symptoms of IBS, see your doctor. He or she may want you to have some tests, such as a barium enema and X-ray, to rule out more serious ailments (see **abdominal pain chart,** page 144). In the meantime, self-care can help:

- If you have **diarrhea,** see page 183.
- Keep a record of what you eat and note which foods seem to cause problems. Avoid those foods if you can.
- Change your diet. Cut down on fatty foods. See if it helps to avoid likely troublemakers such as eggs, dairy products, spicy foods, cabbage and broccoli, caffeine, and diet foods with sorbitol (an artificial sweetener).
- Try slowly adding more high-fiber foods to your diet (raw fruits and vegetables, bran, whole wheat, and beans). Some people find this helps, but others find it can make the problem worse.
- Eat smaller meals 4 or 5 times a day to make digestion easier.
- Don't smoke. Avoid smoky places.
- Include exercise and relaxation in your daily life.
- Seek therapy or try a stress-reduction program if you suspect that stress is a cause of the problem.

when to call the doctor

Call for a prompt appointment:

- If you notice pain in your lower left abdomen, with fever and maybe a change in your bowel movement pattern; diverticulitis may be the problem.
- If you get a fever with diarrhea, or you wake up during the night with diarrhea and

you have been losing weight. These may be signs of inflammatory bowel disease.

Call for advice and an appointment:

- If your stools contain blood or mucus, if your stools look different, or if you notice a change in how often you have bowel movements. You may have colon polyps or colon cancer.
- If any bowel problems get in the way of your normal daily life.

how to prevent it

- The causes of irritable bowel syndrome are unknown. The best approach is to take care of yourself by eating well and easing stress.

complementary choices

- Take 1 or 2 coated peppermint-oil capsules between meals, 3 times a day, or drink peppermint tea.
- Take gingerroot capsules or drink ginger tea to soothe the intestinal tract. Chamomile, valerian, and rosemary teas also help reduce spasms.
- Practice relaxation techniques such as yoga and meditation. Acupressure and acupuncture may also reduce symptoms.

for more help

Organizations: American Gastroenterological Association, 7910 Woodmont Ave., 7th Floor, Bethesda, MD 20814. 301-654-2055, M–F 8:30–5 EST; *www.gastro.org/digestinfo. html.* At Web site, click on *Gas in the Digestive Tract.*

■ International Foundation for Functional Gastrointestinal Disorders, P.O. Box 170864, Milwaukee, WI 53217-8076. 888-964-2001, M–F 8:30–5 CST; *www.iffgd.org.* Provides support and brochures on bowel problems.

■ Intestinal Disease Foundation, 1323 Forbes Ave., Suite 200, Pittsburgh, PA 15219. 877-587-9606, M–F 9–5 EST. Offers support, educational programs and fact packets, and names of doctors near you.

■ National Digestive Diseases Information Clearinghouse, 2 Information Way, Bethesda, MD 20892-3570. 301-654-3810, M–F

8:30–5 EST; *www.niddk.nih.gov/health/digest/ pubs/irrbowel/irrbowel.htm* for an online brochure on irritable bowel syndrome.

Newsletter: *Nutrition Action,* from the Center for Science in the Public Interest, 1875 Connecticut Ave. NW, Suite 300, Washington, DC 20009-5728. 202-332-9110, M–F 9–5:30 EST; *www.cspinet.org/nah/index.htm.* $24 per year (10 issues). Offers clear, useful advice on good nutrition and diet.

Books: *Good Food for Bad Stomachs,* by Henry D. Janowitz, M.D. Provides sample dietary programs to help avoid irritable bowel syndrome and other intestinal problems. Oxford University Press, 1998, $13.95.

■ *Breaking the Bonds of Irritable Bowel Syndrome: A Psychological Approach to Regaining Control of Your Life,* by Barbara Bradley Bolen, Ph.D. Discusses how to manage symptoms through stress reduction and diet. New Harbinger, 2000, $14.95.

muscle cramps

signs and symptoms

- A sudden tightening of a muscle, with sharp pain.
- A muscle that is hard to the touch.
- At times, twitching of the muscle.
- Heat cramps: sudden, severe spasms in the arms, legs, and sometimes the abdominal muscles.

A muscle cramp can happen anytime—in bed, during a walk, after working in the garden. The muscle contracts with great force and stays this way, most often for about a minute, before relaxing.

Muscle cramps occur mostly in the legs, often after exercise in the heat or when a limb is stuck in an awkward position for a long time. They may also result from an imbalance in minerals and fluids caused by dehydration. Abdominal cramps may be caused by lower back problems or menstruation. Medical conditions such as Parkinson's disease, untreated thyroid problems, or diabetes also can lead to cramps.

Muscle cramps are rarely serious, but heat cramps can be a sign of heat exhaustion. With dizziness or confusion, they can signal the onset of heatstroke, which can be fatal.

what you can do now

- Stretch. For calf muscles, stand a little away from a wall and put your hands or forearms against it. Keep your feet flat on the floor and put your right foot forward, with leg bent, and extend your left leg behind you. Move your hips toward the wall until you feel the stretch in your calf. Hold for 10 to 20 seconds, and repeat on the other side.
- Massage. Begin at the edges of the cramp and move in toward the center, squeezing the muscle gently.
- For a stubborn cramp, immerse the area in warm water while stretching and massaging the muscle.
- If you have heat cramps, get out of the sun and sip cool water or a sports drink.
- For menstrual cramps, take warm baths or put a hot-water bottle or heating pad on your abdomen. Try ibuprofen to ease pain.

when to call the doctor

Call 911 or go to an emergency room **right away:**
- If you get a severe, cramping pain in your chest, shoulders, or arms; this can signal a heart attack.
- If you have heat cramps with dizziness or confusion; you may have heatstroke.

Call for advice and an appointment:
- If cramps are long-lasting or frequent.

how to prevent it

- Drink 6 to 8 glasses of water every day.
- Stretch often, and especially before bed.
- Warm up and stretch before exercising.
- To prevent heat cramps in hot weather, drink a small glass (about 4 ounces) of cool water before and after exercise and every 15 minutes during exercise. (Drinking lots of cold water at once may cause stomach

upset.) If you use a sports beverage, drink one low in sugar.
- Take 400 IU of vitamin E daily and eat foods rich in potassium, such as bananas, to prevent muscle cramps.

for more help

Web site: Duke University Healthy Devil Online, *h-devil-www.mc.duke.edu/h-devil/women/ women.htm*. Discusses causes of menstrual cramps and suggests treatment.

nausea & vomiting

signs and symptoms

Nausea and vomiting sometimes happen with:
- Diarrhea.
- Abdominal cramps or pain.
- Fever, weakness, and fatigue.
- Headache.
- Loss of appetite.

Although nausea and vomiting are common and usually aren't serious, they can worry you. In children and young adults, they most often result from the viral infection commonly called stomach flu. In these cases, vomiting and diarrhea often go away within 2 or 3 days, but weakness and fatigue may last about a week.

In older people, medicines and ulcers are more often the culprits (see **ulcers and gastritis,** page 218). Less common causes include bacterial and parasitic infections, food **allergies** (see page 162), and drinking too much alcohol.

Another cause is food poisoning, which you can get from eating food tainted with viruses, bacteria, or chemicals. In this case, you could also have abdominal cramps and diarrhea, headache, dizziness, or fever and chills. The vomiting may leave you dehydrated.

Mild food poisoning lasts only a few hours or at worst a day or two, but some types—such as botulism and certain forms of chemical poisoning—are severe and may be fatal unless you get prompt treatment.

what you can do now

If you think you might have severe food poisoning or chemical poisoning:

- Call the local poison control center listed in the front of your phone book. Trained staff members can help you decide whether you need medical help. (If you can't find the local center in your phone book, call information, a local hospital, or 911.)
- For food poisoning, ask others who ate the same food whether they got sick. Try to get a sample of the food, which can be tested if your symptoms get worse or don't go away.

If you have mild vomiting and diarrhea:

- It's best not to take over-the-counter antinausea or antidiarrhea medication for 24 hours, unless a doctor advises it. Vomiting and diarrhea are the body's way of getting rid of whatever is causing the problem. But if you do need relief after a few hours, it's safe to take Pepto-Bismol (it will turn your stools black). Also, children may need medication because they become dehydrated more quickly.
- Sip clear fluids. Suck on ice chips or Popsicles if nothing will stay down.
- Once you can keep fluid in your stomach, drink clear liquids for the next 12 hours or so. Then, for a full day, eat bland foods—such as rice, cooked cereals, baked potatoes, and clear soups—if your stomach will take them.
- Watch for signs of dehydration, especially in infants, children, and older adults. You can lose lots of fluid from repeated vomiting. Symptoms include dry mouth, sticky saliva, dizziness or weakness, dark yellow urine, and sometimes extreme thirst. For advice about replacing lost fluids, see **diarrhea,** page 183. If you can't keep liquids down and are becoming badly dehydrated, you will need to go to a hospital to get enough fluids into your body.
- Get plenty of rest until symptoms are completely gone.

when to call the doctor

Call 911 or go to an emergency room **right away:**

- If, along with vomiting and abdominal pain, you have blurred vision; muscle weakness; a hard time breathing, speaking, or swallowing; or trouble moving or feeling your muscles. These may be signs of botulism, a rare but sometimes fatal type of bacterial food poisoning.
- If you have symptoms of chemical food poisoning—vomiting, diarrhea, sweating, dizziness, very teary eyes, great amounts of saliva, mental confusion, and stomach pain—about 30 minutes after eating. Pesticides or tainted food may be to blame. This type of poisoning can be deadly.
- If you vomit blood or anything that looks like coffee grounds. These are signs of bleeding in the esophagus or stomach.

Call for a prompt appointment:

- If you have bloody or black, tarry stools. This can signal internal bleeding.
- If you develop signs of dehydration—dry mouth, sticky saliva, dizziness or weakness, dark yellow urine, and, sometimes, extreme thirst. Dehydration is serious in infants.
- If you have intense pain or swelling in the abdomen, rectum, or anus. You may have an abdominal disorder (see **abdominal pain chart,** page 144).

Call for advice:

- If your symptoms come back after treatment; you may have another problem such as an intestinal parasite.
- If your vomiting and diarrhea are severe and last longer than 2 or 3 days.
- If you have a fever of 101.5 or higher.
- If a prescribed drug might be the cause.

How to prevent it:

To avoid catching viral stomach flu:

- Keep your immune system strong with plenty of rest, exercise, and a healthy diet.
- Wash your hands often.

To prevent food poisoning:

- Don't thaw frozen meat on the kitchen counter. Let meat thaw in the refrigerator, or thaw it quickly in a microwave oven and cook it right away. Be sure that frozen food (especially poultry) is fully thawed or defrosted before cooking. This will help it cook all the way through so that the heat can kill any bacteria.

- Quickly refrigerate food that can spoil. Set your refrigerator at 37 degrees, and never eat cooked meat or dairy products that have been left out longer than 2 hours.
- Avoid raw meat, fish, or eggs. Cook all these foods well.
- At picnics (or anywhere else), don't eat moist foods that have been out 2 hours or more, or long enough to become warm.
- Using soap and hot water, wash your hands and any utensils, cutting boards, or countertops that are touched by uncooked meat, fish, or poultry.
- Be sure that all members of your household wash their hands with soap and water after using the toilet and before fixing food or eating.
- Don't eat any food that looks or smells spoiled, or any food in bulging cans or cracked jars—a sign that the contents have gone bad.
- Don't eat any wild berries, mushrooms, or other plants unless you know for sure what they are.

osteoporosis

signs and symptoms

- A broken bone (may be the first symptom), often in the spine, hip, ribs, or wrist.
- Stooped and round-shouldered posture; loss of height (usually occurs after age 70).
- Severe backache.

Osteoporosis means "porous bones." When you're young, your skeleton acts as a calcium bank for the rest of your body, taking in new deposits that help replace old bone. By the time you reach your mid-30s, though, it's easier to lose bone mass than to gain it. From then on, bones tend to become less dense and more brittle.

Osteoporosis is most common in people over 70 and in women after menopause, when levels of bone-protecting estrogen drop. If you're thin, if you smoke or drink, or if others in your family have osteoporosis, you may have a high risk as well. It can get worse without symptoms until a bone breaks—often in the spine, causing severe backache and a stooped posture.

Major bone breaks may require surgery and bed rest, which can lead to further weakness and to ailments such as blood clots or pneumonia.

That's the bad news. The good news? You can prevent osteoporosis, and if you have it, you can slow its progress. Self-care, including weight-bearing exercise and calcium supplements, is important. Hormone therapy for menopausal women can cut the risk of fractures in half, but it may also increase the risk of breast cancer. Your doctor may prescribe physical therapy along with drugs that prevent bone loss or help build new bone.

what you can do now

- Ask your doctor about a bone density test; it can show whether you have lost bone.
- Get plenty of exercise. It lowers your risk of losing bone. And it can strengthen bones that have begun to thin. Weight-bearing exercise is best—racket sports, step aerobics, or climbing stairs. Strength training (lifting weights) also increases bone mass.
- Make sure you get lots of calcium and vitamin D in your diet. If you are past menopause, get at least 1,500 milligrams of calcium per day; men, younger women, or women on hormone replacement therapy should get 1,000 mg per day.
- If you're not sure your diet has enough calcium, take over-the-counter calcium supplements. Some common antacids also are good sources. Check the label to see how much "elemental" (usable) calcium a supplement or antacid contains. (If you have a problem with kidney stones, talk with your doctor about calcium supplements; they may not be for you.)

- If you have osteoporosis that causes pain, take over-the-counter painkillers (see **pain relief** box, page 207).
- To prevent falls, take the following precautions: Install handrails on stairs and grab bars in the bathroom. Cover slippery floors with carpet, rubber mats, or nonskid wax. Use bright lamps and night-lights.

when to call the doctor

- If you fracture a bone.
- If you have stubborn pain in your back, ribs, spine, or feet.
- If you have a backache or are getting a curved back ("dowager's hump").

how to prevent it

- All the steps outlined in What You Can Do Now will help. Also:
- Try to gain a few pounds if you're underweight; being too thin puts you at risk.
- If you smoke, quit, and if you drink, don't drink much. Have no more than 1 drink a day (a "drink" is a 5-ounce glass of wine, a 12-ounce beer, or a 1.5-ounce shot of 80-proof liquor).
- If you are going through menopause, consider hormone replacement therapy, which prevents bone loss and cuts the risk of fractures in half. It may increase breast cancer risk in some women.

for more help

Organizations: Arthritis Foundation, 1330 W. Peachtree St., Atlanta, GA 30309. 800-283-7800, 24-hour recording, or 404-872-7100, M–F 9–5 EST; *www.arthritis.org.* Offers lists of local chapters.
- National Institutes of Health, Osteoporosis and Related Bone Diseases National Resource Center, 1232 22nd St. NW, Washington, DC 20037-1292. 202-223-0344

or 800-624-2663, M–F 9–5:30 EST, *www. osteo.org.* At Web site, click on *Bone Health Information* and then on *Osteoporosis.* Click on *Bone Links* for resources.
- National Osteoporosis Foundation, 1232 22nd St. NW, Washington, DC 20037-1292. 202-223-2226, M–F 9–5:30 EST, or 800-223-9994, M–F 7AM–midnight EST; *www. nof.org.*

Books: *The Osteoporosis Solution,* by Carl Germano, R.D., with William Cabot, M.D. Discusses the causes and prevention of osteoporosis. Kensington, 2000, $14.
- *The Osteoporosis Book,* by Nancy E. Lane, M.D. Oxford University Press, 1998, $27.50.
- *150 Most-Asked Questions About Osteoporosis: What Women Really Want to Know,* by Ruth S. Jacobowitz. William Morrow, 1996, $10.

overuse injuries

signs and symptoms

The tip-off to an overuse injury is pain that gets worse with activity. Often, it follows this pattern:
- At first, there is dull pain and general fatigue (the normal effects of exertion).
- Pain becomes sharper and more local (it's felt mostly in one place, such as the knee, hip, or arm).
- Pain lingers from one day to the next, often with swelling.
- Pain or swelling makes it hard to do the activity that caused it.
- Pain or swelling makes it hard to do normal activities of daily living, such as walking or standing.

Overuse injuries result from using bones, muscles, tendons, or joints in the same way, over and over again, without enough rest—often in the repeated motions of a sport. Runners are more likely than others to get overuse injuries of the knees and feet. For weekend warriors, throwing a ball or swinging a tennis racket can be hard on the shoulders and elbows. But injuries can be caused by any repeated motion, such as typing, or by activities you do now and then, such as trimming the hedge for the first time in the spring.

Overuse injuries can take longer to heal than other kinds. Without rest and therapy, they may come back or cause more serious problems, such as **arthritis** (see page 165).

what you can do now

- Stop or change what causes pain.
- Use the **RICE** treatment (see box, page 208) on the sore spot.
- Take an over-the-counter painkiller (see **pain relief** box, page 207) for pain and swelling. But even if this helps, don't assume that it's okay to return to the activity that caused the pain in the first place. Allow plenty of time for the injury to heal.
- When pain and swelling have eased, slowly resume your normal activities. If doing this causes more pain, however, stop and rest some more. Find other things to do that don't hurt. For instance, if walking hurts your knee, try swimming until the pain in the knee is gone.

when to call the doctor

- If a week of home care doesn't help.

how to prevent it

- Allow at least 48 hours between hard workouts such as running, tennis, or swimming.
- Don't increase the time or intensity of a sport more than about 10 percent at one time. For example, if you walk or run 10 miles a week, increase your distance no more than about 1 mile each week.
- Know your body. Change your activities if you have a problem. For instance, people with flat feet may get knee or foot trouble from running; they can try swimming or tennis instead.
- Use the right gear. If you walk or run, your shoes should be sturdy enough to help absorb the shock. (If you have foot problems, ask your doctor about orthotics, shoe inserts that can help prevent knee and foot injuries.)
- If a certain motion makes trouble, change your technique. You may want to learn a new swimming stroke if you're prone to shoulder problems, for instance.
- Vary your routine so you don't keep working the same muscles and joints over and over. Jog one day, say, and swim the next.
- Warm up before exercise. Stretch gently and walk briskly for a few minutes. Warmed muscles, ligaments, and tendons are less likely to get hurt.
- Make sure your work site is comfortable and properly set up (see **carpal tunnel syndrome**, page 171).

tennis elbow

Anyone who uses the arms and elbows in sports or on the job can get tennis elbow. It results when the forearm is snapped, rolled, or twisted, or when people lift heavy objects with the elbow locked and the arm extended. In tennis, it can occur when the grip is wrong.

The remedies for tennis elbow and tendinitis are the same. But the symptoms of tennis elbow may last from 6 to 12 weeks. The best home care is rest and over-the-counter painkillers, then gentle exercise. You can also try wearing a Velcro tennis-elbow strap, sold in sporting goods stores, to support muscles and tendons. Don't wear the strap for long periods, though, because it can reduce blood flow.

Prevent tennis elbow the same way you prevent tendinitis. If tennis is the cause of your pain, try a more flexible racket or one with a slightly larger grip; ask a coach to help you change your grip to ease the stress on your elbow.

pain relief: the big four

In this era of high-tech medicine, over-the-counter pain relievers still rank as wonder drugs. They ease pain, reduce fever, and are almost always harmless when used as they should be. You can get 3 of the basic 4—aspirin, acetaminophen, and ibuprofen—just about everywhere as generics, identical to name brands.

Of course, you should use any drug with care. Some cautions:
- Pregnant women should ask their doctors before taking any medicine.
- Don't take any of these together, or along with other painkillers.
- Ask your doctor before taking any of these with other drugs. Be sure to read the labels.
- Ask your doctor before taking any of these with an anticoagulant or with an antacid or acid blocker. Some combinations can cause bleeding.

acetaminophen
(Common brand name: Tylenol) For fever and pain but not for inflammation. It's the only one of the 4 that doesn't prolong bleeding and that can be taken with acid blockers (such as Pepcid or Tagamet) or antacids (Mylanta, Maalox). It's advised for people having dental work or other treatment that causes bleeding, and for those with ulcers, frequent nosebleeds, or other bleeding problems. It's safest for children because it isn't linked to Reye's syndrome. Reye's syndrome is a rare disease that typically affects young people, from infants to teens. It causes vomiting and sometimes leads to delirium, coma, and even death. It is connected with aspirin taken during viral infections such as chicken pox and the flu. **Cautions:** Taking larger-than-advised doses of acetaminophen for several weeks or with alcohol can cause liver damage. Daily use for several months may damage the kidneys.

aspirin
(Common brand names: Anacin, Bayer, Bufferin) For fever, pain, and inflammation.

Some people take an aspirin every day to guard against heart attack, stroke, and colon cancer. Ask your doctor about the best approach for you. **Cautions:** Aspirin can cause stomach upset—take it with meals or try buffered or coated types. Don't take it with stomach-acid drugs.

More than the other 3, aspirin makes blood less able to clot. As a result, it makes bleeding harder to stop. Don't take it if you have ulcers or other bleeding problems, or for about 5 days before oral or other surgery. (If you take aspirin every day, ask your doctor if it's okay to quit.) Aspirin can also trigger asthma attacks. It's linked to Reye's syndrome: Never give aspirin to a child or teenager who might have an illness caused by a virus.

ibuprofen
(Common brand names: Advil, Motrin, Nuprin) For pain, inflammation, and fever. Very good for menstrual and other cramps, arthritis, and muscle aches. **Cautions:** Ibuprofen can cause bleeding in people with ulcers if taken for more than 2 weeks or if taken with stomach-acid drugs. It can cause stomach upset (take it with meals or milk) and may trigger asthma attacks. Don't take ibuprofen if you've had an allergic reaction to any other painkiller. Also, ibuprofen may cause fluid buildup. Daily use for several months can cause kidney problems.

naproxen sodium
(Common brand name: Aleve) For fever, minor aches and pains, muscle pain, arthritis, and menstrual cramps. Naproxen works longer than the other 3 painkillers. For chronic pain, that's important, but for most pain naproxen may be more than you need. **Cautions:** Follow dose limits carefully. Don't give it to children under 12. Don't use it in the last 3 months of pregnancy. Don't take naproxen if you've had an allergic reaction to any other painkiller. Naproxen can cause mild heartburn, or stomach upset or bleeding (drink an 8-ounce glass of water with each dose).

first aid for injuries: R·I·C·E

RICE stands for **Rest, Ice, Compression,** and **Elevation.** This is the best treatment for an overuse injury or a sprain. Start it as soon as you notice symptoms. If begun right away, it can save you days or even weeks of pain.

rest

Try not to use the injured part until the pain and swelling go away (often 1 to 3 days).

ice

Apply ice as soon as you can to reduce swelling and pain. Place a damp towel over the injured spot and a plastic bag full of ice on top of it. A bag of frozen peas also works well. Hold the cold pack in place for 10 to 30 minutes, then leave it off for 30 to 45 minutes. Repeat as often as you can. You should use ice for at least 3 days; for severe bruises, up to 7 days. For chronic pain, use ice whenever you have symptoms.

compression

Use an elastic bandage to apply gentle but firm pressure until the swelling goes down. Wrap the bandage in an upward spiral, starting a few inches below the injured area. Apply even pressure to start, then wrap more loosely after you've passed the injured area. (To use ice and pressure at the same time, wrap a bandage over an ice pack.)

elevation

For the first 1 to 3 days, keep the injured area raised above the heart to help drain any excess fluid from the area.

Note: Also for the first 1 to 3 days after an injury, to reduce swelling:
- Do not apply heat (hot showers, compresses, or baths).
- Do not work the injured part.
- Do not massage the injury.
- Do not drink alcohol.

for more help

Web site: The American Academy of Family Physicians' Running: Preventing Overuse Injuries, *familydoctor.org/handouts/147.html.* Describes stretches for runners.

Books: *Anybody's Sports Medicine Book,* by James G. Garrick, M.D., and Peter Radetsky, Ph.D. An illustrated guide to preventing, understanding, and treating sports-related injuries. Ten Speed Press, 2000, $16.95.
- *Complete Guide to Sports Injuries,* by H. Winter Griffith, M.D. Perigee Books, 1997, $16.95.

palpitations

signs and symptoms

Rapid heart rate:
- A nagging awareness of your heartbeat.
- A fluttering, thumping, pounding, or racing beat.
- Shortness of breath, chest pain, light-headedness, or fainting.

Slow heart rate:
- Fatigue, light-headedness, shortness of breath, or fainting.
- Nausea.

Palpitations are caused by changes in the electrical impulses that control the heart muscle. Nearly everyone has an uneven heartbeat now and then; it's usually harmless. But a frequent or lasting change in the heart's rhythm can cause problems.

The older you are, the greater your chances of having palpitations. Anxiety, stress, thyroid problems, and some drugs, including nicotine, caffeine, and alcohol, can also set them off. But the most important causes are **high blood pressure** (see page 199) and artery disease (see **heart disease,** page 192). These health problems can damage the heart muscle, causing a "short circuit" in its electrical system.

Mild palpitations can often be controlled with drugs or surgery. Sometimes devices such as pacemakers are put into the chest to control more severe palpitations.

what you can do now

Call your doctor for a prompt appointment if you have palpitations often—even once a day—if they make you feel dizzy, or if they're bad enough that you become very aware of your heartbeat.

when to call the doctor

Call for a prompt appointment:
- If you have fainting spells.
- If you notice a strange heartbeat and feel light-headed or dizzy.
- If you have uneven heartbeats that are intense, painful, or more than fleeting.
- If you are taking drugs your doctor has given you for palpitations and you notice a new, uneven heartbeat pattern or you are nauseated, vomit, faint, or have diarrhea or a rash.

how to prevent it

- Cut out caffeine (in coffee, tea, chocolate, and caffeinated soft drinks).
- Don't smoke, and stay away from alcohol, decongestants, diet pills, and stimulant drugs such as cocaine or amphetamines.

Do what you can to keep your heart in good shape:
- Get plenty of exercise, such as brisk walking, jogging, swimming, or bicycling, to help control your resting heart rate.
- Find a healthy outlet for **stress** (see page 215). Try a relaxation technique such as meditation, yoga, or deep breathing.
- Eat balanced, low-fat meals. Your doctor may also suggest mineral supplements; calcium, magnesium, and potassium help control the heartbeat.

for more help

Organization: American Heart Association, 800-242-8721, hours vary; *www.american heart.org.* Staff answers questions and sends out brochures.

Web sites: The Franklin Institute Online's The Heart: An Online Exploration, *sln.fi. edu/biosci/heart.html.* This user-friendly tour of the heart and blood system provides links to other heart-related sites. For more information on palpitations, click on *Search* and type *arrhythmia.*
- Heart Information Network, *www.heart info.org.* A comprehensive online guide to keeping your heart healthy.

pelvic inflammatory disease

signs and symptoms

Often PID has no symptoms. Sometimes it can cause:
- Mild to severe aching in the lower abdomen, sometimes with backache.
- Pain during intercourse.
- Fever, sometimes with chills.
- Absent or irregular periods, or very heavy bleeding.
- Heavy or foul-smelling discharge from the vagina.
- Frequent urination with burning pain.
- Nausea and vomiting.
- Trouble getting pregnant (chronic or prior PID).

Pelvic inflammatory disease (PID) is an infection of the female reproductive organs, including the ovaries, the fallopian tubes, the cervix, and the uterus. Untreated, it can result in fatal illnesses, such as blood poisoning or infection of the abdominal cavity. It can also cause infertility or ectopic pregnancy (in which a fertilized egg settles outside the uterus).

PID is often caused by the bacteria that produce gonorrhea and chlamydia (see **sexually transmitted diseases** chart, page 158). It may also be brought on by other bacteria that get into the upper genital region through sexual intercourse, abortion, miscarriage, childbirth, or hysterectomy.

Sexually active teens, women with more than one sex partner, and those with a partner who has sex with others are most likely to get PID. Some experts believe that frequent douching may also increase the risk by pushing bacteria farther up into the reproductive system. Intrauterine devices (IUDs) increase the risk. Birth control pills, however, hinder the passage of bacteria and may slightly lower the chance of getting PID or may keep it from getting more severe.

PID can be treated with antibiotics, but it often comes back and may become chronic (you may have it for a long time, with symptoms that come and go). When antibiotics don't help, a doctor may have to remove or repair infected tissue.

what you can do now

After diagnosis:
- Take all of the drugs your doctor prescribes, even if symptoms are gone.
- If gonorrhea or chlamydia caused your PID, make sure your partner is treated. Otherwise, he may reinfect you.
- Don't have sex until all symptoms are completely gone.
- Get plenty of bed rest.
- If needed, take an over-the-counter painkiller such as ibuprofen.

when to call the doctor

- If you have symptoms of PID.

how to prevent it

- Practice safe sex to protect yourself from STDs by using a barrier method, such as a condom.
- Have regular medical checkups if you are sexually active.
- To prevent infection after you have had pelvic surgery or a minor gynecologic procedure, don't douche or have intercourse for a week.

for more help

Organizations: American College of Obstetricians and Gynecologists, Resource Center, 409 12th St. SW, P.O. Box 96920, Washington, DC 20090-6920. 202-638-5577, M–F 9–5 EST; *www.acog.org*. Send a business-size self-addressed stamped envelope; ask for the brochure on PID.
- National STD Hotline, Centers for Disease Control and Prevention, P.O. Box 13827, RTP, NC 27709. 800-227-8922, 24-hour line; *www.ashastd.org* for general information or *www.iwannaknow.org* for teen questions about STDs. Staff answers questions, sends out written information about STDs, and refers callers for testing.

Web site: Duke University Healthy Devil Online, *h-devil-www.mc.duke.edu/h-devil/women/women.htm*. Covers PID, the STDs that cause it, symptoms, treatment, contraception, and pelvic exams.

premenstrual syndrome

signs and symptoms

- Bloating and weight gain.
- Breast swelling or tenderness.
- Headaches.
- Dizziness.
- Fatigue.
- Decrease or increase in sex drive.
- Outbreaks of acne.
- Mood swings, bad temper, nervousness, or depression.
- Food cravings.
- Diarrhea or constipation.

Premenstrual syndrome, or PMS, affects many women some of the time, and some women nearly every month. It is marked by a range of physical and emotional changes that begin 1 to 2 weeks before a woman's period and stop when her period starts. The symptoms can be mild or severe. Some women feel just a little low on energy, while a small number get so depressed or tense that they can barely function.

No one knows for sure what causes PMS. It may result from changes in hormone levels, monthly changes in brain chemicals, or poor diet.

what you can do now

- Change your diet. The week before your period, skip salt, sugar, and caffeine (found in coffee, tea, sodas, and chocolate). Limit fats, and add grains, fruits, and vegetables.
- Cut out alcohol in the week before your period—it can worsen headaches, fatigue, and depression.
- Eat small meals often—6 times a day—and snack frequently to maintain a steady level of blood sugar.
- Exercise daily. Raising your body temperature helps your body balance hormones.
- Reduce **stress** (see page 215). Practice yoga or meditation. Try taking a stress reduction course.
- Take good care of yourself. Get enough sleep. Take warm baths. Get a massage.
- Try PMS medication or an over-the-counter painkiller to help with bloating, cramps, and aches.
- Take 50 to 100 milligrams of vitamin B6 and 250 mg of magnesium daily; increase gradually if necessary. This may help relieve PMS symptoms.
- Get enough calcium, zinc, copper, and vitamins A and E. Some amino acids and enzymes may also help.
- Join a PMS support or self-help group.

when to call the doctor

- If you've followed the advice above, but your symptoms still bother you.

how to prevent it

There is no way to prevent PMS, but taking steps to control your diet and to get enough rest and exercise can help soften the impact.

complementary choices

- The herb chaste tree may help balance your hormones and reduce anxiety and depression. You can buy it as berries, powder, capsules, and tinctures. To make a tea, pour 1 cup boiling water onto 1 teaspoon ripe berries and let steep for 15 minutes. Drink 3 times a day.
- Dandelion seems to ease bloating and breast swelling. Steep 1 tablespoon dried or 2 teaspoons fresh leaves per cup boiling water. Drink up to 4 cups a day. You can also sprinkle fresh leaves in salads or blend in juices.
- Another herb, skullcap, may help calm tension and irritability. Mix one-half to 1 teaspoon of the liquid form into 8 ounces of water. Or steep 2 teaspoons dried leaves in 1 cup boiling water for 10 to 15 minutes.

Consult your doctor before taking any of these herbs.

for more help

Organizations: National Women's Health Network, 514 10th St. NW, Suite 400, Washington, DC 20004. 202-628-7814, M–F 9–5:30 EST; *www.womenshealthnetwork.org.* Staff answers questions on PMS and sends fact packet for a small fee.

- PMS Research Foundation, Box 14574, Las Vegas, NV 89114. Offers resource information. Write and describe your specific concerns or symptoms, and enclose $5, to receive related resource materials.

Web site: Duke University Healthy Devil Online, *h-devil-www.mc.duke.edu/hdevil/women/women.htm.* Covers PMS and cramps.

Books: *Once a Month: Understanding and Treating PMS,* by Katharina Dalton, M.D. Discusses common symptoms and offers self-help tips. Hunter House, 1999, $15.95.

- *Self-Help for Premenstrual Syndrome,* 3rd edition, by Michelle Harrison, M.D. Explains how to manage PMS, with current information and advice. Random House, 1999, $15.

sleep disorders

signs and symptoms

Insomnia:

- Trouble falling asleep.
- Waking often during the night.
- Early waking.
- Being sleepy often during the day.
- Trouble staying focused.

Obstructive sleep apnea:

- Loud bursts of snoring and gasping that jerk the sleeper (as well as anyone sleeping nearby) awake.
- Morning headaches.
- Daytime sleepiness with trouble staying focused.
- Short temper, bad moods.

Narcolepsy:

- Falling asleep all of a sudden and with no control in the daytime.
- Sudden loss of muscle control triggered by strong emotion or fatigue.
- Vivid dreams or visions when falling asleep or waking up.
- Fatigue.

Restless legs syndrome:

- Creepy, crawly, or painful feelings in the legs, most often when trying to fall asleep or during sleep.
- Constant urge to move feet and legs.
- Jerking of legs (and sometimes arms) that you can't control.

Sleep disorders range from mild insomnia to severe sleep apnea. They affect as many as 70 million Americans.

Short-term insomnia is chiefly caused by stress, emotional upset, hormone fluctuations, or a change in schedule. Long-term trouble with sleep may be a sign of a medical problem, such as a thyroid disorder, chronic bronchitis or emphysema, Parkinson's disease, Alzheimer's disease, or alcohol or drug abuse. Another major cause is **depression** (see page 177). Treating the basic ailment, and creating restful bedtime routines, can often help.

Obstructive sleep apnea is most common among overweight men who sleep on their backs. The muscles in the throat sag, briefly closing off the airway. The effort to catch a breath wakes the sleeper. This process goes on all night long. People with sleep apnea don't get enough deep sleep and feel tired during the day. Obstructive sleep apnea can cause serious health problems over time, including heart disease. People deprived of sleep may become depressed or have other personality changes.

People with **narcolepsy** may fall deeply asleep almost anywhere, anytime. Not much is known about the ailment, but it seems to run in families. It can be treated with prescribed stimulants and antidepressants.

People with **restless legs syndrome** are bothered by odd feelings, most often in the legs, at night when they are still awake or trying to fall asleep, or even after they've been asleep for a while. Those with this ailment may feel tired the next day, especially if they can't get back to sleep or if they get out of bed and walk around to relieve discomfort. No one knows what causes restless legs syndrome, but it, too, seems to run in families.

what you can do now

Insomnia:

- Follow a calming bedtime routine: Drink warm milk, listen to soothing music, or read a book.
- Use your bed only for sleep and sex, not for working or watching TV.
- Don't thrash. If you can't fall asleep, get up and read until you feel sleepy.
- If you have chronic insomnia, try sleep restriction: At first, allow yourself only 4 hours of sleep a night. Once you are able to sleep through 4 hours, slowly add 15 to 30 minutes until you reach your goal. Be sure to get up at the same time every day.

Obstructive sleep apnea:

- Sew a tennis ball into the back of your pajamas so you don't sleep on your back.
- For mild snoring, try an over-the-counter nasal strip, which widens your nostrils and eases breathing.

- Ask your dentist about a retainerlike device that moves your tongue and lower jaw forward. Or ask your doctor about a special device called CPAP (continuous positive airway pressure) that pumps air to you through a mask. Surgery is also an option.

Narcolepsy:
- Schedule one or more daytime naps at regular times.

Restless legs:
- Your doctor can prescribe a drug that may relieve the twitching and discomfort.

when to call the doctor

- If you notice symptoms of obstructive sleep apnea or narcolepsy, especially if you feel sleepy all the time.
- If you have had insomnia for more than 2 weeks.
- If you are taking prescription drugs. Some can cause insomnia.

how to prevent it

- Avoid drinks with caffeine for at least 6 hours before bedtime.
- Don't drink alcohol or smoke for at least 2 hours before bedtime.
- Exercise often, but not within 3 hours of bedtime.
- If you have sleep apnea and are overweight, lose the extra pounds.
- Make sure your bedroom is quiet and dark and has plenty of air.
- Don't take a nap in the late afternoon or early evening.
- Get up each day at the same time, no matter when you go to sleep.

complementary choices

Insomnia:
- Research shows the scent of lavender helps people sleep. Try a lotion or room spray.
- Valerian seems to ease mild insomnia. Take 300 to 400 milligrams before bedtime (look for products with 0.8 percent valerian extract). Results may take a week.

catching up to jet lag

When you change time zones quickly, your sleeping patterns are out of sync with the local time. Jet lag can leave you drowsy and confused.

If you will be staying more than 2 days in a new place, you can avoid many of the symptoms. (It's hard to adjust on trips of 2 days or less.) Here's what to do:
- A few days to a week before leaving, adjust your schedule to the new time zone. Get up and go to bed as if you were already there.
- If you arrive in the daytime, spend some time outdoors. The sunlight helps reset your inner clock.
- Avoid alcohol, caffeine, rich and sweet foods, and too much talking before bed. All can keep you awake.
- Bring earplugs and a blindfold to block out noises and lights when you're sleeping.
- Wake up at the right local time, even if your day's plans don't require it.

- Kava may help. Try a supplement with 30 to 50 percent kavalactones; take 150 to 300 mg an hour before bedtime.

for more help

Organizations: Narcolepsy Network, 10921 Reed Hartman Way, Suite 119, Cincinnati, OH 45242. 513-891-3522, M–F 8–2 EST; *www.narcolepsynetwork.org*. Offers brochures and names of support groups.
- National Sleep Foundation, 1522 K St. NW, Suite 500, Washington, DC 20005. 202-347-3471, M–F 8:30–5:30 EST; *www. sleepfoundation.org*. Write for free brochures on sleep disorders.
- Restless Legs Syndrome Foundation, P.O. Box 7050, Dept. WWW, Rochester, MN 55902-2985. 507-287-6465, M–F 8:30–5:30 CST; *www.rls.org*. Send a 55-cent-stamped self-addressed envelope for a brochure on restless legs syndrome.

Web sites: National Center on Sleep Disorders Research, *www.nhlbi.nih.gov/about/ncs dr/index.htm.* Has a "Test Your Sleep I.Q." quiz, and lists publications and resources.

■ The Sleep Medicine Home Page, *www. cloud9.net:80/~thorpy.* Offers links to research centers and support groups.

■ The Sleep Well, *www.stanford.edu/~ dement.* Offers tips for good sleep and a test to determine if you're sleep-deprived.

Books: *Say Good Night to Insomnia,* by Gregg D. Jacobs, Ph.D. Describes how to end insomnia in 6 weeks. Owl Books, 1999, $13.

■ *The Complete Idiot's Guide to Getting a Good Night's Sleep,* by Martin Moore-Ede, M.D., Ph.D., and Suzanne LeVerte. Covers simple ways to manage sleep disorders. Macmillan, 1998, $16.95.

sore throat

signs and symptoms

- Pain when talking or swallowing.
- Throat that looks red all over or in streaks when you say "aahhh."
- Swollen, tender glands in the neck.

Sometimes:

- Fever.
- Headache.
- Earache.
- Hoarseness or "lost voice."

Strep throat:

- Sore throat that comes on quickly, with fever, swollen neck glands, headache, or bright red tonsils, sometimes with white pus spots.

Mononucleosis:

- Same symptoms as strep throat, plus fatigue and loss of appetite.

Most sore throats result from a virus—from flu, a cold, or a sinus infection. Dirty air, allergies, tobacco smoke, and the dry air of winter heating can also bring them on. Even shouting can cause soreness.

A few sore throats come from bacteria—usually streptococcus (strep). Strep throat is most common in children. Because strep can invade other parts of the body and cause serious trouble such as rheumatic fever or a kidney infection—and because it's impossible to find without a test—see your doctor promptly if you suspect you have it. A doctor can take a throat culture or give you a rapid strep test. If you have strep, antibiotics should knock it out.

Children often get painful sore throats with measles and chicken pox. A sore throat can also signal problems such as epiglottitis (a serious infection of the larynx) or mononucleosis.

what you can do now

- Drink lots of liquids. Warm ones such as soup or herbal tea are soothing.
- Gargle with warm salt water every few hours. (Mix 1 teaspoon salt in 8 ounces warm water. Don't swallow.)
- Don't smoke, and avoid smoky places.
- Take a nonaspirin painkiller to ease pain and inflammation. (Never give aspirin to a child or teenager who has a cold, chicken pox, the flu, or any other illness you suspect of being caused by a virus; see **pain relief box,** page 207.)
- Suck on throat lozenges or cough drops to keep your throat moist.
- Use a vaporizer or humidifier to moisten bedroom air.
- For laryngitis, rest your voice by not talking or whispering. Don't clear your throat.

when to call the doctor

Call 911 or go to an emergency room **right away:**

- If you can't swallow liquids or you have trouble breathing.

Call for a prompt appointment:

- If you have a fever that's higher than 101 degrees.
- If the glands in your neck are swollen.
- If your tonsils are bright red or have spots of white pus on them.

- If your sore throat lasts longer than the 5-to-7-day span of a cold.

how to prevent it

- Don't smoke. Stay away from smoky places and dirty air, fumes, and dust.
- Stay away from people who have strep throat or a sore throat.
- Do what you can to prevent colds and **flu** (see page 186).

for more help

Organizations: American Academy of Family Physicians, P.O. Box 11210, Shawnee Mission, KS 66207-1210. 800-274-2237, M–F 8:30–5 CST; *www.aafp.org.* Call for health information. At Web site, click on the link *familydoctor.org,* then search for *sore throat.*

- American Academy of Otolaryngology–Head and Neck Surgery, 1 Prince St., Alexandria, VA 22314. 703-836-4444, M–F 8:30–5 EST; *www.entnet.org.* Send a business-size self-addressed stamped envelope with your request for a brochure on sore throats. At Web site, click on *Patient Info* and then *Sore Throats.*

stress

signs and symptoms

Physical:

- Frequent headaches.
- Trouble sleeping.
- Fatigue.
- Digestive illness.
- Skin problems.
- Back or neck pain.
- Poor appetite or overeating, or heavy drinking.

Psychological:

- Anxiety, tension, or anger.
- Withdrawal from social life.
- Pessimism or cynicism.

- Boredom.
- Bad temper or resentment.
- Loss of ability to concentrate or perform as usual.

Stress is our reaction to anything—good or bad—that upsets our balance. Stressful events trigger the body's release of the hormones, including adrenaline, that provide a quick supply of oxygen and energy.

But these hormone surges, if sparked again and again, can deplete the body's ability to bounce back and can cause problems such as ulcers, high blood pressure, and loss of appetite. Constant stress also puts you at risk of **headaches** (see page 190), **chronic fatigue syndrome** (see page 174), **depression** (see page 177), and digestive ailments. Stress can also upset your body's immune system and lower your resistance to disease.

Stress often comes from painful situations you feel you can't control: job burnout, money problems, grief, or divorce. Minor stresses range from arguments to traffic jams. But even a good event, such as marriage, a job promotion, or a new baby, can trigger stress. Other causes include illness, loneliness, pain, and the drive to be perfect.

what you can do now

- Do things that calm you. Take walks or long, hot baths. Talk with friends, or rent movies that make you laugh.
- Exercise 30 minutes a day at least 3 times a week. You'll reduce your level of stress hormones and gain a sense of well-being.
- Spend some time outdoors. Research suggests that contact with nature can help reduce stress.
- Enroll in a stress reduction course. Ask your doctor to refer you, or check with the local hospital. Also, some employers offer courses or will send you to one.
- Learn relaxation techniques. These include deep breathing, stretching exercises, yoga, visualization, and meditation.

when to call the doctor

- If you are anxious, depressed, or troubled beyond routine stress (see **depression,** page 177).
- If you have symptoms of stress with any of these: new sleep patterns, mood swings, loss of sex drive, crying jags, exhaustion, great difficulty with minor tasks, agitated or slow movement, or a change in menstrual cycles. You may have a form of clinical depression.
- If your symptoms are long-lasting and prevent you from enjoying life.

how to prevent it

- Figure out what causes your stress and where you can make changes. Set reachable goals for yourself and be forthright with other people about what you can and can't do, and will and won't do.
- Don't try to be perfect. If you are juggling too many things, let a ball or two drop. Your house doesn't have to be absolutely spotless, and you don't always have to be the last one to leave the office. Practice giving yourself a break.
- Take a slow-paced, pressure-free vacation, leaving your work behind.

for more help

Organizations: American Institute of Stress, 124 Park Ave., Yonkers, NY 10703. 914-963-1200, M–F 9–5 EST; *www.stress.org.* Offers a monthly newsletter and a $35 informational packet.
- National Mental Health Association, 1021 Prince St., Alexandria, VA 22314-2971. 800-969-6642, 24-hour recording, or 703-684-7722, M–F 9–5 EST; *www.nmha.org.* Sends free pamphlets on stress and other mental health issues, provides counseling, and lists services and support groups.

Book: *Why Zebras Don't Get Ulcers: An Updated Guide to Stress, Stress-Related Diseases, and Coping,* by Robert M. Sapolsky. W. H. Freeman, 1998, $14.95.

sunburn

signs and symptoms

- Red, "burned" skin (even in dark-skinned people).
- Pain and (sometimes) blisters.

Not too long ago, a suntan—or even a slight burn—was considered a sign of good health. Now we know it's the body's attempt to protect itself from the sun, and a sign of skin damage.

That's because some rays of sun—called ultraviolet A and B (UVA and UVB)—damage skin cells. If you're out in the sun year after year, even if you never burn, the result is wrinkles and perhaps **skin cancer** (see facing page).

A sunburn raises the risks. People of all skin colors can get sunburned, but those with fair skin are the most likely to develop long-term skin damage or skin cancer from it.

what you can do now

- Soothe the burned skin with a cool bath or a compress.
- Try ice for pain. Take one cube and melt it slightly so that it has no rough edges. Glide it over the burn until it melts, keeping it moving to avoid skin damage. Repeat every hour as needed for pain.
- Try lotions or gels with aloe vera to soothe pain and speed healing.
- Use an over-the-counter painkiller. Aspirin works best because it blocks a chemical the body makes in response to burns. (Never give aspirin to a child or teenager who has chicken pox, a cold, the flu, or any other illness you suspect of being caused by a virus; see **pain relief** box, page 207.)
- Consider a lotion or spray that contains benzocaine for pain relief. Caution: It may cause an allergic response. Don't use it if you have skin allergies or if allergies run in your family.
- Watch for signs of dehydration—dry mouth, sticky saliva, dizziness or weakness,

skin cancer

In the United States, 1 person in 5 will have skin cancer during her or his lifetime. The good news is that it can nearly always be cured if caught in time. And because sunlight is the major cause, most skin cancer can be prevented.

The 3 main kinds of skin cancer are:

basal cell carcinoma

This is the most common type. Often found on the face, it develops slowly and, most of the time, doesn't send cancer cells to other parts of the body. The symptoms are:
- A pearly or shiny skin growth, often with a dent in the center and raised edges, that expands over time.
- A patch of skin that itches, bleeds, hurts, or forms a scab.
- An open sore that fails to heal in a month, or one that closes and then reopens.

squamous cell carcinoma

This usually appears on the face, lips, or rim of the ear. It grows quickly and can form large masses. If ignored, it can spread to other parts of the body. The symptoms are:
- Reddish or brownish rough, scaly patches on skin that has been exposed to sunlight.
- A stubborn, scaly patch that sometimes crusts or bleeds.
- A raised growth that looks like a wart and sometimes bleeds.
- A firm, fleshy lump that grows bigger and bigger.

malignant melanoma

This is the most harmful type of skin cancer. A cancer of the cells that produce melanin, it often spreads to other parts of the body and can be fatal. The symptoms are:
- A mole that looks different than it used to. It may become scaly or ooze, bleed, or enlarge.
- A dark area of the skin that feels itchy, or sudden growth of a "bubbly" mole.
- Dark spots or moles that have the following "ABCD" traits: Asymmetrical, Border blurry, Color uneven, Diameter larger than a pencil eraser.

See a doctor promptly if you have any of the symptoms of skin cancer. The earlier skin cancer is detected, the better your chances that treatment will cure it.

Call for a prompt appointment if you have an itchy mole, or a dark spot or bump that changes color, bleeds, or oozes. Call for advice if you see any of the signs of skin cancer; if what looks like a pimple crusts over, doesn't go away, and gets bigger; or if you develop a lump on or beneath the skin that is often exposed to the sun and doesn't go away after 2 weeks of home treatment with warm compresses.

To catch problems early, check your skin thoroughly at least once a month. Use a mirror for hard-to-see places, or ask a partner to look.

Consider having your moles mapped if you were severely sunburned as a child or if you have a fair complexion, a family history of skin cancer, or more than 40 moles. To create a map, a dermatologist records the position, appearance, and size of each mole. The map will make it easy to spot changes that could be early warnings of malignant melanoma.

for more help

- The American Academy of Dermatology, 930 N. Meacham Rd., Schaumburg, IL 60173-4975. 888-462-3376, 24-hour recording, or 847-330-0230, M–F 8:30–5 CST; www.aad.org. Call or send a business-size self-addressed stamped envelope for a pamphlet on skin cancer. At Web site, click on Patient Information, then Patient Education, then Skin Cancer for facts about skin cancer.
- American Cancer Society, 800-227-2345, 24-hour staffed line; www.cancer.org. Gives referrals; information on support groups, treatment options, and events; and a list of American Cancer Society offices near you.
- National Cancer Institute's Cancer Information Service, 800-422-6237, M–F 9–4:30 your time, cis.nci.nih.gov. In English and Spanish. Offers brochures, information on standard treatment options, access to a database of clinical trials, and names of cancer-related resources near you.

and dark yellow urine—especially if the sunburned person is a child. Give water or a **rehydration** drink (see box, page 184).

- Watch out for heatstroke and heat exhaustion. **Caution:** If you suspect heatstroke, don't give the person anything to drink.

Later:

- If skin peels, use a lotion to add moisture and ease itching. Lotions with aloe vera are soothing at any point.
- If you must go back into the sun, keep the burn from getting worse by covering up and using sunscreen with an SPF (sun protection factor) of at least 15.

when to call the doctor

- Call 911 or go to an emergency room **right away** if you see signs of heat stroke.
- Call for advice if the skin blisters. Don't cover the blisters.

how to prevent it

- Apply a sunscreen of SPF 15 or higher 30 minutes before you go outside (to give it time to bond to the skin). You need protection whenever you plan to be out more than a few minutes, even in winter and when it's overcast.
- Reapply sunscreen every 2 hours, even if it's waterproof (no matter what their SPF, waterproof sunscreens by current law have to protect for just 80 minutes when wet, and they're not necessarily sweatproof). **Caution:** If you have allergies or tender skin, test the sunscreen on a small spot to see if you react. You might want to avoid sunscreens with PABA, or try a product with titanium dioxide. Don't put sunscreen on the faces of babies younger than 6 months—it can get in their eyes or mouth. Keep infants out of the sun.
- When possible, avoid being outdoors between 10 AM and 2 PM, when the sun's rays are most intense.
- Wear protective clothing and a hat with a wide brim. But remember, you can get a sunburn through most clothes. The average white T-shirt has an SPF of 9 at most,

and that drops to 3 if the shirt is wet. A few companies manufacture special clothing that blocks UV rays.

- Don't go to tanning salons; they use harmful ultraviolet light.
- Don't use suntan oil; it doesn't protect your skin.
- Do a skin self-exam every month. If you are light-skinned, have freckles, burn without tanning, or have a family history of skin cancer, see your doctor for a checkup and to learn the danger signs (see box on **skin cancer,** page 217).

for more help

Organizations: American Academy of Dermatology, 930 N. Meacham Rd., Schaumburg, IL 60173-4975. 888-462-3376, 24-hour recording, or 847-330-0230, M–F 8:30–5 CST; *www.aad.org.* Call or send a business-size self-addressed stamped envelope for pamphlets on skin cancer. At Web site, click on *Patient Information* and then on *Skin Savvy.*

- National Institute of Arthritis and Musculoskeletal and Skin Diseases Information Clearinghouse, 877-226-4267, 24-hour recording, or 301-495-4484 M–F 8:30–5 EST; *www.nih.gov/niams.* Request the "Sun and Skin" packet.

ulcers & gastritis

signs and symptoms

- Pain in the upper abdomen.
- Nausea.
- Vomiting.
- Loss of appetite.
- Belching or gas.
- Heartburn.
- Dark or bloody stools.

Stomach ulcers are sometimes called peptic ulcers. They are holes or breaks in the lining of the stomach, in the esophagus (the tube between the throat and the stomach), or in the duodenum (the upper part of the small intestine). Experts used to blame most ulcers on stress, but now the prime suspect is a germ—a common bacterium called *Helicobacter pylori*. Overuse of painkillers such as aspirin and ibuprofen can also cause ulcers. Other factors may include:

- **Stress** (see page 215).
- Smoking and heavy drinking.
- Too much stomach acid.
- Too little mucus to protect the stomach lining.

Stomach ulcers are fairly easy to treat. If bacteria are the problem, antibiotics (sometimes with another drug) will take care of them.

The bacteria that cause ulcers can also cause gastritis—inflammation of the stomach lining. In some people, but not all, gastritis may cause symptoms that are like those of indigestion, such as upper abdominal pain, nausea, and vomiting.

Although the symptoms are like those that some people get from overeating or from eating fatty or spicy foods, gastritis is not caused by any of these things.

Your doctor may advise over-the-counter antacids or acid blockers for gastritis that isn't too serious. If he or she suspects bacteria, you will most likely need antibiotics. Untreated gastritis can cause severe damage.

what you can do now

- Don't take aspirin, ibuprofen, or other nonsteroidal anti-inflammatory drugs. Try acetaminophen instead (see **pain relief** box, page 207).
- Drink lots of water and other liquids to prevent dehydration, but avoid milk, which can increase acid.
- Take antacids or acid blockers.
- Eat smaller meals and eat more often. Stay away from any foods that cause symptoms.
- Don't drink alcohol, or don't drink much.
- Don't smoke. Avoid smoky places.
- Do relaxation or stress-reduction exercises.

when to call the doctor

Call 911 or go to an emergency room **right away:**

- If you throw up blood or anything that looks like coffee grounds. This is a sign of bleeding in the esophagus or stomach.
- If you faint or feel faint, chilly, or sweaty. These symptoms may signal blood loss, one cause of shock.

Call for a prompt appointment:

- If you have sharp pain with ulcer symptoms. The ulcer may be perforated—making holes or rips in your stomach or upper intestine.
- If you have an ulcer and are weak and pale. You may have anemia from a bleeding ulcer.
- If your stools are deep red or black, or have blood on them. These can be signs of internal bleeding.

Call for advice and an appointment:

- If you have sharp stomach pain.
- If you have symptoms of a stomach ulcer or gastritis that last more than 2 weeks.

how to prevent it

- Cut down use of aspirin and ibuprofen.
- Avoid foods that upset your stomach.
- Do what you can to reduce stress.
- To prevent an ulcer from coming back, follow your doctor's advice about any ulcer drugs you are taking.

for more help

Organization: National Digestive Diseases Information Clearinghouse, 2 Information Way, Bethesda, MD 20892-3570. 301-654-3810, M–F 8:30–5 EST; *www.niddk.nih.gov/health/digest/pubs/ulcers/ulcers.htm* for an online brochure on ulcers. Call or write for a free fact sheet and packet on gastritis and the helicobacter bacterium.

Web site: Centers for Disease Control and Prevention's fact sheet on peptic ulcers, *www.cdc.gov/ncidod/dbmd/hpylori.htm.*

Book: *Good Food for Bad Stomachs,* by Henry D. Janowitz, M.D. Offers sample diets to help ease gastritis and other digestive problems. Oxford University Press, 1998, $13.95.

urinary problems

signs and symptoms

- Burning or stinging when urinating.
- Urge to urinate often, but with only small amounts passed each time.
- Cloudy, strong-smelling, or bloody urine.
- Yellow discharge from the urinary tube (urethra).
- Pain in the lower abdomen or lower back.
- Pain during intercourse.

Many problems can make urination painful, but urinary tract infections are the most common.

Although normal urine contains no bacteria, bacteria always live on your skin and in the anal area. These germs can get into the urinary tract and travel up the tube (urethra) between the bladder and the outside of the body. They can then grow in the bladder and cause pain, swelling, and redness. This infection is called cystitis. It's the most common urinary tract infection.

The urethra itself can get infected; so can the kidneys if bacteria reach them.

Adult women are more likely than others to get urinary tract infections. Sexually active women are most at risk. That's because the urethra is near the vagina; during intercourse, germs can move into the urethra, and then to the bladder. Women who use diaphragms may be more likely than others to get these infections; the device can irritate the urethra.

People with **diabetes** (see page 181) and weakened immune systems also have a higher risk of infection. So do those with kidney stones or other urinary problems, and people who must use catheters. Risk of a urinary tract infection goes up as you grow older.

Though these infections can be painful, they are easy to cure with antibiotics.

what you can do now

- Drink lots of water in the first 24 hours—at least 8 to 10 glasses, more if you can. Doing so will dilute your urine and help wash out the germs. (But don't drink lots of water if you're going to see the doctor. This can dilute any urine samples you may be asked to give, making it harder to find the cause of your problem.)
- When you have symptoms, avoid juices high in acid, such as cranberry juice.
- Stay away from drinks with caffeine or alcohol in them, and foods with a lot of spices such as black pepper.
- Take a hot bath or use a heating pad to help relieve pain or itching.
- Don't have intercourse until all of your symptoms are gone.

when to call the doctor

Call for a prompt appointment:
- If you have a sharp pain that comes in waves, starting in the back below the ribs and moving toward the groin. You may have a kidney stone.
- If you have a fever that gets worse quickly, with sudden, intense pain in your back near or above your waistline. You may have a kidney infection.
- If your urine looks bloody or very cloudy.
- If you have painful urination and any discharge from the vagina that seems strange. You may have a **sexually transmitted disease** (see chart, page 158).
- If it hurts to urinate, and you have tenderness and a dull ache or pain in your lower back and abdomen, have pain during intercourse, or sometimes miss menstrual periods or have very heavy ones. You may have endometriosis (see **menstrual irregularities chart,** page 156) or **pelvic inflammatory disease** (see page 209).

Call for advice and an appointment:
- If it is painful to urinate or you have other symptoms of a urinary tract infection.
- If your symptoms don't go away or if they come back despite treatment.

how to prevent it

- Drink 8 glasses of fluids—mostly water—each day. Cranberry juice can help keep an infection from starting, but only if you drink at least a *quart* every day.

- Try supplements of vitamin C (ascorbic acid); they may slow bacterial growth.
- Urinate when you have the urge to go. Empty your bladder every time.
- Wash before and after sex. Ask your partner to do the same.
- Urinate right after sex; this helps flush out bacteria that may have entered the urinary tract.
- Take showers instead of baths.
- Don't use bubble bath or scented soaps. Use a mild, scent-free detergent to wash underwear; scented or harsh products can irritate the skin around the urethra.
- Wear cotton-crotch underwear and loose-fitting clothes.
- Wash genitals with plain water once a day. Soap can be irritating.
- If you use a diaphragm, wash it after each use with warm, soapy water, then rinse and dry it. If you continue to have infections, ask your doctor to help you make sure the diaphragm fits well. If that doesn't help, try another type of birth control.
- To keep the urinary tract free of bacteria, always wipe yourself from front to back after using the toilet.

for more help

Organizations: The American Foundation for Urologic Disease, 1128 N. Charles St., Baltimore, MD 21201. 800-242-2383 or 410-468-1800, M–F 8:30–5 EST; *www.afud.org.* Write or call for brochures.
■ Interstitial Cystitis Association of America, 51 Monroe St., Suite 1402, Rockville, MD 20850. 800-435-7422, M–F 8–5 EST; *www.ichelp.org.* Call or send a business-size self-addressed stamped envelope for information on cystitis.
■ National Institute of Diabetes and Digestive and Kidney Diseases, 301-496-3583, M–F 8:30–5 EST; *www.niddk.nih.gov.* Sends information on kidney and urinary tract problems. At Web site, click on *Health Information*, then on *Urologic Diseases*, and choose from list of topics.
Books: *Conquering Bladder and Prostate Problems: The Authoritative Guide for Men and Women,* by Jerry G. Blaivas, M.D. Describes symptoms, tests, and treatments for many specific conditions. Perseus, 1998, $26.95.
■ *You Don't Have to Live With Cystitis,* by Larrian Gillespie, M.D. Offers approaches that can put a stop to urinary tract infections. Avon Books, 1996, $12.

vaginal problems

signs and symptoms

Yeast infection:

- Redness, itching, and sometimes burning during urination.
- Pain during intercourse.
- White, cheesy, odorless discharge (sometimes).

Bacterial vaginosis:

- Watery, grayish white or yellow discharge with a fishy odor.
- Mild burning or irritation.

Contact dermatitis:

- Redness and itching of the vulva (the outer genital area).

The term *vaginitis* refers to many irritations of a woman's genital area.

A **yeast infection** is the most common (see **fungal infections,** page 187). It's caused by overgrowth of a fungus normally found in the vagina. It can be brought on by pregnancy, diabetes, use of antibiotics, and sometimes use of the Pill. Some experts believe that feminine hygiene products also cause it. If you get frequent yeast infections, your doctor can prescribe antifungal pills.

Bacterial vaginosis occurs when bacteria normally found in the vagina grow out of control or when bacteria normally found in the rectum get into the vagina. Poor health, poor hygiene, or clothing made of material that does not allow air to reach the skin can make it more likely.

Contact dermatitis may be caused by chemicals in latex condoms, spermicides, or diaphragms; feminine hygiene sprays; colored or scented toilet tissue; soaps, detergents, or fabric softeners; and deodorant tampons or sanitary pads (see **dermatitis,** page 179). Your doctor can prescribe an ointment that will help bring relief.

what you can do now

For all vaginitis:
- Don't have intercourse for 2 weeks, or until all soreness is gone.
- Don't scratch. Use cool compresses or sitz baths to ease itching.
- Use plain yogurt with live acidophilus cultures (check the label) to make a compress or to put in the vagina. You can apply it as a douche, or with a spoon or applicator made for vaginal treatments.
- Keep your vulva clean, and dry it well after urinating or showering. You can use a hair dryer set on low to blow warm, dry air on the sore area—just be careful of the heat.
- Wash all underwear in mild, fragrance-free soap or detergent (soap made for baby laundry is good) and rinse twice. Don't use fabric softener or bleach.

Yeast infection:
- If you are sure that you have a yeast infection, use an over-the-counter antifungal cream made for yeast infections. Be sure to use all of the cream as directed, even after your symptoms are gone.
- The infection can spread, so stop having sex until you finish treatment. Your sexual partner also may need treatment to keep from reinfecting you.

when to call the doctor

Call for a prompt appointment:
- If you have bleeding between menstrual periods or after menopause; a firm, raised lesion or bump on the vulva or inside the vagina; or vaginal pain and itching that doesn't go away. These may be signs of cancer of the vagina or vulva.
- If you notice a vaginal discharge that is yellow or green and foul-smelling. This may be a symptom of a **sexually transmitted disease** (see chart on page 158).

Call for advice and an appointment:
- If you have symptoms of bacterial vaginosis. Your doctor can treat the infection with an oral antibiotic. It can spread, so be sure your partner is also treated.
- If you have any vaginal symptoms for the first time, or if they recur more than twice a year.
- If symptoms don't go away after treatment, or are severe.

how to prevent it

- Wipe from front to back after a bowel movement to avoid spreading bacteria from the rectum to the vagina.
- Don't use scented toilet paper, perfumed soaps, or feminine hygiene products.
- Change tampons and sanitary pads at least 4 times a day.
- Clean diaphragms, cervical caps, and spermicide applicators well after each use.
- Don't wear tight pants, clothing that can trap moisture, or underwear or panty hose with a crotch that's not cotton.
- If you are taking antibiotics, ask your doctor whether you should use an antifungal cream in your vagina to prevent a yeast infection.
- Try eating a cup of yogurt that has live cultures every day (check the label). Studies show that yogurt may prevent yeast infections.
- Check your vulva monthly for changes.

for more help

Organization: National Women's Health Network, *www.womenshealthnetwork.org.* Staff answers questions and sends facts about vaginitis and yeast infections.

Web site: Duke University Healthy Devil Online, *h-devil-www.mc.duke.edu/hdevil/women/women.htm.* Covers vaginal and urinary tract infections.

Book: *Our Bodies, Ourselves for the New Century: A Book by and for Women,* by the Boston Women's Health Book Collective. An updated version of the classic guide to women's health. Touchstone, 1998, $24.

medical advisors

ERNIE CHANEY, M.D.
Professor Emeritus, Department
of Family & Community Medicine,
University of Kansas School of
Medicine–Wichita

DAVID CHERNOF, M.D., F.A.C.P.
Associate Clinical Professor of Medicine
(Hematology/Oncology), University
of California Los Angeles Medical Center;
former Senior Medical Director,
Blue Cross of California

R. RON FINLEY, B.S.PHARM., R.PH.
Lecturer, Department of Clinical Pharma-
cy, School of Pharmacy, University of
California, San Francisco

GREGORY GRAY, M.D., PH.D.
Chairman, Department of Psychiatry,
Charles R. Drew University of
Medicine & Science, Los Angeles

MARGARET HAMMERSCHLAG, M.D.
Professor of Pediatrics & Medicine,
Director of Pediatric Infectious
Diseases, State University of New York,
Health Sciences Center, Brooklyn

STEPHEN HANAUER, M.D.
Chair, Section of Gastroenterology
& Nutrition, University of Chicago
Medical Center

JOHN HECKENLIVELY, M.D.
Vernon C. Underwood Chair of
Ophthalmology, Jules Stein Eye
Institute, University of California
Los Angeles Medical Center

**RONALD L. KAUFMAN, M.D.,
M.B.A., F.A.C.P.**
Director of Medical Services, Clinical
Services Department, Office of the
President, University of California

DENIS KOLLAR, M.D.
Staff Emergency Physician,
Department of Emergency Medicine,
Citrus Valley Medical Center,
West Covina, California

JOHN M. LUCE, M.D.
Professor of Medicine & Anesthesiology,
University of California San Francisco

RONALD J. PION, M.D.
Clinical Professor (Obstetrics &
Gynecology), University of California
Los Angeles Medical Center;
Chairman and CEO, Medical
Telecommunications Associates, Inc.

**STEPHEN N. ROUS, M.D.,
F.A.C.S., F.A.A.P.**
Professor of Surgery (Urology),
Dartmouth Medical School;
Chief of Urology, V. A. Medical Center,
White River Junction, Vermont

ROWENA SOBCZYK, M.D.
Georgia Institute of Technology Student
Health Services, Atlanta, Georgia

MICHAEL A. WEBER, M.D.
Professor of Medicine, State University
of New York, Health Sciences Center,
Brooklyn

BARRY W. WOLCOTT, M.D.
Senior Vice President, Chief Medical
Officer, Access Health Group, McKesson-
HBOC, Broomfield, Colorado

GAYLE E. WOODSON, M.D.
Professor, Department of
Otolaryngology, University of
Tennessee, Memphis College
of Medicine